Alcohol Patterns and Problems

Series in Psychosocial Epidemiology

Volume 5

Andrew E. Slaby, M.D., Ph.D., M.P.H.
General Editor

SERIES IN
PSYCHOSOCIAL
EPIDEMIOLOGY

VOLUME 5

ALCOHOL PATTERNS & PROBLEMS

EDITED BY
Marc A. Schuckit

Rutgers University Press
New Brunswick, New Jersey

Publication of this book has been supported in part by a grant from the Metropolitan Life Foundation.

Library of Congress Cataloging in Publication Data
Main entry under title:

Alcohol patterns and problems.

(Series in psychosocial epidemiology; v. 5)
Bibliography: p.
1. Alcoholism—Addresses, essays, lectures.
I. Schuckit, Marc A. II. Series. [DNLM: 1. Alcoholism.
W1 PS79E v.5 / WM 274 A35255]
RC565.A44335 1985 362.2'922 84–3453
ISBN 0–8135–1060–0
ISBN 0–8135–1061–9 (pbk.)

Contents

Introduction to Studies in Psychosocial Epidemiology

Rising costs of mental health care and interest in the development of a national health insurance that should include mental health services has heightened concern both for ways by which health planners may evaluate the extent of behavioral problems as well as for means by which the efficacy of various treatment modalities may be assessed. Questions of paramount importance include: If there are two or more ways to treat an illness, which is the most effective? If two therapeutic modalities are equally effective, which is the most efficient? If equally efficient, which is the least costly? Questions regarding the prevalence and incidence rates of specific psychiatric illness in communities are comparably being raised by those delegated with the task of making policy recommendations for programs of primary prevention and treatment. What is the natural history of an untreated behavioral problem and how is the problem affected by normal growth and development? What does a knowledge of the natural history of a disorder of mood, thought, and behavior tell us about its etiology and how may it lead to methods of prevention? If an illness is not preventable by currently available knowledge, what interventions may be made in its natural history to arrest and possibly reverse its course? Mental health is now big business and failure to look at specific population needs when planning programs and to build in ways of evaluating cost, efficiency and effectiveness results in considerable psychological and economic cost to millions of patients and their families as well as to taxpayers in general.

Epidemiology includes a number of technical skills that may be put to use in answering some of the questions facing health planners today. Traditionally, epidemiology has been seen as the study of disease patterns in populations. Epidemiologists have provided useful data that have led to effective programs to prevent a number of infectious diseases including malaria, smallpox, and poliomyelitis. Epidemiology has, however, played a minor role in psychiatric research until relatively recently. Epidemiologic studies in mental health tended to be descriptive and to focus on the prevalence and incidence of symptoms in broad categories of illness such as "neuroses" or "psychoses." Some infectious and chronic disease epidemiologists, in fact, question whether epidemiology can be used to tackle psychiatric problems. The Society for Epidemiologic Research does not have a section on psychosocial epidemiology, and publication of papers in social and psychiatric epidemiology in the main journal of epidemiology is infrequent. Principal organs of dispersion of knowledge in psychosocial epidemiology have been *Psychological Medicine* and the *Archives of General Psychiatry*. The former journal, published quarterly, has editorial board members that are sophisticated in epidemiology and probably publishes the greatest number of articles in this area. However, it is a British journal with limited readership in the United States. On the other hand, the *Archives of General Psychiatry*, a publication of the American Medical Association, is fairly widely read in the United States. It publishes a number of high quality papers in epidemiology but has a broad mandate and therefore is limited in its ability to publish more.

The *Series in Psychosocial Epidemiology*, of which this is the fifth volume, is to serve several important functions for epidemiology, psychiatry, and related areas in public health. The objectives include:

1. Providing a forum for discussion of research strategies in the evaluation of mental health problems in the community and of asssessing effectiveness of psychiatric treatment interventions;
2. Serving as a teaching tool for students in medical schools and schools of public health, hospital administration, social work, and nursing as well as for students in departments of psychology, sociology and especially epidemiology;
3. Keeping prospective researchers alert to problems needing investigation in the area of psychosocial epidemiology;

4. Serving as a vehicle to bring together research in the area of psychosocial epidemiology;
5. Providing a means of continuing education for epidemiologists working in the field; and
6. Providing a means for discussions on how the results of epidemiologic and related behavioral research might be brought to bear on the development of state and federal health policy decisions.

To achieve these ends, each monograph will have a theme of particular interest to investigators in the field of psychosocial epidemiology, such as the study of children, the study of stressful life events, and needs assessment. For each volume in the series a guest editor will be chosen with an established reputation in the field to direct the selection of the individual contributors and to write the introductory article. In general, the lead article will (1) contain a discussion of methodological considerations in research of a given area (i.e., experimental design, sampling, instruments used, analysis of data, economic considerations, and ethical decisions in planning studies), (2) critically review existing studies, (3) present information on the current state of the field, and (4) suggest directions for further research.

Volumes in the series to follow this one on alcohol studies will focus on community surveys, needs assessment, genetics, aging, ethics of epidemiologic research, drug use, and the methodology of natural experiments. Earlier volumes in the series focused on studies of children, stressful life events, and help-seeking behavior. Barbara Dohrenwend and Bruce P. Dohrenwend, Felton Earls, Stanislav V. Kasl, David Mechanic, Jerome Meyers, Lee N. Robins, Catherine E. Ross, Marc Schuckit, Laurence R. Tancredi, Ming T. Tsuang, George Warheit, and Myrna M. Weissman are the current guest editors. In addition to the introductory article and papers selected by investigators in the field, each volume will contain, whenever possible, an editorial appearing as the Afterword written by a representative of the World Health Organization, as well as a Foreword written by myself. The representative of WHO, chosen by Dr. Norman Sartorius, Director of the Division of Mental Health, will focus on what is being done internationally in the topic area discussed, what should be done cooperatively and independently to advance the field, what WHO feels are research priorities in the field, and what particular methodologic problems in research in the area exist in pretechnological and Third World nations. I will direct my editorial to the present state of epidemiologic research in the area, the directions the Center for Epidemiological Studies at the National Institute of Mental Health would like to see research take, and the relationship of research in the field to the formation of health policy.

The mandate of this series is challenging and the task is great, but with the help of the guest editors and other contributors, and with feedback from readers, the series can fulfill the need for an organ that draws together researchers, students, and health policymakers in an effort to reap from research in psychosocial epidemiology conclusions that lead to effective and consumer-responsive health policy and programs of preventive psychiatric care.

A.E.S.

Foreword

Alcoholism and alcohol abuse are two of the world's leading social problems. In addition to the great cost of loss of human life and serious physical injury in alcohol-related accidents (automobile, airplane, industrial and domestic), drownings, fires, suicides and homicides, there are numerous other social, psychological, and physical consequences. Families and love relationships disintegrate and careers of promise are compromised when an individual finds it impossible to wrest him- or herself free from the uncontrollable use of alcohol.

Alcohol has widereaching effects on all body systems. Excess use is associated with high rates of cancer at all levels of the digestive tract, but especially of the esophagus and stomach. Inflammation of the stomach (gastritis) and pancreas (pancreatitis), ulcer disease, hepatitis, and cirrhosis occur more frequently with heavy alcohol use. Chronic ingestion of alcohol results in deterioration of the peripheral nerves of the hands and feet in 5% of alcoholics and a number of temporary and permanent organic mental syndromes due either to the direct toxic effects of alcohol or to related vitamin deficiencies such as Wernick-Korsakoff's syndrome (due to thiamine deficiency) are seen in somewhat less than 5% of individuals who are chronic abusers of alcohol. It is estimated that between 15% and 30% of permanent organic mental syndromes seen in nursing home patients may be attributed to alcohol use. Alcohol-induced cardiovascular disease is seen in an estimated one-fourth of alcoholics. Other physical consequences include muscle wasting (particularly of the shoulders and hips) and decreased production of all types of blood cells.

Using serious life problems as a criterion for alcoholism, it has been estimated that between 5% and 10% of the adult American male population will suffer from the illness at some point during their lifetime. Because of the high incidence of physical pathology associated with heavy alcohol use, 20% to 35% of male medical and surgical patients are alcohol abusers. Nearly 3% of total personal expenditures (totaling billions of dollars annually) are spent on alcohol. The cost to the country in terms of lost productivity, property damage, health care, and social welfare is billions of dollars more.

A quarter to one-half of young men experience transient alcohol-related problems such as missing work due to excess alcohol use, driving violations under the influence, and personal arguments. Over two-thirds of American men drink more than just occasionally with the male to female ratio about 1.3 to 1. With the rates of alcohol abuse rising among both women and adolescents, we can anticipate a significant change in this ratio over time. While per-capita consumption peaks between 16 and 25 years of age and decreases with age, the average *alcoholic* experiences his or her first alcohol-related life problem in the late twenties and early thirties. Most alcoholics first seek treatment or are brought to it in their early forties after more than a decade of difficulties. If alcohol abuse continues, the individual may expect to die about 15 years earlier than he/she would have normally if they had not continued to drink to excess.

Despite the magnitude of health-related problems, alcoholism research has been fraught with numerous methodologic problems that have caused many empirically minded epidemiologists to shun research in this area and caused health policy makers to view most results of alcohol investigators with skepticism. Not the least of the problems has been the difficulty in defining the problem. Approaches used have included the quantity-frequency-variability approach (attempting to gather information on statistically normative and deviant drinking patterns), the psychological dependence approach (based on a series of subjective experiences relating to drinking problems such as having a drink before going to a party), and the approach used by most physicians based on the occurrence of withdrawal or abstinence symptoms when an individual stops drinking.

A fourth and increasingly favored approach to definition is use of occurrence of serious social or health problems related to alcohol such as marital separation or divorce, multiple arrests, or physical evidence that alcohol has been harmful to the individual's health such as the presence of cirrhosis or cardiomyopathy. Before one can determine the incidence or prevalence of alcoholism for legislators interested in appropriate allocation of limited resources for prevention programs, research, or treatment, we must first know how to define the problem.

Population estimates and evaluation research are further thwarted by the fact that alcoholism is not a unitary disease. Alcoholism may be a *primary* problem with a relatively straightforward course or a problem secondary to a number of other psychiatric problems. Secondary alcoholism is most frequently seen with sociopathy and affective illness. Approximately 20% of women and 5% of men meeting the criteria for alcoholism have episodes of affective illness prior to their first major alcohol problem. Comparably, 20% of male alcoholics and 5% of female alcoholics can be diagnosed as primarily antisocial with secondary alcoholism. An understanding of the effect of concomitant psychological illness (in the instances of affective illness and sociopathy) or physical illness (in the case of alcohol-induced organic mental syndromes) on how an individual responds to treatment is necessary when samples are selected for research and when outcomes of various treatment approaches are evaluated.

Finally, an awareness of the natural history of untreated alcoholism is necessary before the value of a specific or nonspecific therapeutic intervention can be assessed. The risk at any stage of life of being a drinker (*not* an alcoholic) is higher for people with more education and higher socioeconomic status and those of Italian or Jewish ancestry. The usual *alcoholic*, however, is more frequently of lower socioeconomic status, lower education, and of French or Irish extraction. The modal alcoholic alternates periods of abstinence or very little drinking with periods of serious alcohol misuse. In any given month, one-half of alcoholics will be abstinent. Alcoholics have about 10% to 30% chance of reaching remission without treatment ("spontaneous remission"). An understanding of the fact that the average alcoholic has spontaneous periods of abstinence and marked decrease in drinking alternating with heavy drinking is critical to those interested in the evaluation of the cost-efficiency and effectiveness claims of various proponents. Assumed therapeutic triumphs may be merely an artifact of the natural history of the illness.

The volume is edited by Marc A. Schuckit, a leader in the epidemiology of alcohol use. His introduction presents an overview of basic methodologic approaches. The emphasis is on methodology in order to acquaint readers, many of whom are health policymakers rather than primary researchers, with issues that must be considered in interpreting results from any epidemiologic study of substance abuse. Dr. Schuckit makes a clear distinction between the epidemiology of drinking practices (the number of people who drink and their characteristics), studies of drinking problems (some of which are evanescent and not predictive of future serious problems), and alcoholism (implying persistent and serious alcohol-related difficulties). In his paper, problems of definition, instrumentation, sampling, validity and reliability, and ethical issues in alcohol-related research are examined. A section on research protocols compares the relative effectiveness of the key informant (or casefinding) approach, the social indicators approach, the rate under treatment approach, and survey methods. Dr. Schuckit concludes that in the final analysis it is not possible to give a sample statistic about the rate of drinking, alcohol-related problems, or alcoholism. Rough estimates are misleading when generalized to different population subgroups or different areas of the country. Other papers include one by Michael Polich and Charles Kaelber on national sample surveys and one by Popham et al. on heavy alcohol consumption and physical health problems.

In subsequent chapters, special attention is given to studies of specific populations. Elizabeth Morrissey discusses the unique methodologic problems in studies of alcoholism, alcohol abuse, and problem drinking in specific populations. Douglas Kolb and Eric Gunderson review some research on alcohol abuse and rehabilitation in the United States Navy. Roberta Ferrence discusses methodologic issues in the study of driving impairment and alcohol-related collisions. Ann Streissguth and Ruth Little address the issue of the effects of heavy drinking during pregnancy on offspring. Robert Popham, Wolfgang Schmidt, and Stephen Israelstam review the epidemiologic evidence relating heavy alcohol use to physical health problems. Robert Moore discusses the prevalence of alcoholism in medical and surgical patients. Irving Rootman, writing from the Division of Mental Health of the World Health Organization, concludes this volume with an afterword discussing research on alcohol-related problems from an international perspective.

Basic and evaluative research in the area of alcoholism and alcohol use and abuse is not easy, nor is interpretation of results always obtained. This volume, however, can serve as a first and major step forward for students, researchers, and health policymakers interested in a better understanding of the problems of epidemiologic research in the area of alcoholism. They should be able to use that understanding to design better studies and arrive at more empirically-based policy decisions.

A.E.S.

Reference

Schuckit, M.S. *Drug and Alcohol Abuse: A Clinical Guide to Diagnosis and Treatment.* New York: Plenum Press, 1979.

Chapter 1

Overview: Epidemiology of Alcoholism

MARC A. SCHUCKIT

This chapter will set the scene for the rest of the book. The goal is to place the issue of the epidemiology of alcoholism into perspective by identifying methodologic issues and briefly presenting some results.

To do this adequately it is necessary to first make some distinctions. In general the emphasis in this text is on methodology in order to acquaint the reader with the issues that must be considered in interpreting results from any epidemiologic study, especially those dealing with substance abuse. When relevant data are presented the emphasis is primarily on studies carried out in English, particularly those from North America.

Alcoholism is the main topic both in this chapter and the book in general. Unfortunately, it is rare for any two studies to use identical criteria for this disorder or to adequately distinguish it from related topics. Thus a distinction is made here between the epidemiology of *drinking practices* (the number of people who drink and their characteristics), studies of *drinking problems* (some of which are evanescent and do not predict serious future problems [Cahalan & Cisin, 1968; Fillmore, 1974]), and *alcoholism* (implying serious and persistent alcohol-related difficulties).

It is assumed the reader of this text will approach the material with some level of sophistication and background in both epidemiology and alcoholism. Those who wish a general introduction into the field of alcoholism might consider the text, *Drug and Alcohol Abuse* (Schuckit, 1984), or introductory books written by Mendelson and Mello (1979) or Estes and Heinemann (1982). For a clearly written and straightforward approach to basic epidemiology readers should consider perusing the fine text by MacMahon and Pugh (1970).

The chapter introduces a series of methodologic issues that

must be considered in either carrying out epidemiologic research in alcoholism or in interpreting the results of other research studies. A brief overview of research design is followed by a discussion of the relative costs versus benefits of each approach, an exposition on definitions, an overview of assets and liabilities of various research instruments and sample selection techniques, a brief discussion of data analysis, and finally a review of ethical, validity, and reliability issues. The last section is a brief introduction into each of the four methodologic approaches or research protocols: key informants (where "experts" are polled), social indicators (using public records such as cirrhosis rates), rate of individuals under treatment, and survey techniques. Within each of these subsections, a brief review of relevant results is presented. The information given in this introductory chapter is intended to aid in interpreting and placing in perspective each of the following chapters in the monograph.

Basic Methodologic Issues

General Considerations

There are two general rules: (1) no study can answer questions about everything, so each investigator is faced with a series of decisions as to the specific questions at hand; (2) no research methodology is perfect, but the final approach comes from a careful consideration of the assets and liabilities in each step of the research project ranging from the time reference chosen to definitions, instrumentation, sample selection, and more.

Each subsection raises an issue that must be considered by the investigator. For example, he must understand the assets and liabilities as well as the relevant limitations and interpretations resulting from the way the sample was selected and the completeness of the collected data. He must choose, for example, between the lower cost and the probable less validity of a phone survey versus a face-to-face interview. Furthermore, he must determine whether to address the status of things at one point in time or look at the time course of problems as might be done in a longitudinal study.

The conclusion reached at each decisions point ideally depends on a form of cost-benefit analysis. The equation will consider how much money and manpower are available as well as the time constraints. Generally, although not always, the more of these assets the more complete the answer will be.

Ideally, the amount of time or money applied will be influenced by the use planned for the data. For example, a key informant method may be most appropriate in determining professional attitudes, a rate-of-individuals-under-treatment design may be most useful for health care planning and bed utilization determinations, while the more costly survey technique using individual interviews may be most important in ascertaining the actual extent of a problem in society. If, however, the money and time necessary to carry out an adequate survey are not available, one might obtain similar data, although at the risk of a potential lower validity, through any of a variety of approaches using social indicators such as public death records.

Other important factors to be considered in the equation are ethical issues. The potential risks to individuals surveyed in face-to-face interviews might preclude the use of this methodology in some cases. For example, in a group of felons awaiting trial an anonymous questionnaire might offer less risk of asking individuals to incriminate themselves.

Time Frame for the Study

In deference to cost issues, most investigators have chosen to study alcoholism cross-sectionally, i.e. at one point in time. Thus the distribution of alcoholism in a given population is determined by any of a variety of means as it occurred on a specific day, month, or year. Study of populations prospectively over time—longitudinal investigations—can give important data about changes occurring in any population (Kandel,1978).

A variety of risks are associated with *cross-sectional* studies. The time chosen for determination of the alcoholism rate may have special characteristics and thus the results may have limited generalizability. One recent example is the possible bias in a survey of the rate of drinking problems (not necessarily alcoholism) in a group of high school seniors in April, a time that (due to fast approaching graduation and frequent dances and off-campus activities) may not be representative of drinking practices and problems at other times of the year (Rachal et al., 1976;

Davies, 1962). Depending on the methodology used, cross-sectional studies can give useful information.

It is possible to apply some of the cross-sectional methodologies to similar populations at two or more different times to determine trends over the years in a *longitudinal* study. Unfortunately, while such studies are sorely needed (Gibbons, 1954; deLint & Schmidt, 1968) their relative high cost and the necessity of allocating monies over an extended period of time make the true longitudinal study relatively rare.

In summary, while a great need exists for longitudinal studies, cost constraints have limited most studies to a cross-sectional type. Although there are limitations with this approach, careful selection of the time of sampling can help eliminate possible biases from the results.

Definition of Alcoholism

No matter which method of study is used, the results may depend upon the definition of alcoholism invoked, as shown in table 1. Investigators should clearly state their specific criteria (deLint & Schmidt, 1971; Knupfer, 1967) as it is important for

TABLE 1
Variation in Rates of Severe Problem Drinking as a Function of Diagnostic Criteria (%)

Problem area	*Men*	*Women*	*Sex ratio*
Excessive intake	4.9	1.8	2.7 to 1
Interpersonal problems	4.9	0.3	16.3 to 1
Excessive intake plus addiction or coping	2.1	0.3	7.0 to 1
Self-perceived problems plus addiction or coping	2.6	0.2	13.0 to 1
One or more problem areas	9.5	4.0	2.4 to 1

Note: Reprinted with permission of authors from Estes and Heinemann, 1977. These data were obtained from an area probability sample of noninstitutionalized adults in San Francisco. The definitions for each problem category include one or more of the following elements: (1) excessive intake, (2) mental disturbance, (3) social/economic disruption, or (4) loss of control over drinking.

the reader to fully understand the results reported. Historically, four sets of indicators have been used to separate criteria into groups although each has undergone considerable refinement over the years. These include definitions based on the quantity, frequency, and variability of drinking—a measure of consumption; definitions based on psychological dependence; alcoholism defined by medical complications or physical dependence; and alcoholism as it related to life problems (Schuckit, 1984; Haglund & Schuckit, 1982).

The *quantity/frequency/variability* definitions suffer the drawback that it may be hard to standardize what is "normal." For example, an average of four drinks a day may be almost normal for an 18-year-old-blue-collar worker but pathological for a 68-year-old man (Schuckit & Gunderson, 1974). Also, interpretation of the specific quantity and frequency of alcohol intake is usually done retrospectively and involves a good deal of conjecture on the part of the respondent.

Psychological dependence implies that the individual is very uncomfortable unless alcohol is available. While all alcoholics manifest psychological dependence, determination of this attribute is very subjective.

The third possible approach, based on the appearance of *physical withdrawal* signs, may not be noted in the average alcoholic who drinks on evenings and weekends, although he or she may demonstrate any of a series of life problems related to alcohol (Schuckit, 1984; Victor, 1966). Therefore, this definition used alone may be too restrictive.

The *life problems definition* of alcoholism is based on the premise that drinking to the point of incurring serious life difficulties indicates that the individual had warning that alcohol was causing problems but would not or could not stop drinking. Thus, an alcoholic is an individual who demonstrates any one of a series of life problems related to alcohol including a marital separation or divorce, multiple arrests, physical evidence that alcohol has harmed his health, or a job loss or layoff related to drinking (Schuckit, 1984).

Once an alcoholic diagnosis has been established, the next logical step is to differentiate between primary and secondary disorders. In *secondary alcoholism* the individual demonstrates a significant psychiatric disorder prior to the onset of alcoholism (Schuckit, 1984, Goodwin & Guze, 1984) and this is likely to run a complex or unpredictable course (Schuckit, 1978, 1984), making projections of future health care needs difficult. Unfortunately, it is rare for epidemiologic studies to take these factors into consideration.

Research Instruments

The methods of gathering and recording data are also very important. The final choice must rest with the goals of the study and the constraints of time, money, and personnel. When using social indicators or rate under treatment approaches, the instruments are relatively straightforward and involve numerous ways of organizing the extraction of data from official records. The specific instruments become of more central importance in studies using interviews or questionnaires such as those invoked in the key informant and survey methods.

The investigator must make a variety of decisions on instrumentation. As described below, these include: (1) whether the questions should be asked in a structured or more free-floating manner; (2) whether a face-to-face or phone interview or a self-administered questionnaire is more appropriate; (3) if a questionnaire, whether it should be given to an individual or a group or mailed; and (4) whether a short standardized questionnaire would be appropriate.

Initially, the researcher must determine whether to gather the data by using a *structured* or an *unstructured* format. In a structured format each question is carefully worded so each respondent is asked exactly the same inquiries in the same order. This approach requires that the investigator think through all the possible answers ahead of time and develop a coding manual whereby the data can be transformed for later analysis by a computer. In the unstructured interview the researcher is guided by some global questions and is more free to modify the interview for each person, probing where necessary. In general, large scale investigations appear to generate more valid and reliable data when interviewers follow a structured format and are encouraged to probe for additional and qualifying information when appropriate (Saghir, 1971). This is the most logical approach if one wants to be sure that identical criteria are being applied to all respondents.

It is not always possible to conduct face-to-face interviews, so the decision as to whether to use an individually administered or group-administered questionnaire must be made. The questionnaire offers the benefits of being faster and requiring less personnel to administer, but has the drawbacks of not allowing the investigator to probe inadequate answers and of having no way to be certain that the subject understands each question. The administration to a group makes it relatively easy to gather information from large numbers of individuals over a fairly short period of time.

In giving questionnaires to a group it is important to make a distinction between anonymous questionnaires (theoretically encouraging the respondent to be totally honest but also increasing the chances that he may give "silly" or inappropriate answers) and those where the respondent is assured of confidentiality but advised that respondent names will be recorded. Anonymous questionnaires have the additional drawback of not allowing the investigator to correlate information gathered on the questionnaire with data obtained from records and precludes future followup of individuals. While anonymous questionnaires are less costly to administer, they also decrease the ability of the investigator to create a rapport with the patient or subject, which in turn may lessen the validity of the information obtained.

Questionnaires can also be administered by mail, which is very economical. It is probable, however, that even with relatively thorough followup methodology (e.g., repeated mailings, followup by personal letter, and phone calls) only rarely will studies result in higher than 70% response rate (King, 1970) while group-administered questionnaires usually result in 90%–95% cooperation.

One type of questionnaire that deserves special mention is the relatively short, simple check list, which is reported to diagnose alcoholism. The most widely used check list is the Michigan Alcohol Screening Test (MAST) (Brady et al., 1982, Favazza & Cannell, 1977). At best the MAST can only be considered as a highly standardized screen that allows one to identify groups of individuals who demonstrate alcohol-related difficulties and are at elevated risks for fitting of the diagnostic criteria for alcoholism as outlined above.

In summary, most investigators feel that face-to-face interviews provide the best information and also allow the interviewer to record information about the subject's appearance and behavior and, when appropriate, to probe. An added advantage is that an interview can also be conducted by telephone. The major drawback to this approach is that it is the most costly.

Sample Selection

Ideally, one would study through interviews, questionnaries, etc., every individual relevant to the question being asked. As this is usually impossible, most investigations use an identifiable subgroup or sample of individuals and attempt to gather as much relevant information from as high a percentage of the sample as possible. If enough people within the group are studied (probably an excess of 80%) the results probably reflect the "truth" about the sample. However, the results will only be generalizable to other groups or the population at large if the original sample was carefully chosen.

As with individuals, samples have unique characteristics. These involve most treatment and demographic or descriptor attributes, including such things as patient versus nonpatient status, volunteers versus paid subjects, men versus women, individuals of different socioeconomic strata (SES), and individuals of different age groups. For example, a particular study may be generalizable to other volunteer, nonpatient males with an average age in the mid-30s (range, 21–45) living in a middle-class neighborhood of a city of 1–5 million individuals, but have little potential relevance to black, rural, young females.

This does not mean that one cannot carry out worthwhile studies. The implications are that all relevant descriptive information about subjects must be carefully reported so readers can determine the biases involved and interpret the results accordingly (Edwards, 1973). Table 2 relates information from different survey studies and breaks down results by sex, urban versus rural background, and SES data demonstrating how different results can occur even with this small number of sample characteristics. Two epidemiologic investigations can therefore present vastly different findings if the samples selected for study are significantly different.

In carrying out epidemiologic research, the investigator in-

TABLE 2
Alcoholism Survey Findings

Samples[a]	Percent reporting serious consequences of drinking[b] Men	Women	Sex ratio
Large cities	3.2	0.9	3.6 to 1
	7.7	1.7	4.5 to 1
Urban and rural	—	—	—
	—	—	—
Blue-collar workers	7.3	2.0	3.7 to 1
College students	21.0	6.4	3.3 to 1
U.S. military	7.0	—	—

Note: Reprinted with permission of authors from Estes and Heinemann, 1977.
[a]Samples were derived from populations in the United States.
[b]Variations in diagnostic criteria account for some of the rate fluctuations.

vokes a series of compromises based on the specific questions asked. These include:

1. Determination of the most relevant *target pool* from which to select subjects based on whether the results should reflect a cross-section of individuals in our society or whether they may be more relevant if they relate to a specific subgroup, for example, black women.
2. Once the target is selected, a specific group felt to be representative of that target is chosen. Thus someone interested in drinking practices among male collegians in middle-class private schools might begin with a university in his home town.
3. Once a specific target sample has been selected, an effort must be made to ensure the *sample* actually studied is representative of the target group itself. If the target group, e.g., male collegians in a specific university, is too large to study for time-related or financial reasons, a sample felt to be representative of the entire target group can be selected. One method is to use a totally random selection method whereby each individual has an equal chance of being chosen for interview or questionnaire. The difficulty here may

be that there are relevant subgroups that are not equally represented within the population, for example, freshmen may comprise 40% rather than the expected 25% of the student body in a particular college. The investigator might then choose to do a stratified random sampling, choosing individuals at random within each stratum year, e.g., 25% of the sample could come from the freshmen group, 25% from the sophomore group, and so on.

4. General population surveys face similar problems. If the target group is supposed to be a representative sample of individuals residing in Milwaukee, Wisconsin, how can a randomly selected or random stratified sample, whichever is more relevant for the question being asked, be chosen? Each of a series of methods has its own assets and liabilities, therefore, investigators must carefully consider and spell out decisions, e.g., whether election polls are used to generate names, whether individuals are chosen based on their block of residence, how single versus multiple dwellings are considered, or whether more transient individuals are excluded (Edwards, 1973).
5. Even with all this done, the results are only representative of a specific sample or target group if a very high percentage of those who are eligible are actually used to generate information. This is because individuals who are more difficult to contact may have special characteristics; for example, their unavailability may reflect the fact that they have a higher rate of alcoholism and thus are less cooperative (Stanton, 1977; Lasagna & von Felsinger, 1954). In general, the greater the percentage of individuals who were selected for study but for whom data are unavailable, the less valid the results.

In summary, an important attribute of epidemiologic research is the sample under investigation. While no epidemiologic study can be conducted without compromises, a careful understanding of such factors as how the target population was selected; whether a random, stratified random or entire sampling assignment was used; and the percentage of chosen individuals who were actually contacted must all be known before the results can be interpreted.

Reliability and Validity

It is apparent by now that no study is perfect. The compromises that must be made to carry out a "do-able" investigation all threaten to a greater or lesser extent the possibility that one would obtain the same results by replicating the same study (*reliability*) and raises the possibility that the answers do not represent the "truth," i.e., are not *valid*. On the other hand, two different studies arriving at divergent results may both be valid, the differences reflecting sample selection, instrumentation, time frame of the study, etc. The problem is complicated even further by the fact that cross-sectional studies using the same methodology on the same population may arrive at different results because drinking practices, problems, and even alcoholism may not be static phenomena but may change within any individual over time (Schuckit, 1984; Fillmore, 1974; Cahalan 1972; Ludwig, 1972). This section will discuss factors that can affect the validity and reliability of epidemiologic studies so the reader can try to gauge the probable accuracy of any specific investigation.

Reliability

Reliability is a complex phenomenon that can be measured in a number of different ways (Celentano & McQueen, 1978a, 1978b). I choose to follow the definition of MacMahon & Pugh (1970) where the key question is whether the investigator would obtain the same answer to the question if the methodology were to be repeated again with the same population. Problems with reliability can occur for a variety of reasons: the question may have been poorly worded and interpreted differently by the subject on the two separate occasions; unintentional "hints" were offered by different interviewers about what answer was desired; a subject genuinely forgot something he knew on the first interview. Additionally there may be changes in individual reluctance to report socially undesirable behaviors (Edwards, 1973) as well as the possibility that the practice being queried is past behavior the subject no longer considers relevant because his attitudes have changed. Therefore, investigators must carefully specify the probable length of time between an event and the query. In addition to the factors outlined above, it must be recognized that within any specific study different questions may have different levels of reliability, based on the degree of complexity of the question.

Nonetheless, most studies report relatively high levels of reliability for questions regarding drinking practices, problems, and even alcoholism. Thus. when a group of outpatient male alcoholics were retested with the same instrument after 6 weeks, their reports of drinking frequency had a reliablility of 0.79–0.98 i.e., for 80% or more, the answers were similar on both occasions (Sobell, Sobell, & VanderSpek, 1979). Other investigators looking at alcoholics' self-reports of drinking have reported reliabilities as low as 0.60–0.70 (Armor et al., 1976). Edwards and others in studying drinking practices in nonalcoholic populations discovered a reliability of 0.75 after 2–3 months (Edwards et al., 1973). Even when one is dealing with individuals involved in a great deal of socially unacceptable behavior, convicted felons for example, the reliability for major events as studied 8–9 years later can be as high as 0.75 (Guze & Goodwin, 1972) with rates even higher for those criminals with the greatest antisocial involvement. Those with divergent answers are just as likely on the second interview or questionnaire to report high levels of involvement as they are to minimize their original answers (Sobell & Sobell, 1975).

In summary, considering all the difficulties that can interfere with a person's understanding of the question, memory of past events, and the possibility that individuals will try to report their most socially acceptable behavior, the reliability of most alcohol related studies is relatively high, probably 75% or higher. The distortion of results occurring from decreases in reliability does not seem to show a definite pattern as there seems to be parity between the number who increase or decrease their estimates on the second questionnaire or interview.

Validity

The only way to be certain the results of a study regarding drinking practices, problems, or alcoholism is valid is to have a totally unbiased investigator use crisp and totally unambiguous criteria, administer a perfect research instrument, and follow and record the activities of each research subject 24 hours a day.

In the real world such an impossible task is probably unnecessary for it is only required that the data be valid enough to give the best answer possible for the question being posed. Thus the "truth" resulting from a study is at best an approximation.

As with reliability, validity can also be defined a number of different ways. One good way is to use an approximation based on a comparison or ratio of the value obtained for the whole sample (for instance, the average number of days a week the sample drank) and the best approximation of the true value, producing a ratio called the aggregate validity (Pernanen, 1974). Because the true value is unknown the denominator becomes the most difficult part of the equation and some compromises must be made in its calculation. If the investigator chooses to try to establish validity by comparing results from an interview with those obtained from official records he should be cognizant that it is probable only 10%–25% of actual events become part of official records, e.g., police records (Edwards, 1973). Similarly, when answers on drinking practices given by an individual are compared with the data for the same person but gathered from a resource person (e.g., the spouse), the usual result is that patient or subject reports higher levels of alcohol involvement than the resource person. This probably reflects the fact that the resource person cannot observe the individual for 24 hours a day any more than the investigator can, and therefore, will miss much of the drinking behavior. The "true value" is rarely known for sure, and validity is estimated by comparing results from an individual with the best "guestimate" based on all additional data sources.

Results can be valid to a greater or lesser extent—validity is rarely an absolute value. The level of validity can be lowered because of errors in sampling (for instance inadvertently skipping certain households in a population survey), cluster effects (e.g., resulting from over-representation of certain areas such as skid row areas), nonresponses (e.g., not following up those individuals who are harder to locate as they may have much higher levels of the problems (Nilsson & Svensson, 1971), forgetting by the respondent (something which tends to increase with lapsed time and complexity of the question), direct lying (which also depends upon the social desirability of the question or the perceived loss of benefits by telling the truth), as well as a host of other factors (Pernanen, 1974).

It becomes apparent that validity can be impaired by many factors in addition to the possibility that the subjects may deliberately evade the truth. For example, the level of validity of nonthreatening ideas such as those that establish socioeconomic strata may be as low as 75%, perhaps reflecting misunderstanding, sampling errors, etc. (Mulford & Miller, 1963; Rubington, 1972).

Reports on drinking behavior have a fairly high level of estimated validity when the results of interviews or questionnaires are compared with official records or data from resource persons. There is, for instance, at least 75% agreement between husband and wife on smoking, drinking, and dietary history (Kolonel et al., 1977), which increases to 91% if the question is one of simple correlation between whether an individual admits to having drunk recently rather than the specific amount imbibed (Armor et al., 1976).

The more global the question asked, the greater the chance of agreement between subject and ancillary data sources. For example, using a gross measure of quantity and frequency of drinking a 96% agreement between the reports of husbands and wives was found. The disagreement, if any, was likely to be one of the patient reporting more than the spouse (McCrady, Paolino, & Longabaugh, 1978). The level of agreement, however, obviously decreases as the question becomes more specific, as for example, if the investigator wanted to pin down the intake of the exact number of ounces of alcohol per day (McCrady et al., 1978).

There are some differences in validity based on the type of subject or patient involved, with the heaviest drinkers being the ones most likely to minimize their alcohol intake (Sobell, Maisto, Sobell & Cooper, 1979; Sobell, Sobell & Vanderspek, 1979; Sobell & Sobell, 1975). When the reports of alcoholics are compared with official driving and police records the correlation is at least 0.65, with the subjects tending to report more than is obvious from the records (Sobell & Sobell, 1973; Sobell, Sobell & Samuels, 1974). Finally, in an attempt to approximate the ideal conditions described in the beginning of this section on validity, Hartford and others (Hartford, 1976) correlated unobtrusive observations of drinking behavior of a group of "normal" subjects in a bar with the later self-reports of drinking behavior in that atmosphere and found a 75% level of validity.

Similar high levels of validity, as best they can be approximated, have been established for other forms of substance-related or deviant behavior. Maddux and Desmond (1975) report a 71% agreement between interviews and official records in a group of 34 heroin users, and Clark (1966) established an 82% validity for questionnaires and a 92% validity for interviews in 40 male subjects (Robins & Braroe, 1964).

In summary, the aggregate validity is difficult to establish, at least in part, because the actual "truth" is rarely known. The most that can be determined is that the level of validity appears to be relatively high, usually in excess of 75% and may be as high as 90% if more global questions are asked. It should be noted that as defined here, a study that is valid is also reliable, although the reverse is not necessarily true.

Ethical Issues

This section is included to make sure that an issue that should be self-evident is not neglected. No form of patient or subject contact is without possible dangers (Ingelfinger, 1977; Dickson, 1978). The potential problems have recently been reviewed (Berger & Stallones, 1977; Spingarn, 1974; Gordis & Gold, 1980) and will, only be highlighted here. Ethical issues are not simple. Not only must the rights of individual subjects be protected, the obligations to nonsubjects, those who may suffer from the difficulties in the future and might be helped by this research, must also be considered (Modell, 1960). The final task, therefore, is to ensure that the aggregate potential harm is far less than the aggregate potential gain and that any risks to individual subjects are known to them and are warranted.

In general, epidemiologic research carries limited potential dangers. One specific problem involves confidentiality, a breech of which could result in self-incrimination should the answers be obtained by legal authorities, or embarrassment should personal information be released to friends or acquaintances. It is possible to establish safeguards of confidentiality by implementing procedures such as: (1) using code numbers on the interviews or questionnaires so other data handlers do not know to whom the information relates; (2) limiting access to research files to only those with a "need to know," which means only those most intimately involved in the project; and (3) keeping the data in locked file cabinets (American Psychiatry Association, 1975). A second problem is possible loss of dignity should the interview or questionnaire be insulting or carried out in a callous manner (Reiss, 1977), or a threat to self-esteem that might conceivably involve some danger of psychological harm.

Actually, the risks are relatively low and instances of injury very uncommon (Curran, 1978; Cardon et al., 1976). When interviews are carried out by careful researchers, subjects are prone to report later that they found the process helpful and that it cleared up issues with which they themselves had been wrestling (McCabe, 1977).

One major step in protecting subjects' rights is to be certain that the individuals fully understand the process in which they are asked to participate and that they give truly informed consent (Berger & Stallones, 1977; Alfidi, 1971). Another necessary step is to avoid using subjects who cannot understand the instructions or who might be experiencing coercion (e.g., mentally retarded individuals or prisoners) unless special safeguards are instituted.

Whenever possible, incriminating questions should be avoided. Special tactics might be required. For example, one can safely ask whether a subject has ever been arrested for a specific crime (something that would already be a matter of record for the police) and avoid asking direct questions as to whether they had committed a specific crime. Should the latter be required it may be necessary to obtain a specific exemption from the relevant law enforcement agencies to ensure that no subpoena can be issued at a later date or to make provisions for keeping incriminating records in a safe deposit box outside of the country (Curran, 1977).

In light of the information just outlined, for most epidemiologic studies it appears that the danger to nonsubjects (i.e., those who might gain from the study by obtaining more expert help in the future should the project be neglected) is usually greater than the danger to subjects. In fact, the laws protecting public records and research subjects are quite thorough and intricate and the level of resulting restraint may be inappropriate (Gordis & Gold, 1980; Chalkley, 1977). Obtaining approval from governing groups (e.g., human subjects committees) is difficult because researchers may be treated as if they are guilty of violating patient rights before any studies are carried out, requiring the investigator to go through intricate procedures to prove his innocence (Meyer,1977). The result has been that epidemiologic research, especially projects examining substance misuse or antisocial behavior, is becoming more and more difficult to do (Brody, 1975; Chalkley, 1977). It is fairly certain that careful application of the legislation presently on the books is more appropriate than the addition of further layers of protection (Gordis & Gold, 1980). To help ensure protection of subjects and to further encourage important epidemiologic research it is important to develop a national policy of making research files immune from subpoena (Gordis & Gold, 1980). While there has been some movement in this direction, it has tended to be piecemeal and inadequate (Curran, 1977; Culliton, 1976).

Other Relevant Factors

This review of basic methodologic issues is far from exhaustive. Results can be affected by a host of additional factors including the biases of the investigators, a funding source with expectations of desired results, and the time of year the study is carried out.

One other factor deserves to be mentioned. Once the study format has been developed and the data gathered, data processing and analysis remain to be done. For a study to be maximally effective, the mode of data handling should be clearly established before the first datum is recorded. While it is certainly beyond the scope of this review to discuss the intricacies of determining the level of significance, and the assets and liabilities of various simple and multivariant techniques, those methods must be given close scrutiny before the results can be fully interpreted.

Summary

Research results are a product of a combination of factors. Proper investigations can be carried out only after a variety of decisions are made which attempt to balance the specific question being asked, the money and time available, and relevant ethical issues. The product is a variety of compromises on time frame, definitions, instrumentation, data analytical procedures, and other factors, with a resulting level of validity and reliability. In carrying out epidemiologic research or interpreting the results of other studies, each of these factors must be kept in mind, not to decide whether a study is perfect but how the biases shade the results and the final level of reliability and validity. The next section places these issues in additional perspective by reviewing four major types of research, protocols encompassing different combinations of time frames, definitions, instrumentations, and sampling procedures.

Research Protocols

Overview

Most studies of the epidemiology of alcoholism use one of four general approaches: the key informant approach or case-finding technique; the social indicator method; the rate of alcoholics under treatment; or the survey method. In the following sections the methodologies involved in each of the research approaches will be presented with a brief example of the data generated. The reader should turn to each of the relevant subsequent chapters contained in this monograph for an indepth discussion of the results.

Key Informant Approach or Case-Finding Technique

Definition

The key informant methodology or case-finding approach (Furst & Beckman, 1979) surveys a limited number of key or "expert" individuals in order to gather either their impressions or limited data on the scope of alcoholism in a population. The goal when using this method is to establish an estimate of the extent of the problem. The most common subjects are health care deliverers or related professionals such as physicians, social workers, or clergy, but the approach can be extended to police, press, and other public institutions. The key informant methodology can be used to establish quick estimates of health care needs (Beigel et al. 1974). Unfortunately, because a relatively small number of individuals are asked to give their opinions, frequently unsubstantiated by data, this methodology is fraught with difficulties, not the least of which is the need to choose truly informed experts as subjects and then to make sure the data is gathered from a high percentage of those selected.

Assets and Liabilities

The major assets of this approach are that it is relatively inexpensive, it is an easy way to measure prevailing opinions in key individuals, and it can be accomplished in a relatively short time. However, these assets are usually more than counterbalanced by a probable low level of validity (Solomon, et al., 1980). Few individuals identified by the key informant as "problems" are known to treatment agencies and many known to the latter are not identified by key informants (Edwards et al., 1973). An additional difficulty, demonstrated in table 3, is the fact that only a minority of "experts" polled usually respond.

Some Relevant Examples

Estimates of alcohol related difficulties using the key informant technique are shown in table 4. Markedly divergent results are seen when different populations are used, but overall, almost 1% of males (i.e., 10 per 1000) and slightly more than 0.1% of females are identified as alcoholics by this approach. The prevalence of alcoholism measured by this technique is consistently lower than from either social indicators or survey results, a finding not surprising in light of the liabilities of this approach.

TABLE 3
Key Informant Protocol Results

	Physicians (%)	*Psychiatrists* (%)
Response rate to poll	43	42
Practitioners contacting alcoholic patients	90	56
Rate of alcohol disorders among hospitalized patients	47.3[a]	20.5[b]

Note: Reprinted with permission of authors from Estes and Heinemann, 1977.
[a]Admissions to a California general hospital with accompanying alcohol disorder.
[b]First admissions with alcohol disorder to psychiatric hospitals in California.

TABLE 4
Estimates of Alcohol-Related Difficulties from Key Informant Protocols

			Results (rate/1000)	
Source	***Year***	***Informants***	***Male***	***Female***
Edwards	73	Courts, press, emergency rooms, employees, clergy, voluntary agencies, physicians, hospitals, AA, social workers, general practitioners, hospital	2.8	0.1
Parr	57	Private physicians	1.1	
Hawker, et al	67	Employees	3.5	0.09
Pollak	71	Private physicians	9.8	2.2

Social Indicators Approach

Definition

This methodology uses readily available social data or statistics to estimate the prevalence of alcohol related problems or alcoholism. While any of a variety of public statistics could be used, those most frequently invoked include rates of commissions of crimes, mortality (usually alcohol death rates), rates of specific alcohol-related disorders such as cirrhosis (morbidity), or alcohol sales and/or evidence of rates of consumption.

Assets and Liabilities

The major benefits of this approach are (1) its relatively low cost compared to survey techniques, (2) relatively quick performance when the public data are already available, and (3) repeatability within a given locale when attempting to observe changes over time. The major drawback is that it is at best an estimate of problems and vulnerable to differential reporting methods and varying practices in different locales or in the same city or province over time.

Some Relevant Examples

The usual methodologies involve estimates of alcohol problems or alcoholism rates based on morbidity or illness statistics (e.g., cirrhosis), figures based on alcohol consumption rates, attempts at estimating local figures by combining censes and large survey data, use of official government registers or criminal justice records, and death or mortality figures.

1. Estimates based on morbidity (illness or problems).

In order for this method to work it is necessary to establish that there is a close correlation between the given morbid state and the use of alcohol. The most often invoked statistic is the rate of cirrhosis, where it has been established that somewhere between 25%–65% of cirrhotics would qualify for a diagnosis of alcoholism (Hodgson & Thompson, 1976). Thus, overall it is probable there is a correlation of 0.5 or better between alcohol consumption and the rate or cirrhosis in different countries (deLint & Schmidt, 1971).

The most often used formula correlates alcoholism rates with cirrhosis (Andreano & Li, 1974; Jellinek & Keller, 1952). The original formula specifies the relationship between liver cirrhosis, mortality, and alcoholism among heavy drinkers. Simply stated, the prevalence of alcoholism (A) is determined by the equation: $A = (PD/K)R$, where P is the proportion of deaths attributable to alcoholism, D is the number of deaths from liver cirrhosis in the specified period, K is the annual death rate from cirrhosis among alcoholics with medical complications, and R is the ratio of all alcoholics to all alcoholics with complications (Furst & Beckman, 1979; Haglund & Schuckit, 1982; Schmidt & Popham, 1978; Walsh and Walsh, 1973; Popham, 1970; Schmidt & deLint, 1970). Jellinek warned against taking the formula too literally and there have been numerous proposed modifications (Popham, 1970).

The advantages of this approach include its relatively low cost and ease of use, of great potential benefit in health care planning (Popham, 1970). However, the approach has been criticized by Jellinek (1959) and others (Douglass, 1973) for several reasons: the formula may not directly relate to a variety of definitions of alcoholism but more closely indicates levels of problem drinking (Schmidt & deLint, 1970; Walsh & Walsh, 1973); it may be inaccurate or less accurate in relatively abstentious geographic areas; it may be particularly unsuitable for areas of small population (Furst & Beckman, 1979); and it may be vulnerable to differences in associations between drinking, alcoholism, and cirrhosis within various ethnic or socioeconomic groups. An example of some of the potential biases is demonstrated by the fact that Ireland is rated relatively high in prevalence of alcoholism by a variety of methods but is noted to have a relatively low rate of alcoholism if the Jellinek formula is imposed (Walsh and Walsh, 1973).

Table 5 illustrates in a shorthand way the estimated numbers of alcoholics in the United States over the years. These figures have generated estimates of the prevalence of alcoholism in the nation of up to 9 million problem drinkers, including 5 million alcoholics (Bailey et al. 1965; Efron et al., 1974; Gorwitz, 1970; Kaij, 1970; Keller & Efron, 1958).

2. Consumption or sales figures (deLint & Schmidt, 1971).

   In this approach the level of per capita consumption of alcohol as ascertained from public tax or sales statistics is used to estimate the prevalence of alcohol-related difficulties and, perhaps, alcoholism. For this approach to work one must assume there is a direct correlation between the average intake in a population and the number of individuals imbibing at an excessive rate and then must further assume this correlates with the level of alcoholism.

TABLE 5
Examples Based on the Jellinek Formula

Year	*Total Number*[a]	*Rate per 1000 population over age 20*
1940	2,632,000	30.50
1945	2,876,000	30.90
1972	5,500,000	42.00

Note: Reprinted with permission of authors from Estes and Heinemann, 1977.
[a]Jellinek formula, ratio of complicated to noncomplicated for 1972 = 5.1.

The most often used formula is that of Ledermann (Schmidt & Popham, 1978; Furst & Beckman, 1979), an approach based on the assumption that the amount of alcohol consumed can be used to estimate the number of persons whose health is at risk from excessive consumption. The Ledermann formula also assumes the distribution of alcohol consumption is described by a continuous, unimodel, positively skewed, log-normal curve implying that drinkers and alcoholics are part of the same continuum (deLint & Schmidt, 1971). The cutoff of those individuals who are at exceptionally high risk, based on data from alcohol treatment programs, is 14.7 centiliters of alcohol daily which translates to 116 grams or 5 ounces of absolute alcohol or approximately 12 ounces of 80 proof scotch per day.

The advantages of this approach are the same as those discussed for the Jellinek formula. On the other side, the Ledermann equation has been criticized for a variety of reasons mainly centering around the dangers involved in using a mean to imply distribution (Moore & Gerstein, 1981; Parker & Harman, 1977) and the fact that "dangerous" levels of consumption change with a number of factors including age, e.g., the average 70-year-old alcoholic is only drinking four drinks per occasion (Schuckit & Pastor, 1979). One aspect of the equation receiving the most adverse comment has been the log-normal curve, which is not felt to represent realities of consumption (Furst and Beckman, 1979). In addition, the formula appears to be insensitive to the manner in which expenditures may relate to expendable income—the amount of income available after necessities are paid (Walsh & Walsh, 1973)—and the approach probably obscures relevant subgroups within a population (Parker and Harman, 1977). No high-level of correlation between the Ledermann data and survey data has yet been established (Celentano & McQueen, 1978).

Table 6 when compared to table 5 gives some examples of information generated on the rate of alcoholism when the Jellinek formula or the Ledermann formula is used. The results confirm differences in alcoholism rates for different ethnic groups as well as regional differences within the United States as well as in comparisons between countries

TABLE 6
Examples of Estimates Based on the Ledermann Formula

Rates of alcoholism based on drinking ≥15 ml absolute alcohol per day	
Country	***Rate/1000***
France	0.94
Italy	0.59
Canada	0.27
U.S.A.	0.22
England, Wales	0.20

Note: Based on table from deLint and Schmidt, 1971.

when the Jellinek approach is invoked. Using all available data, the rate of alcoholism appears to be between 3%–5% for men and 1%–2% for women with this approach. Using the Ledermann formula, where alcoholism is inferred from a probable intake of 15 milliliters of absolute alcohol per day or more (30 ml ≃ 1 oz) the rate appears to be about 2% for most countries including the United States with higher levels for Italy and France.

3. Synthetic estimates (Furst & Beckman, 1979).

Synthethic estimators are any of a group of devices used to give estimates of a target statistic for a specific limited area. The general approach consists of using descriptive data for the characteristics of individuals within an area in combination with average values for the specific statistics which were gathered on a national or regional level (Steinberg, 1979). This approach can be useful in program planning and is a way local administrators can use data about their own area in conjunction with national survey information to generate an estimate of drinking practices, problems, or alcoholism in their locale.

One method involves breaking down the local population and the national or regional data into subsets based on sociodemographic subgroups. For example, the investigators could make a table of local cross-classifications by sex, race, age, employment states, etc., then generate a second table cross-classified by the census or national data divided into the same subgroups. Multiplying the tables of problem drinking by demographic category with the table of the specific population breakdown within the sub-area being studied produces a third table consisting of the expected distribution within that subpopulation (Furst & Beckman, 1979). Thus it can be seen this is not a separate methodology in itself but rather a modification of the social indicators survey or consumption/sales approach.

The major asset is one of low cost as well as a recognition of the fact that many survey techniques were developed for large areas and may not be as accurate if applied directly to smaller populations. The results can at best be considered as a rough estimate for a variety of reasons: (1) in order for the method to work properly it is assumed the specific demographic patterns studied account for the differences in problem drinking or consumption; (2) the approach does not compensate for the fact that specific subgroups relevant to the small subarea may have been underestimated in the larger data block; and (3) synthetic estimates do not allow an investigator to determine whether the smaller area being studied is atypical in any important way (Levy, 1978).

4. The use of official registers or justice system data.

   This might have been considered an example of the "rate under treatment" approach but is discussed here because of the lack of official government recognition of the number of people receiving treatment. A number of Scandinavian countries maintain official registers of individuals who have been identified as having alcohol problems. These rarely reach the level of sophistication of establishing a rigorous criteria for alcoholism itself but can be used as an estimate of the general scope of alcohol-related difficulties (Kaij, 1960; 1970). In the United States such registers are rare with the closest approximation being the now abolished Monroe County register of individuals coming into contact with the mental health system (both public and private) including those with labeled alcohol problems (Zax, et al., 1967). In a similar manner one could use justice system records to document the number of individuals involved with each of a variety of specific alcohol-related crimes (e.g., public intoxication or driving under the influence of alcohol) and some areas might also offer data about the number of crimes, especially violent crimes, where alcohol was felt to play a role. In interpreting the justice system information, however, one must recognize that a single drunk driving arrest, being involved in a rowdy party, or the commission of a crime while intoxicated does not necessarily mean the individual had persistent alcohol-related problems justifying the label primary alcoholic (Schuckit, 1979).

The major advantages of the official registers approach are the ease of gathering data, decreased costs, and the probability that the register (which was developed for administrative reasons) will be available over the years for generation of comparison data. On the other hand, the investigator is at the mercy of the public record keeper, and his level of thoroughness. Also there is no guarantee that other areas use similar procedures in generating their registers, resulting in a problem with comparability of data. This method also suffers from justice system and police biases in whether individuals of different socioeconomic strata, races and age are arrested and processed, as well as the specific social control pressures and manpower availability in any locale during any one period of time (DeFleur, 1975). These difficulties are highlighted by the findings that only 20% of a sample of severe alcoholics were actually registered by a temperance board (Kaij, 1970) and that two-thirds of alcoholics identified by a survey were not known to the board (Hagnell & Tunving, 1972).

5. Mortality data.

These are related to the excess morbidity and illness in alcoholics (Klatsky, et al., 1981) which has been used to generate formulas such as the Jellinek equation. Data on alcohol-related deaths, usually taken from death certificates, can be used as another estimate of alcohol-related problems. This information has been gathered from violent deaths (Cleary, 1979; Cahalan, 1970), suicides (Schmidt & Popham, 1978), and poisoning deaths (for example, alcohol poisoning) (Ispen et al., 1952). In each of these instances an official autopsy is usually required with resulting data on toxicology determinations including alcohol.

Once again this method can be carried out with official statistics enabling the investigator to reap benefits from their ongoing nature and the relative low cost of the data extraction. On the other hand the information requires a type of "fudge factor" to estimate whether the presence of alcohol in the deceased indicates that alcohol was a serious contributing factor in the death. It takes an additional jump in logic to determine whether an actual alcohol involvement in the difficulty indicated the presence of other serious or pervasive alcohol-related difficulties that might be labeled alcoholism. Nonetheless, in one study there was a fairly consistent correlation between alcohol-related deaths, suicides, cirrhosis, and rates of alcohol consumption in a Canadian province (Schmidt & Popham, 1978).

Rate-Under-Treatment Approach

Definition

In this methodology hospital, clinic, emergency room, and other treatment setting data are gathered in order to establish an estimate of alcohol-related problems or alcoholism. The information can be organized so that only first contacts with treatment programs are counted (the incidence rate), or it can be used to determine the number of individuals in contact with treatment agencies for alcohol-related problems at any given time (prevalence), or it can be studied longitudinally to determine the lifetime risk for difficulties within a given locale. The studies can be carried out retrospectively by retrieval from records or prospectively by interviewing a group of patients coming into a treatment program with a questionnaire, a structured interview, or a brief diagnostic checklist such as the Michigan Alcohol Screening Test (MAST). Such studies can be done in an alcohol hospital (Rimmer & Chambers, 1971; Rimmer et al., 1972; Tamayo & Feldman, 1975), a general medical or surgical facility (Poikolainen, 1980; Moore, 1971), through emergency units (Reichler et al., 1983), sometimes using the Drug and Alcohol Warning Network (DAWN), or during routine physical exams (Klatsky et al., 1983), with each method probably giving different results.

Assets and Liabilities

The major assets of this approach are that, while potentially more expensive than the use of public registers, it is much less

TABLE 7
Examples of Results of First Admissions For Alcoholism as a Percentage of Total Admissions to State and Private Psychiatric Hospitals

	1950	*1960*	*1967*
With psychoses[a]			
State			
Men	8.83	12.14	16.03
Women	2.10	2.96	4.23
Private			
Men	8.82	12.00	14.89
Women	1.93	3.32	2.95
Without psychoses[b]			
State			
Men	48.73	42.87	40.26
Women	17.34	13.66	13.15
Private			
Men	61.47	29.90	14.94
Women	19.35	8.45	4.33

Note: Reprinted with permission of authors from Estes and Heinemann, 1977.
[a] Acute and chronic brain syndrome with alcoholism.
[b] Alcohol addiction.

costly than most surveys and is well adapted for establishing treatment facility utilization rates and developing estimates for future treatment slot needs. On the other hand, subjects are rarely queried in enough depth to determine whether the alcohol-related problem in fact represents alcoholism. The method further suffers from the vicissitudes of insurance coverage, where many alcohol-related diagnoses may not even be mentioned in official records so that the patients will be covered by their insurance companies, and the difficulty whereby only a minority of alcoholics seek hospitalization and actually receive a diagnosis. In one study only 21 of 165 alcohol-related death victims had been treated by agencies (Gunderson & Schuckit, 1975; Gorwitz, 1970). Finally many administrative decisions relating to hospital bed occupancy and the attitudes of personnel toward alcoholics may severely affect how one program may appear to have different rates of "alcoholism" admissions than another, even though the populations served may have identical rates of problems (Stanton, 1977).

TABLE 8
Examples of Results of Comparison of Treatment Population Analysis Findings

	Type of facility		% With alcohol disorder[a]	
Authors	*General medical*	*Psychiatric*	*Men*	*Women*
Tamayo, Feldman	X		—	—
Barcha, Steward, Guse	X		34.8	8.7
Moore	X		18.0	5.5
Moore		X	50.0	22.0

Note: Reprinted with permission of authors from Estes and Heinemann, 1977.
[a]This classification does not imply uniform diagnostic criteria for determining the problem level in a facility. Rather, it indicates a range of alcohol and alcohol-related disorders diagnosed in a sample of facilities. Both case record data and patient interview data are represented.

Some Relevant Examples

Tables 7 and 8 outline the type of information that can be generated through rate-under-treatment studies. It can be seen there is a potential variation between different types of facilities, differences which might reflect study methods, administrative practices, or actual prevalence rates. In general, the highest rate of alcohol-related problems, or perhaps alcoholism, is obtained when either interviews or short alcohol-related questionnaires such as MAST are used on general medical or surgical wards where as many as 50% of males and 20% of females may qualify for a diagnosis of alcoholism (Moore, 1972), reflecting the increased rate of many serious medical problems in alcoholics (Schuckit, 1984). These latter findings of prevalence of disorder are markedly different from the first admission rates noted in table 7, reflecting the fact that the incidence of a chronic disorder such as alcoholism as measured by first admission rates (where each case is only counted once) will be markedly lower than the prevalence; cases that develop tend to remain within the population for an extended period of time. In addition, admission to a psychiatric hospital with an alcohol-related diagnosis would be expected to occur much less often than admission to a general medical or surgical facility for an alcohol-related physiological problem. Once again it becomes apparent that two studies with markedly different results may both be correct, with the answers reflecting different methodologic approaches and definitions, even when one standardizes for the general approach such as rate under treatment.

One other rate-under-treatment approach is worth mentioning. As a mixture of morbidity data and rate under treatment, there a number of nationally coordinated data bases including the Drug and Alcohol Warning Network (DAWN) and the Automated Management Information System (AMIS). Through these approaches, emergency room or alcohol- and drug-related treatment programs are required to periodically fill out a report which is then included in national statistics. While this information is readily available and similar methodologies are supposedly being used in different locales, not enough in-depth information is generated to be certain that specific criteria for alcoholism or drug abuse are met. Implementation of the guidelines tends to be quite different within different locales, and this approach suffers from the same difficulties involving potential insurance coverage as is seen for other rate-under-treatment approaches (Edwards, 1973).

Survey Methods

Definition

In the survey method, data are gathered on drinking practices, alcohol-related problems, or alcoholism by direct contact with subjects, usually in the general population. The results of this investigation, as much or more than others, depend on the specific instrument (e.g., questionnaire versus structured, semi-structured or unstructured interview), sampling techniques (e.g., manner of random or stratified random sampling), whether one or multiple informants are used for each household (Smart & Liban, 1982), definitions of problems of alcoholism (Weissman et al.,1980), or whether individuals are contacted in person or by phone. Sociodemographic data are important as the rate of alcohol-related problems is probably highest in the 18–25-year-old group, while alcoholism is elevated in the 35–50 year olds. Also the occurrence of difficulties or alcoholism decreases slightly with increasing socioeconomic strata

(Rubington, 1972). The rate of alcohol-related difficulties and alcoholism is probably higher in men than women (Schuckit & Morrissey, 1976; Humphrey et al., 1983), and there are marked differences in drinking practices with different areas of the country (Cahalan & Cisin, 1968) as well as fluctuations within the time of year (Johnson, 1973). In evaluating such investigations one must know whether the investigator is attempting to study drinking practices, drinking problems, or alcoholism (Wechsler et al., 1978; Haglund & Schuckit, 1982).

Assets and Liabilities

This approach is potentially the most thorough of the research methodologies, if the study is done carefully. Because more detailed information can be gathered, it also has the greatest chance of revealing subtle nuances of differences between population subgroups. On the other hand, to be effective these complex studies must be done meticulously and therefore have the highest cost of any of the alcohol epidemiology approaches. One inherent problem is that most of these investigations are done at one point in time (cross-sectionally) and may obliterate the very important fluctuations in drinking practices and problems that occur within any individual over time as well as ignore the possibility of spontaneous remission of alcoholism (Fillmore, 1974; Cahalan & Cisin, 1968; Smart, 1975/1976; Ludwig, 1972). However, repeated cross sectional evaluations with similar samples over time can help overcome some of these problems (Fitzgerald & Mulford, 1981).

Some Relevant Examples

Table 9 outlines a sample of surveys carried out in different locales between 1965 and 1978. This table directly points out how the rate of problems varies with differing methodologies. For example, Clark's study in 1960 would have related a rate of 0.3%–2% for any one specific problem related to alcohol; this increases to a rate of 6.2% if any individual qualifies for a label based on having had difficulty in any one of multiple areas; and rises up to 27% if very "loose" criteria for alcohol-related difficulties are invoked. Some of the studies relate prevalence of those individuals fulfilling relatively strict criteria for alcohol-

TABLE 9
Examples of Results from Alcohol Problems and Alcoholism Surveys

			Rate/1000		
Source	*Year*	*Subject & definition*	*Male*	*Female*	*Both*
Marconi	1955	Santiago, Chili	83	6	
Essen Moller	1956	Rural Sweden	13.5	30	
Manis-Hunt	1957	Small Town, USA (lifetime problem)			43
Bruun	1960	Finland (drunken driver)	114		
Mulford	1960	Iowa (1^+ problem)			116
Mulford	1962	Iowa (1^+ problem)			67
Mulford	1964	National Survey (1^+ problem)			100
Bailey	1965	NY Urban (problems)			19
Mulford	1966	Chicago Suburb (problem)			50
Clark	1966	San Francisco (problem)			62
Haberman	1967	NYC (problem)			62
Cahalan	1968	NYC (problem)	130	50	
Kaij	1970	Sweden (problem)	130		
Chalke	1971	?	70		
Edwards	1972	London suburb (problem)	64	6	
Hagnell	1972	? (problem)	100		
Edwards	1973	London suburb (problem)	61	8	
Mulford	1974	Psychiatric patients (CAGE)	390	150	
Favazza	1977	USA students (MAST)	280	150	
Saunders	1978	Scotland, Wales (problem)	52	5	
Winokur	1978	Medical surgical patients (problems)	50	4	

ism, while others (e.g., Chalke, 1976) relate looser problem areas such as "compulsive drinkers," etc., and deal with problems in a population at one given time. Still others relate the lifetime prevalence of ever having experienced problems. Differences occur even when similar criteria are used. For example Mulford (1963) related a 6.7% rate of individuals reporting at least one or more interpersonal alcohol-related problems, while similar methodologies carried out in 1960 related a rate of 11.6%. These large differences are much more likely to reflect methodological issues rather than an actual halving of the rate of alcoholism. Thus the best one can ask for from the various alcoholic surveys are "ballpark figures" of the actual rate of the difficulty and some more solid estimates of differences be-

TABLE 10
An Example of Survey and Social Indicator Comparisons

Authors	*Survey sample (U.S.)*	*Problem drinkers, initial survey (%)*	*Change at followup (%)*	*Jellinek rate (%)*[a]	*Difference (%)*[b]
Bailey; Haberman; Alksne	Urban	1.9	—	5.5	+3.6
Manis; Hunt	Urban	4.3	—	2.4	−1.9
Mulford; Wilson	Urban	5.0	—	5.1	+0.1
Clark	Urban	6.2	—	6.6	+0.4
Haberman; Scheinberg	Urban	6.2	—	5.5	−0.7
Mulford; Miller	Statewide	11.6	−4.0	2.8	−8.8
Cahalan	National	9.5	+3.0	4.2	−5.3
Mulford	National	10.0	—	4.2	−5.8

Note: Reprinted with permission of authors from Estes and Heinemann, 1977.
[a]As calculated for state and national totals.
[b]Percentage of increase or decrease in the rate attributable to the Jellinek formula.

tween various population subgroups by sex and socioeconomic strata and race when the same methodology is used.

So, it is very difficult to scan these studies and come up with a consensus of the actual rate of alcohol related problems or alcoholism. It is possible, however, to conclude that regardless of methodologic constraints, the rate of alcohol-related problems or alcoholism appears to be a good deal higher in men than women, and that the rate of difficulties is relatively high, especially for men where it may approach 10% or more.

A Comparison of Different Methods

With the great amount of variability within research approaches, it is not surprising to note that there are divergent results when different basic approaches are used. Table 10 represents a brief overview of a comparison between at least two methodologies, the survey and the Jellinek formula.

Such a summary of survey findings is complicated by the diversity of methods and study samples in the published literature. The two methodologies reported here yield similar results for urban areas, but state and national comparisons diverge. This may reflect the variations in accuracy of statewide or national mortality reports on which the Jellinek formula depends. Using all available data, when review is limited to groups with severe problems, survey findings indicate a 2%–4% rate of serious alcohol-related impairment with a four to one ratio of men to women problem drinkers in the total population. Certain subgroups show a much higher problem level (e.g., college samples or military groups) but probably lower rates of alcoholism (Haglund & Schuckit, 1982). Direct inferences regarding the treatment needs of these heavy drinkers cannot be made until a further examination of a typical course of their illness has been undertaken and the impact of situational factors is understood.

Another comparison of different methodologies was reported by Edwards et al. (1973) where survey and key informant results were compared. Using agency personnel the probable rate of alcoholism is 8.6 per thousand for men age 16 or over with comparable rates for women of 1.3 and an overall rate of 4.7 per thousand. Using a survey (thus not depending solely upon those individuals known to specific agencies in the same area), the results are 61.3 per thousand for men and 7.7 for women with an overall rate of 31.3 per thousand. The different results, however, may cover different individuals as some may be known to key informants, others may only be known through public agencies, and yet others may have only been picked up through treatment samples. Perhaps one approach to the dilemma of trying to determine which finding is most relevant may be to carry out multiple approaches within any one specific area, keeping track of the names of the individuals involved so that redundancy can be eliminated.

Summary

I have briefly presented a number of factors that must be addressed in order to carry out careful epidemiologic research into drinking practices, alcohol-related problems, or alcoholism. Distinctions between various approaches, the definition of the problem, sample selection procedures, data analytic techniques, etc. can greatly affect results and are important no matter what the research protocol.

The four basic protocols that can be used in alcohol-related epidemiologic research include surveys of key informants, social indicators, establishing the rate of individuals under treatment, and various survey techniques. Each of these has its own assets and liabilities with greater ease or less cost generally resulting in a lowered level of probable validity. Nonetheless, the more rapid or less expensive approaches can be of great importance when the question being asked relates to opinions of individuals in the field or to bed utilization practices.

In the final analysis it is not possible to give a simple statistic about the rate of drinking, alcohol-related problems, or alcoholism. Rough "ballpark" figures may be misleading about different population subgroups or different areas of the country. The best "guesstimate" would include a rate of drinking for the vast majority of the population, transient alcohol-related problems in a significant minority, perhaps as high as 40%, and probably alcoholism in 5%-10% of men and 1%-5% of women.

I hope the reader will now be able to approach each of the following chapters in this monograph carefully. It will be important to weigh as many of the factors outlined in this chapter as possible to put the research findings into perspective.

References

American Psychiatric Association: Conference and Third Parties Task Force Report 9, June 1975.

Alfidi, K.J. (1971). Informed consent, a study of patient reaction. *J.A.M.A.* 216:1325–1329.

Andreano, R.L. & Li, J.Y. (1974). Death rates from liver cirrhosis in alcohol monopoly and free-market states. *Quart. J. Stud. Alc.* 35:649–654.

Armor, D.J., Polich, J.M. & Stambul, H.B. (1976). Alcoholism and treatment. Prepared for the National Institute on Alcohol Abuse and Alcoholism, Santa Monica, CA: Rand Corp.

Bailey, M.B., Haberman, P.W. & Alksne, H. (1965). The epidemiology of alcoholism in an urban residential area. *Quart. J. Stud. Alc.* 26:19–40.

Barcha, R., Stewart, M.A., Guze, S.B. (1968). The prevalence of alcoholism among general hospital ward patients. *Am. J. Psychiat.* 125:681–684.

Beigel, A., Hunter, E.J., Tamerin, J.S., Chapin, E.H. & Lowery, M.J. (1974). Planning for the development of comprehensive community alcoholism services: I. The prevalence survey. *Am. J. Psychiat.* 131:1112–1121.

Berger, P.M. & Stallones R.A. (1977). Legal liability and epidemiologic research. *Am. J. Epidemiol.* 106:177–183.

Brady, J.P., Foulks, E.T., Childress, A.R. & Pertschuk, M. (1982). The Michigan alcoholism screening test as a survey instrument. *J. Operat. Psychiat.* 13:27–31.

Brody, E.B. (1975). The freedom of medical information. *J.A.M.A.* 233:145–146.

Cahalan, D. (1970). Problem drinkers; a national survey. San Francisco: Jossey-Bass.

Cahalan, D. (1972). Problem drinking among American men aged 21–59. Paper presented at the 30th International Congress on Alcoholism and Drug Dependence, Amsterdam.

Cahalan, D. & Cisin, I.H. (1968). American drinking practices: summary of findings from a national probability sample. I. Extent of drinking by population subgroups. *Quart. J. Stud. Alc.* 29:130–151.

Cardon, P.V., Dommel, F.W. & Trumble, R.R. (1976). Injuries to research subjects. A survey of investigators. *New Eng. J. Med.* 295: 650–654.

Celentano, D.D. & McQueen, D.V. (1978a). Reliability and validity of estimators of alcoholism prevalence. *J. Stud. Alc.* 39:869–878.

Celentano, D.D. & McQueen, D.V. (1978b). Comparison of alcoholism prevalence rates obtained by survey and indirect estimators. *J. Stud. Alc.* 39:420–424.

Chalke, H.D. (1976). Alcohol and history. *J. Alcoholism* 11:128–149.

Chalkey, D.T. (1977). Federal constraints: earned or unearned? *Am. J. Psychiat.* 134:911–913

Clark, J.P. & Tifft, L.L. (1966). Polygraph and interview validation of self-reported deviant behavior. *Am. Soc. Rev.* 3:516–523.

Clark, W. (1966). Operational definitions of drinking problems and associated prevalence rates. *Quart. J. Stud. Alc.* 27:648–668.

Cleary, P.D. (1979). A standardized estimator of the prevalence of alcoholism based on mortality data. *J. Stud. Alc.* 40:408–418.

Culliton, J.B. (1976). Confidentiality: court declares researcher can protect sources. *Science* 193:467–469.

Curran, W.J. (1977). Confidentiality of NIH research-project records. *New Engl. J. Med.* 296:1273–1274.

Curran, W.J. (1978). Legal liability in clinical investigations. *New Engl. J. Med.* 298:778–779.

Davies, D.L. (1962). Normal drinking in recovered alcohol addicts. *Quart. J. Stud. Alc.* 23:94–104.

DeFleur, L.B. (1975). Biasing influences on drug arrest records: implications for deviance research. *Am. Soc. Rev.* 40:88–103.

deLint, J. & Schmidt, W. (1968). The distribution of alcohol consumption in Ontario. *Quart. J. Stud. Alc.* 29:968–973.

deLint, J. & Schmidt, W. (1971). The epidemiology of alcoholism. In *Biological Basis of Alcoholism*, ed. Y. Israel. New York: Wiley & Sons, Inc.

deLint, J. & Schmidt, W. (1971). Consumption averages and alcoholism prevalence: a brief review of epidemiological investigations. *Br. J. Addict.* 66:97–107.

Dickson, P. (1978). *The Official Rules,* New York: Dell Publishing Co., Inc.,

Douglass, R.L. (1973). A strategy to measure the prevalence of late symptomatic alcoholism. *HITLAB Rep.* 3:7–13.

Edwards, G., Hawker, A., Hensman, C., Peto, J. & Williamson, V. (1973). Alcoholics known or unknown to agencies:epidemiological studies in a London suburb. *Br. J. Psych.* 123:169–183.

Edwards, G. (1973). Epidemiology applied to alcoholism. A review and an examination of purposes. *Quart. J. Stud. Alc.* 34:28–56.

Efron, V., Keller, M. & Gurioli, C. (1974). *Statistics on Consumption of Alcohol and on Alcoholism.* New Brunswick, NJ: Rutgers Center of Alcohol Studies.

Estes, N. & Heinemann, E. (1977). *Alcoholism: Development, Consequences and Intervention.* St. Louis: C.V. Mosby.

Favazza, A.R. & Cannell, B. (1977). Screening for alcoholism among college students. *Am. J. Psychiat.* 134:1414–1416.

Fillmore, K.M. (1974). Drinking and problem drinking in early adulthood and middle age. An exploratory 20-year follow-up study. *Quart. J. Stud. Alc.* 35:819–840.

Fitzgerald, J.L. & Mulford, H.A. (1981). The prevalence and extent of drinking in Iowa, 1979. *J. Stud. Alc.* 42:38–47.

Furst, D.J. & Beckman, L. (1979). Mortality and consumption data: stability of estimates for small areas. Paper presented to Alcohol and Drug Problem Association Annual Meeting.

Gibbons, R.J. (1954). Alcoholism in Ontario: a survey of an Ontario county. *Quart. J. Stud. Alc.* 15:47–52.

Goodwin, D.W. & Guze, S.B. (1984). *Psychiatric Diagnosis.* New York: Oxford University Press.

Gordis, L. & Gold, E. (1980). Privacy, confidentiality, and the use of medical records in research. *Science* 207:153–156.

Gorwitz, K. (1970). Some epidemiological data on alcoholism in Maryland: based on admissions of psychiatric facilities. *Quart. J. Stud. Alc.* 31:423–443.

Gunderson, E.K.E. & Schuckit, M.A. (1975). Hospitalization rates for alcoholism in the Navy and Marine Corps. *Dis. Nerv. Sys.* 36:681–684.

Guze, S.B. & Goodwin, D.W. (1972). Consistency of drinking history and diagnosis of alcoholism *Quart. J. Stud. Alc.* 33:111–116.

Haglund, R.M. & Schuckit, M.A. (1982). The epidemiology of alcoholism. In: *Alcoholism: Development, Consequences and Intvervention,* ed. N. Estes & E. Heinemann. St. Louis: C.V. Mosby.

Hagnell, O. & Tunving, K. (1972). Prevalence and nature of alcoholism in a total population. *Soc. Psychiat.* 7:190–201.

Hodgson, H.J.F. & Thompson, R.P.H. (1976). Cirrhosis in South London. *Lancet* 2:118–121.

Hartford, T.C. (1976). A national study of adolescent drinking, behavior, attitudes and correlates. *J. Stud. Alc.* 37:1747–1750.

Hartford, T.C. (1976). Alcohol consumption in bars: validation of self-reports against observed behavior. *Drinking and Drug Practices Surveyer II.*

Humphrey, J.A., Stephens, V. & Allen, D.F. (1983). Race, sex, marihuana use and alcohol intoxication in college students. *J. Stud. Alc.* 44:733–738.

Ingelfinger, F.J. (1977). Ethics of human experimentation defined by a national commission. *New Eng. J. Med.* 296:44–45.

Ispen, J., Moore, M. & Alexander, L. (1952). Prevalence of alcoholism in the population and among suicides and accidents from poisoning. Massachusetts, 1938–1948. *Quart. J. Stud. Alc.* 13:204.

Jellinek, E.M. (1959). Estimating the prevalence of alcoholism: modified values in the Jellinek Formula and an alternative approach. *Quart. J. Stud. Alc.* 20:261.

Jellinek, E.M. & Keller, M. (1952). Rates of alcoholism in the United States of America, 1940–1948. *Quart. J. Stud. Alc.* 13:49–59.

Johnson, B.D. (1973). *Marijuana users and drug subcultures.* New York: Wiley.

Kaij, L. (1960). *Alcoholism in twins.* Stockholm: Almquist and Wicksell.

Kaij, L. (1970). Biases in a Swedish social register of alcoholics. *Soc. Psychiat.* 5:216-218.

Kandel, D.B. (1978). Convergencies in prospective longitudinal surveys of drug use in normal populations. In: *Longitudinal Research on Drug Use*, ed. D.B. Kandel. New York: Holsted Press.

Keller, M. (1975). Problems of epidemiology in alcohol problems. *J. Stud. Alc.* 36:1442–1451.

Keller, M. & Efron, V. (1958). The rate of alcoholism in the U.S.A., 1954–1956. *Quart. J. Alc.* 19:316–319.

King, F.W. (1970) Anonymous versus identifiable questionnaires in drug usages surveys. *Am. Psychol.* 25:982–985.

Klatsky, A.L., Friedman, G.D. & Siegelaub, A.B. (1981). Alcohol and mortality (A ten-year Kaiser-Permanente experience). *Ann. Intern. Med.* 95:139–145.

Klatsky, A.L., Siegelaub, A.B., Landy, C. & Friedman, G.D. (1983). Racial patterns of alcoholic beverage use. *Alc: Clin. Exp. Res.* 7:372–377.

Knupfer, G. (1967). The epidemiology of problem drinking. *Am. J. Public Health Nation's Health* 57:973–986.

Kolonel, L.N., Hirohata, T. & Nomura A.M.Y. (1977). Adequacy of survey data collected from substitute respondents. *Am. J. Epidemiol.* 106:476–486.

Lasagna, L. & von Felsinger, J.M. (1954). The volunteer in research. *Science* 120:359–361.

Levy, P.S. (1978). Small area estimation-synthetic and other procedures, 1968–1978. Paper presented at NIDA/NCHS Workshop on Synthetic Estimates for Small Areas, Princeton, New Jersey.

Ludwig, A.M. (1972). On and off the wagon. *Quart. J. Stud. Alc.* 33:91–96.

MacMahon, B. & Pugh, T.F. (1970). *Epidemiology: Principles and Methods.* Boston: Little, Brown & Co.

Maddux, J.F. & Desmond, D.P. (1975). Reliability and validity of information from chronic heroin users. *J. Psychiat. Res.* 12:87–95.

McCabe, M.S. (1977). Human rights and interviews. *Arch. Gen. Psychiat.* 34:1369–1371.

Mendelson, J.H. & Mello, H.K. (eds.) (1979). *Diagnosis and Treatment of Alcoholism.* New York: McGraw-Hill.

Meyer, R.E. (1977). Subjects' rights, freedom of inquiry, and the future of research in the addictions. *Am. J. Psychiat.* 134:899–903.

McCrady, B.S., Paolino, T.J. & Longabaugh, R. (1978) Correspondence between reports of problem drinkers and spouses on drinking behavior and impairment. *J. Stud. Alc.* 39:1252–1257.

Modell, W. (1960). The ethical obligations to the nonsubject. *Clin. Pharm. Ther.* 1:137–140.

Moore, M.H. & Gerstein, D.R. (1981). *Alcohol and Public Policy: Beyond the Shadow of Prohibition.* Washington, D.C.: National Academy Press. pp. 61–78.

Moore, R.A. (1971). Alcoholism treatment in private psychiatric hospitals; a natural survey. *Quart. J. Stud. Alc.* 32:1083–1085.

Moore, R.A. (1971). The prevalence of alcoholism in a community general hospital. *Am J. Psychiat.* 128:638–639.

Moore, R.A. (1972). The diagnosis of alcoholism in a psychiatric hospital: a trial of the Michigan Alcoholism Screening Test (MAST). *Am. J. Psychiat.* 128:1565–1569.

Mulford, H.A. & Miller, D.E. (1963). The prevalence and extent of drinking in Iowa, 1961: a replication and an evaluation of methods. *Quart. J. Stud. Alc.* 24:39.

Nilsson, T. & Svensson, P.G. (1971). The alcohol habits and alcohol attitudes of the Swedish people. In: *Svenska Folkets Alkoholvanor* (*Alcohol Habits of the Swedish People*). Stockholm: Statens Offentliga Utredningar, Finansdeparlementet.

Parker, D.A. & Harman, M.S. (1977). The distribution of consumption model of prevention: a critical assessment. Prepared for the NIAAA symposium on normative approaches to prevention at Coronado, CA, April.

Pernanen, K. (1974). Validity of survey data on alcohol use. In: *Research*

Advances in Alcohol and Drug Problems, Vol. 1, ed. R.J. Gibbens, Y. Israel, H. Kalant, R.E. Popham, W. Schmidt, & R.G. Smart. New York: Wiley and Sons.

Poikolainen, K. (1980). Increase in alcohol-related hospitalizations in Finland 1969–1975. *Brit. J. Addict.* 75:281–291.

Popham, R.E. (1970). Indirect methods of alcoholism prevalence estimation: a critical evaluation. In: *Alcohol and Alcoholism,* ed. R.E. Popham. University of Toronto Press.

Rachal, J.V., Hubbard, R.L., Williams, J.R. and Tuchfield, B.S. (1976). Drinking levels and problem drinking among junior and senior high-school students. *J. Stud. Alc.* 37:1751–1761.

Reichler, B.D., Clement, J.L. & Dunner, D.L. (1983). Chart review of alcohol problems in adolescent psychiatric patients in an emergency room. *J. Clin. Psychiat.* 44:338–339.

Reiss, D. (1977). Freedom of inquiry and subjects' rights: an introduction. *Am. J. Psychiat.* 134:891–892.

Rimmer, J. & Chambers, D.S. (1971). Alcoholism II. Influence of sex, socioeconomic status and race. *Quart. J. Stud. Alc.* 32:942–952.

Rimmer, J., Pitts, F.N., Reich, T. & Winokur, G. (1971). *Quart. J. Stud. Alc.* 32:942–952.

Rimmer, J., Riech, T. & Winokur, G. (1972). Alcoholism V. Diagnosis and clinical variation among alcoholics. *Quart. J. Stud. Alc.* 32: 658–666.

Robins, L.N. & Braroe, N.W. (1964). The lay interviewer in psychiatric research. *J. Nerv. Ment. Dist.* 138:70–78.

Rubington, E. (1972). The hidden alcoholic. *Quart. J. Stud. Alc.* 33: 667–683.

Saghir, M.T. (1971). A comparison of some aspects of structured and unstructured psychiatric interviews. *Am. J. Psychiat.* 128:180–184.

Schmidt, W. & Popham, R.E. (1978). The single distribution theory of alcohol consumption. *J. Stud. Alc.* 39:400–419.

Schmidt, W. & deLint, J. (1970). Estimating the prevalence of alcoholism from alcohol consumption and mortality data. *Quart. J. Stud. Alc.* 31:957–964.

Schuckit, M.A. (1984). Alcoholism and affective disorder: diagnostic confusion. In: *Alcoholism and Depression,* ed. D.W. Goodwin. New York: Spectrum Press.

Schuckit, M.A. (1978). The disease alcoholism. *Postgrad. Med.* 64:78–84.

Schuckit, M.A. (1979). *Drug and Alcohol Abuse.* New York: Plenum Medical Book Co.

Schuckit, M.A. & Gunderson, E.K.E. (1974). Deaths among young alcoholics in the U.S. Naval Service. *Quart. J. Stud. Alc.* 35:856–862.

Schuckit, M.A. & Haglund, R.M. (1977). An overview of the etiological theories on alcoholism. In: *Alcoholism: Development, Consequences and Interventions*, ed. N.J. Estes, & M.E. Heinemann. St. Louis, Mosby Co.

Schuckit, M.A. & Morrissey, E.R. (1976). Alcoholism in women: some clinical and social perspectives with an emphasis on possible subtypes. In: *Alcoholism Problems in Women & Children*, ed. M. Greenblatt, & M.A. Schuckit. New York: Grune & Stratton, Inc.

Schuckit, M.A. & Pastor, P.A. (1979). Alcohol-related psychopathology in the aged. In: *Psychopathology in the Aging*, ed. O.J. Kaplan. New York: Academic Press.

Smart, R.G. (1975/76). Spontaneous recovery in alcoholics: a review and analysis of the available research. *Drug Alc. Depend.* 1:277–285.

Smart, R.G. & Liban, C.B. (1982). Alcohol consumption as estimated by the informant method: A household survey and sales data. *J. Stud. Alc.* 43:1020–1027.

Sobell, L., Maisto, S.A., Sobel, M.B. & Cooper, A.M. (1979). Reliability of alcohol abusers' self-reports of drinking behavior. *Behav. Res. Ther.* 17:157–160.

Sobell, L.C. & Sobell, M.B. (1975). Outpatient alcoholics give valid self-reports. *J. Nerv. Ment. Dis.* 161:32–42.

Sobell, L.C. & Sobell, M.B. (1973). Validity of self-reports in three populations of alcoholics. *J. Consult. Clin. Psychol.* 46:901–907.

Sobell, M.B., Sobell, L.C. & Samuels, F.H. (1974) Validity of self-reports of alcohol-related arrests by alcoholics. *Quart. J. Stud. Alc.* 35:276–280.

Sobell, M.B., Sobell, L.C. & VanderSpek, R. (1979). Relationships among clinical judgment, self-report, and breath-analysis measures of intoxication in alcoholics. *J. Consult. Clin. Psychol.* 47:204–206.

Solomon, J., Vanga, N., Morgan, J.P. & Joseph, P. (1980). Emergency-room physicians' recognition of alcohol misuse. *J. Stud. Alc.* 41: 583–586.

Spingarn, N.D. (1974). *Confidentiality*, Report of the Conference on Confidentiality of Health Records, Key Biscayne, Florida, American Psychiatric Association.

Stanton, M.D. (1977). Drug use surveys' method and madness. *Int. J. Addict.* 12:95–119.

Steinberg, J., ed. (1979). *Synthetic Estimates for Small Area.* NIDA Research Monograph 24, Rockville, MD: National Institute on Drug Abuse.

Tamayo, M.B. & Feldman, D.J. (1975). Incidence of alcoholism in hospital patients. *Soc. Work* 24:89–91.

Victor, M. (1966). Treatment of alcoholic intoxication and the withdrawal syndrome. *Psychosomatic Med* 28:636–649.

Walsh, B.M. & Walsh, D. (1973). Validity of indices on alcoholism. *Br. J. Prev. Doc. Med.* 27:18–26.

Wechsler, H., Demone, H.W. & Gottlieb, N. (1978). Drinking patterns of greater Boston adults. Subgroup differences on the QEV index. *J. Stud. Alc.* 39:1158–1166.

Weissman, M.M., Meyers, K. & Harding, P. (1980). Prevalence and psychiatric heterogeneity of alcoholism in a U.S. urban community. *J. Stud. Alc.* 41:672–681.

Winokur, G. & Tsuang, M.T. (1978). Expectancy of alcoholism in a midwestern population, *J. Stud. Alc.* 39:1964–1967.

Zax, M., Garner, E.A. & Hart, W.T. (1967). A survey of the prevalence of alcoholism in Monroe County, N.Y., 1961. *Quart. J. Stud. Alc.* 28:316–327.

Chapter 2

Sample Surveys and the Epidemiology of Alcoholism

J. MICHAEL POLICH
CHARLES T. KAELBER

The epidemiology of alcoholism can accomplish two main objectives. First, it can describe the distribution of alcoholism and alcohol abuse in the general population. Second, it can illuminate the causal process by which alcohol abuse develops. At present, survey research has achieved only the first of these two aims: it has compiled a descriptive inventory of the types of alcohol abuse and their correlates, without much exploration of developmental processes. Nonetheless, the results of survey research to date contain important implications for understanding the nature of alcohol-related disorders.

In this paper we seek to bring together the most important survey research on alcoholism and alcohol-related problems in the United States. To maximize our ability to generalize, we concentrate on research that has used national probability samples.[1] Because definitional questions present so many problems in this field, we begin by considering the definitions and methods of measurement found in the literature, followed by a discussion of the methodologic factors that affect survey accuracy. We then review the principal findings of major national surveys between 1964 and 1982. Finally, we suggest directions that could aid future research in moving beyond description to specify the causal factors in the development of alcohol-related disorders.

1. Probability samples are composed of respondents who have been selected by strict random methods to reflect the characteristics of the entire nation, so that generalizations to the national population are possible with known limits of error.

Defining Alcoholism and Alcohol-Related Problems

Definitional questions are very important in the study of alcoholism. This is because many diverse problems can be caused by drinking and because the lines between "problem" and "nonproblem" behavior are indistinct. Survey research has described this diversity in detail, and has shown that alcohol-related problems encompass many phenomena other than the severe disorders seen in alcoholism clinics.

Types of Alcohol Abuse

Broadly speaking, studies of alcohol abuse have identified three types of alcohol-related problems (Knupfer, 1967): (1) *dependence on alcohol*, a condition in which the individual experiences a "need" for alcohol that impairs his ability or desire to regulate drinking; (2) *excessive consumption of alcohol*, meaning intake of a volume deemed unsafe or "deviant"; and (3) *adverse consequences of drinking*—any effects of alcohol that harm the individual. Traditional theories of alcoholism focus on alcohol dependence or addiction. Survey studies, in contrast, usually enumerate cases of excessive consumption or adverse consequences of drinking, paying little attention to dependence. These differences in perspective, termed the "two worlds of alcohol problems" by Room (1977), reflect the wide gap between the features of alcoholism as portrayed in clinical accounts and the picture of alcohol-related problems built up by surveys of the general population.

Dependence and loss of control

Many discussions of alcoholism implicitly or explicitly restrict attention to alcohol dependence, a severe condition often thought to be marked by "loss of control." In one of the most widely known formulations, alcoholism is defined as a disease manifested by the patient's tendency to lose control of drinking (Keller, 1962). Loss of control does not mean "uncontrolled" or "undisciplined" drinking (as, for instance, in an individual who deliberately drinks to intoxication). Rather, loss of control refers to the imputed inability of the individual to refrain from drinking despite his volition. As outlined by Jellinek (1960), an addicted alcoholic may develop a need for alcohol associated with physiologic abnormalities such as changes in metabolism, increased tolerance, and withdrawal symptoms (which appear when alcohol consumption is interrupted). According to this view, the state of addiction creates an impulse to drink that is difficult or impossible to resist. Keller (1972) has argued that the disease concept of alcoholism should include the alcoholic's inability to abstain, in addition to his inability to stop drinking, once started.

Loss of control is a particularly difficult concept to operationalize (Clark & Cahalan, 1976). In the first place, it cannot be observed unless the individual attempts to limit his drinking. Yet measuring the attempt to control drinking, independently of the actual drinking behavior, is extremely difficult. Many studies accept the subject's self-report of loss of control. However, such a measure is inherently subjective, as it requires that the respondent assess his state of mind as well as his behavior, and it seems especially likely to be distorted by denial.

For such reasons, many empirical studies have employed alternative indicators of alcoholism that are linked to the loss of control theory. An inventory of such indicators was incorporated by Jellinek (1946) in his classic "Grapevine" study, an analysis of symptoms retrospectively reported in questionnaires filled out by members of Alcoholics Anonymous. The results were used as the basis for Jellinek's widely cited theory of the progressive stages of alcoholic symptoms (1952). Among the more prominent symptoms in that progression were blackouts, loss of control, morning drinking, and binges; but the list ranged much more widely, including such events as secretive drinking, gulping drinks, preoccupation with alcohol, and even such nonspecific indicators as aggression, anxiety, and "ethical deterioration."

Many specific aspects of the Jellinek model have proven inconsistent with empirical data (Ludwig & Wikler, 1974; Lloyd & Salzberg, 1975), but some recent authors continue to emphasize dependence as a central element of alcoholism. An official formulation was set forth by an expert World Health Organization committee on alcohol-related disabilities (Edwards et al., 1977). The committee found that the "alcohol dependence syndrome" constitutes a core entity that accounts for the persistence of damaging drinking in many persons affected by alcohol. It acknowledged, however, that many other persons experience alcohol-related problems (or "disabilities") without being dependent.

Excessive consumption and other alcohol-related problems

Of course, less restrictive definitions of alcoholism have also been proposed. An early definition of the World Health Organization (1952) identified alcoholics as "those excessive drinkers whose dependence upon alcohol has attained such a degree that it shows a noticeable mental disturbance or an interference with their bodily and mental health, their interpersonal relations, and their smooth social and economic functioning." Thus alcoholism by that definition rested not only on dependence but also on excessive drinking and its adverse effects. Davies (1976) has reiterated the view that alcoholism may be recognized either by dependence or by the harm drinking causes. In practice, physicians faced with the problem of diagnosing alcoholism use a broad array of signals, not just dependence symptoms (Filstead et al., 1976), as reflected in the diagnostic guidelines of the National Council on Alcoholism (1972). However, there are strong reasons to distinguish dependence from other forms of self-destructive drinking. In particular, many individuals suffer serious adverse effects of drinking without experiencing loss of control (Clark, 1976).

For these reasons, much empirical research has emphasized "alcohol-related problems" rather than the syndrome of alcohol addiction. Survey samples have never found more than a minute proportion of respondents who possess the conjunction of symptomatology, physical pathology, and social impairment characteristic of clinical alcohol addiction. Instead, surveys encounter many drinkers who experience serious adverse consequences of drinking but lack signs of dependence. For example, Mulford & Miller (1960c) measured a broad range of "troubles due to drinking," including events such as problems with the police, family discord, and absenteeism from work. This type of measurement was greatly elaborated in the work of Cahalan (1970) and his associates (Cahalan & Room, 1974; Clark & Midanik, 1982).

Surveys have also paid considerable attention to the subject's quantity of alcohol consumption, a factor that is not crucial in the loss of control theory. The complexity and variability of alcohol consumption has led to a proliferation of measures, which are by no means standardized (Bowman et al. 1975). All reports agree, however, that only a small fraction of the population approaches consumption levels commonly found in alcoholic patients. Moreover, although there are substantial correlations between alcohol consumption measures and other indicators of alcohol-related problems, only a small proportion of heavy drinkers possess other attributes related to alcoholism (Mulford & Miller, 1960c).

Measurement Methods

With such diverse definitions, the measurement of an "alcohol-related problem" is a very complex undertaking. Tables 1 to 3 summarize the three main types of alcohol-related problems identified in surveys, with examples of measurement procedures employed.

Table 1 represents measures of alcohol dependence or addiction. Generally, such measures are based on the assumption that alcoholism constitutes an underlying condition or "core entity," as outlined by Edwards et al. (1977). The condition is conceived of as a "need," impulse, or drive to consume alcohol, representing either psychological or physical dependence. The most direct method of measurement is to ask the subject such questions as, "Have you been unable to stop drinking?" Most observers would also accept the occurrence of physical dependence symptoms, including withdrawal symptoms or tolerance, as valid indicators of this condition. Some investigators have attempted to measure "psychological dependence" by inquiring about the subject's reasons for drinking. Psychological dependence is then inferred if the subject reports that he frequently drinks to alter his mood rather than for social reasons (Knupfer, 1967; Cahalan, 1970). Finally, many research studies have fallen back on more diffuse "addictive symptoms" derived from those described in the Jellinek model (Mulford & Miller, 1960c; Clark & Midanik, 1982). It is a truism in the field that these measurements are inadequate, and efforts are under way to improve the measurement of alcohol dependence. (Caetano et al., 1978).

Table 2 represents measurement methods directed at alcohol consumption itself, rather than at the condition of dependence.

TABLE 1
Survey Measures Related to Alcohol Dependence

Concept	*Publication*	*Sample items*[a]
Loss of control	Clark (1976); Cahalan & Room (1974); Clark & Midanik (1982)	Tried to cut down or quit drinking, but was unable to do so. Sometimes kept drinking after I'd promised myself not to. Got drunk at inappropriate times or places. Once I started drinking it was difficult for me to stop before I became completely intoxicated. Was afraid I might be an alcoholic.
Withdrawal/alcohol dependence	Polich (1981); Clark & Midanik (1982)	My hands shook a lot the morning after drinking. I had the "shakes" because of drinking. I took a drink the first thing when I got up in the morning. I have taken a strong drink in the morning to get over the effects of last night's drinking.
Symptomatic drinking[b]	Mulford & Miller (1960c); Clark & Midanik (1982)	I worry about not being able to get a drink when I need one. I sneak drinks when no one is looking. I awakened the next day not being able to remember some of the things I had done while I was drinking. I take a few quick ones before going to a party to make sure I have enough. I neglect my regular meals when I am drinking. I drink for the effect of alcohol with little attention to type of beverage or brand name.
Psychological dependence[c]	Cahalan (1970)	I drink when I want to forget everything. I drink because I need it when tense and nervous. A drink is helpful when I am depressed or nervous. A drink helps cheer me up when I am in a bad mood. A drink helps me to forget my worries.

[a]These items are only a subset of those used to measure the concept in most of the studies. For the complete set, see the original publication.
[b]Termed "preoccupation with alcohol" by the authors. Similar scale termed "addictive symptoms" in Knupfer (1967) and "symptomatic drinking" in Cahalan (1970). Combination of these items and withdrawal items termed "alcohol dependence" in Clark and Midanik (1982).
[c]Similar scale termed "coping use of alcohol" in Knupfer (1967); "escape drinking" in Cahalan, Cisin, and Crossley (1969); and "definitions of alcohol" in Mulford and Miller (1960b).

TABLE 2
Indexes of Alcohol Consumption

Index	*Publication*	*Items and index construction procedure*
Total volume	NIAAA (1974)	Two items per beverage: 1. Frequency of drinking, past 30 days. 2. Number of drinks consumed on a "typical" day when the beverage was drunk. Total volume is computed as a continuous variable, multiplying frequency times quantity for each beverage.
Quantity/frequency scale	Clark & Midanik (1982)	Several items per beverage: 1. Frequency of drinking 1–2 drinks, past 12 months. 2. Frequency of drinking 3–4 drinks. 3. Frequency of drinking 5–7 drinks, 8–11 drinks, etc. until highest amount ever consumed is recorded. Total volume is computed as a continuous variable, summing across all three beverages and computing average consumption per month.
Composite quantity/frequency index	Polich & Orvis (1979)	Two components, for separate drinking patterns: 1. Volume resulting from typical drinking days (total volume index, as computed by NIAAA, 1974). 2. Volume resulting from atypical, heavy drinking days (days on which 8 or more drinks were consumed). Components are summed after weighting for the fraction of days representing each pattern.

TABLE 2 (*continued*)

Index	*Publication*	*Items and index construction procedure*
Volume-variability index	Cahalan et al. (1969)	Four items per beverage: 1. Frequency of drinking the beverage. 2. Frequency (proportion of occasions) when 5 or more drinks were consumed. 3. Frequency of consuming 3–4 drinks. 4. Frequency of consuming 1–2 drinks. Two dimensions of the index are computed: 1. Total volume of consumption (low/medium/high). 2. Maximum amount (5 or more drinks/less than 5).
Binge drinking	Cahalan & Room (1974)	Stayed intoxicated several days at a time. Frequency of being "high or tight" for more than 1 day in a row.

The user of such methods is generally interested in alcohol intake as a causal agent that may generate alcohol-related problems. Several descriptive studies of "drinking practices" have focused on this aspect of alcohol-related behavior (e.g., Cahalan & Cisin, 1968a, 1968b; Cahalan et al. 1969). Consumption indexes have also been used by survey researchers to identify subgroups of the general population who are placed at increased risk of developing other problems (Polich & Orvis, 1979).

Alcohol consumption is a complicated phenomenon because of individual variations in frequency of drinking and in the quantity consumed on various drinking occasions. Thus, some heavy drinkers consume a high volume regularly, while others drink moderately on most occasions but sometimes drink to severe intoxication. The former group might be at risk of liver damage or other physical pathology (Lelbach, 1974), while the latter might be at risk of adverse effects of acute intoxication, such as driving accidents or violence. Also, regular heavy drinkers may be more apt to develop alcohol dependence, whereas episodic heavy drinkers may be more likely to "mature out" of their drinking pattern. Limited empirical evidence suggests that the two patterns do have somewhat different correlates (Knupfer, 1966; Polich & Orvis, 1979), but the significance of the patterns as precursors of long-term problems remains at present only an hypothesis to be tested.

Some measurement schemes focus on overall volume of ethanol consumption per calendar period (day, year, etc.), while others classify subjects according to categorical typologies such as frequent-heavy, occasional-heavy, infrequent, etc. (Mulford and Miller, 1960a). The distinctions made are always arbitrary, because no definitive data exist to demonstrate which consumption patterns are safe or unsafe. Some studies show that risks of physical pathology rise with increasing consumption levels, but the existence of any threshold is in doubt (Lieber, 1979). At present, therefore, it is difficult to define any particular pattern of alcohol consumption as a "drinking problem" in and of itself.

Table 3 shows commonly used measures of the consequences of excessive drinking. These should be distinguished from alcohol dependence because they may not represent an ongoing "condition." Although most of them reflect harm related to drinking, their interpretation is often ambiguous. Cahalan &

TABLE 3
Adverse Consequences of Drinking

Concept	*Publication*	*Sample items*
Interpersonal relations	Cahalan & Room (1974)	Spouse got angry about my drinking. Spouse threatened to leave, or actually left, because of my drinking. Relatives indicated I should cut down on drinking. Drinking had a harmful effect on my friendships and social life. Had trouble with the law about driving after drinking. Had trouble with the law about drinking, where driving was not involved. Drinking was involved in losing a friendship. Got into a fight (because of drinking). Drinking had a harmful effect on my marriage or home life.
Health and injury	Cahalan & Room (1974)	Drinking had a harmful effect on my health. A physician suggested I cut down on drinking. Was in a hospital because of drinking. An illness related to drinking kept me from work for a week or longer. Drinking contributed to my getting hurt in an accident.
Job and finances	Cahalan (1970)	I lost a job, or nearly lost one, because of drinking. People at work indicated I should cut down on drinking. Drinking had a harmful effect on my financial position. Drinking had a harmful effect on my work and employment opportunities.

TABLE 3 (*continued*)

Concept	*Publication*	*Sample items*
Social consequences	Clark & Midanik (1982)	My spouse threatened to leave, or actually left, because of my drinking. Friends indicated I should cut down on my drinking. My drinking was involved in losing a friend or drifting apart from a friend. Police questioned or warned me because of my drinking. I was arrested for being drunk (or for driving after drinking). Drinking contributed to getting involved in an accident in which someone else was hurt or property was damaged. People at work indicated I should cut down on my drinking. Drinking may have hurt my chances for promotion, raises, or better jobs. I lost a job, or nearly lost one, because of drinking.

Room (1974) have emphasized that drinking problems connected with interpersonal functioning, in particular, may be viewed as "problems" of a social unit rather than characteristics of an individual. Data on health status, for example, could be distorted by failure of the medical system to diagnose a problem or to communicate it to the patient. When it comes to measuring the effects of drinking on job or role performance, workers in more privileged occupations may be more insulated from social reaction to their impairment. Homemakers may be better able than others to continue excessive drinking without sanctions. These ambiguities illustrate the conceptual complexities involved in constructing a comprehensive inventory of alcohol-related problems.

Most of the surveys we have reviewed gathered data from structured personal interviews. As opposed to less formal procedures, structured interviews provide a much more standardized method of eliciting information in an objective and quantifiable manner. In the lore of the survey field, personal interviews are generally believed to improve response rates, especially compared with mail methods; they also maximize rapport and ensure flexibility to react to problems of interpretation. On the other hand, the lack of anonymity in personal interviews has led many researchers to ask their most sensitive questions (e.g., problems due to drinking) via a self-administered form filled out by the respondent during the interview. In recent years, telephone interviewing has come into vogue for many survey applications, although few published accounts exist describing alcohol surveys conducted by telephone. The survey literature generally indicates that there are only small "method effects" induced by use of personal, telephone, or self-administration techniques of data collection (Hochstim, 1967; Bradburn & Sudman, 1979). In the present state of knowledge, therefore, there does not seem to be a "quality" reason to prefer one method over another, and a choice may be determined by anticipated response rate or cost.

Accuracy of Survey Measurements

The measures discussed above can provide comprehensive, detailed, and useful data. But are such data accurate? This question is particularly acute for surveys that cover sensitive areas of behavior. General studies of survey methodology reveal only small errors in survey estimates compared with estimates from other sources (Hochstim, 1967; Marquis et al., 1981). However, surveys of drinking face special problems of sampling and possible response error because of the topic and the difficulty of locating deviant drinkers.

Types of Error

Sample and completion rates

Ideally, an epidemiologic study should establish the characteristics of the entire population in a given geographic area. Sample surveys of alcohol-related problems come closer to this ideal than many other methods, but they still retain notable limitations.

First, the sampling frame may be limited. In the United States, survey samples are commonly constructed by area probability methods. In a multistage process, the nation is randomly divided into small areas, down to the level of local primary sampling units; within each sampling unit the dwelling units are enumerated and individuals are randomly drawn from selected dwellings (Kish, 1967). Typically, only households are included. Thus several potentially significant groups are omitted from the sampling frame: (1) transients, who have no established household or address; (2) persons in hospitals, nursing homes, or other inpatient-care settings; (3) persons in prison or jail; (4) college students who live in dormitories; (5) members of the military services who do not live in households in the United States. All of these groups are more likely to contain heavy drinkers than the typical household. In addition, some sampling schemes exclude residents of hotels, rooming houses, and other group quarters. Presumably these omissions bias the sample, mostly in the direction of underrepresenting heavy drinkers, although the result of some omissions (such as older persons in inpatient treatment facilities) may be to overrepresent drinkers.

Second, individual people selected for the target may be unlocatable. In surveys with many callbacks the proportion of unlocatable subjects will be reduced to insignificance, but resources often do not permit such careful followup. Outright refusals because of subject matter are usually overcome by reputable interviewing organizations, but in recent years more households have become unreachable because of security systems or refusal of subjects to open the door to a stranger. The impact of such nonresponse should not be exaggerated; a recent analysis of nonresponse in a sample of alcoholics revealed very little association between nonresponse and alcohol-related behavior (Polich et al., 1981). Nonetheless, the precise effects of nonresponse are inherently difficult to specify, and failure to include all types of persons in the sample probably biases survey sample estimates downward, at least for alcohol consumption (Pernanen, 1974).

Response errors (validity and reliability)

In addition to sampling errors, survey results, like all data, are subject to measurement errors. Even though a proper sample may ensure that the individuals selected are representative of the population, the individuals may give erroneous answers to questions about their drinking. The most obvious potential measurement errors are those of underreporting or overreporting, but other possibilities include forgetting, telescoping, and inaccurate recall of events. The effects of such errors depend crucially on whether they represent bias (lack of validity) or random error (lack of reliability). Measurement bias in a variable leads to error in the sample mean, whereas unreliabilty tends to reduce the apparent strength of association between variables. Bias is clearly defeating for prevalence estimates, but in causal analysis unreliability leads to distortions while bias usually does not.

Evaluations of Survey Error

Most research on measurement error in alcohol surveys has focused on bias in aggregate alcohol consumption. Numerous studies in the United States, Canada, Britain, and Scandinavia have shown that survey reports of consumption, when projected to the total population, yield estimates that reflect only about 50 percent of total beverage sales (Pernanen, 1974). Surveys for the 1970s in the United States showed a "coverage" rate of 44 percent (Armor et al., 1978, p. 185). In the 1960s coverage rates varied among regions by more than a factor of 1.5, with "dry" regions having consistently lower coverage than "wet" regions (Room, 1971).

Diverse reasons can be advanced to explain this aggregate error. In addition to sampling limitations, many early questionnaires had defects now recognized, such as failure to include response categories for very heavy drinkers and failure to measure heavy-drinking occasions along with typical lighter-drinking occasions. Such factors led Room (1971) to conclude that simple improvements in instruments could raise the coverage rate to 67 percent. In fact, one survey which had minimal sampling problems and factored heavy-drinking periods into its consumption measure found an estimated coverage rate of 85 percent (Polich, 1981).

To pin down the sources of error more precisely, a few studies have compared measurements on the same individuals. Edwards et al. (1973), reinterviewing a sample of 2 to 3 months after initial contact, found a high test-retest correlation for frequency of drinking (0.76) and for adverse effects of drinking (0.66), but a low correlation for the quantity consumed per drinking occasion (0.17). Studies that have measured blood alcohol concentrations also suggest possible problems with interview data on the quantity of alcohol consumed. Among drivers randomly stopped for roadside breath tests, self-reports of moderate drinking have been confirmed in most cases (Armor et al., 1978), but similar tests of alcoholics have suggested that at least 25 percent of heavy drinkers underreport the amount they drink (Polich, 1982; Sobell et al., 1979).

Investigations employing other "hard" criteria have been limited to checks of official records on serious problems caused by drinking. Such checks generally corroborated self-reports. Sobell and Sobell (1975) found that fewer than 5 percent of subjects' answers about hospitalization and law enforcement incidents were underreports compared with official records, while 9 percent were overreports. High validity has also been found among court-referred alcoholics, a group presumed to have strong reasons for underreporting (Sobell and Sobell, 1978).

Another source of corroborating information is the report of a "collateral" (someone who knows the subject well enough to give an independent report on his drinking). Such comparisons have found good agreement between self-reports and collateral reports of specific problems and symptoms related to drinking (Guze et al., 1963; Maisto et al., 1979; Knupfer, 1979; Polich, 1982). For example, Polich (1982) found fewer than 15 percent of subjects underreporting dependence symptoms, compared with collateral reports; a self-report, in fact, was more likely to contain admissions of drinking problems than the collateral report.

Unfortunately, this evidence on response errors is quite limited, and much of the available data is drawn from alcoholic groups, where measurement problems may be exaggerated compared with general populations. At present, it seems that reports of concrete "drinking problems" are sufficiently valid for research purposes, whereas reports of alcohol consumption may be substantially understated, at least for some individuals or population subgroups.

Principal National Surveys on Alcoholism

Although much of our current knowledge of alcoholism and alcohol-related problems is derived from local community surveys, a national sample possesses the obvious advantage of generalizability, particularly since American regions and localities are greatly varied in their history of "dry" sentiment, support for Prohibition, and other factors related to drinking. Unfortunately, there are only a few data bases with nationwide coverage. Table 4 lists the principal published national probability surveys on alcohol conducted in the United States between 1964 and 1982. This list excludes polls and other data collection efforts that contained only a small set of questions.[2]

Modern survey research on alcohol began in the mid-1960s, when Cahalan and his associates formed an Alcohol Research

2. Two earlier national surveys (Riley & Marden, 1947; Mulford, 1964) provided descriptions of national drinking practices and suggested a slight trend toward drinking and away from abstention. However, those early surveys used quota samples, in which biases can arise from the latitude allowed to interviewers as they select cases. Comparisons made by some interviewing organizations indicate that carefully constructed quota samples can produce valid results, but many early quota samples were not so carefully done. Most analysts take a conservative view, holding that the possibility of uncontrolled errors in quota samples makes their results more tenuous than those of probability samples (Kish, 1967).

TABLE 4
Principal National Probability Surveys, 1964–1982

Date	*Population*	*N*	*Publication*	*Principal subjects*
1964	Adults, age 21 and older, in households	2746	Cahalan et al. (1969)	Alcohol consumption, sociodemographic correlates, drinking contexts, retrospective changes in drinking, personality correlates, "escape" drinking.
1967	Followup of subsample from 1964 survey	1359	Cahalan (1970)	Definitions of problem drinking; sociodemographic correlates; regression models of problems; change and drinking history.
1969	Adult men, age 21–59, in households	978	Cahalan & Room (1974)	Interrelationships of drinking problems; childhood history, personality, social activity, drug and health habits, and drinking context; periodic vs. steady drinking; neighborhood context.
1971	Adults 18 and over, in households	2205	Harris (1971)	Attitudes toward drinking; knowledge of drinking; alcohol consumption and symptomatic behavior.
1972–1974	Four independent surveys of adults age 18 and over, in households	1590; 1609; 1611; 1595	Harris (1974)	Attitudes toward drinking: knowledge of drinking; exposure to media campaign on drinking; alcohol consumption and signs of drinking problems.

TABLE 4 (*continued*)

Date	*Population*	*N*	*Publication*	*Principal subjects*
1975	Two independent surveys of adults age 18 and over, in households	2157; 1743	Rappeport et al. (1975)	Exposure and reaction to media campaign on drinking; attitudes toward drinking; knowledge of drinking; drinking behavior.
1974	Students in grades 7–12	13,122	Rachal et al. (1975)	Alcohol consumption, drunkenness, drinking problems, sociodemographic correlates, peer and parental influence, drinking context, reasons for drinking.
1978	Students in grades 10–12	4918	Rachal et al. (1982)	
1979	Adults 18 and older, in households	1772	Clark & Midanik (1982)	Alcohol consumption, dependence symptoms, drinking problems, sociodemographic correlates, loss of control, binge drinking, health effects.

Group (now located at Berkeley, California) and conducted a series of national surveys on drinking among adults (Cahalan & Room, 1974). These studies were complemented by surveys on alcohol information and attitudes done for the National Institute on Alcohol Abuse and Alcoholism (NIAAA) and by special surveys of adolescents. Each of these three types of studies had its own particular features that will be discussed in detail.

Alcohol Research Group Surveys

In 1964, the Alcohol Research Group interviewed a representative sample of the U.S. household population aged 21 years and older (table 4). In 1967 a subset of the same sample was reinterviewed, and a new supplemental sample of men age 21 to 59 was selected in 1969. These surveys formed the basis for two landmark works on the use of alcohol in the general population: *American Drinking Practices* (Cahalan et al., 1969) and *Problem Drinkers* (Cahalan, 1970). Two additional followups of the 1967 sample were conducted, along with several community surveys (Cahalan & Room, 1974). Finally, the most recent national survey, conducted in 1979, was carried out by the same group (Clark & Midanik, 1982).

These surveys produced a wealth of systematic information on drinking and its effects. A complete account of the significant findings would far exceed the available space. Some of the results that have received the widest attention are listed below.

1. Drinking, as opposed to abstention, is typical of the American population. The 1979 survey found 25 percent of all males to be abstainers, 54 percent moderate drinkers (an average of less than 2 drinks per day, or 60 drinks per month), and 21 percent heavier drinkers. For females, the figures were 40 percent abstainers, 54 percent moderate drinkers, and 5 percent heavier drinkers (Clark & Midanik, 1982).
2. Drinking problems, as measured by the indices developed in these surveys, are surprisingly common. Studying the severity of alcohol-related problems, Cahalan (1970) found a "high" level of problems in 9 percent of the sample (15 percent of men and 4 percent of women). Adding those with

a "moderate" level of problems, he found a total of 31 percent affected (43 percent of men and 21 percent of women).

3. Heavy drinking has been identified as taking two distinct forms: regular and episodic high consumption. Some individuals maintain a high volume of daily consumption, while others show a low total volume combined with a pattern of heavy consumption on atypical occasions. Cahalan and Cisin (1968b) found more cases fitting the episodic pattern than the regular pattern (23 percent with a "high maximum," 12 percent with a "heavy" overall amount).
4. Sex and age groups differ substantially in drinking behavior. Although trends in the postwar period show an increasing proportion of women drinkers, men are still much more likely than women to be drinkers, to drink heavily, and to experience serious problems as a result of drinking. Members of cohorts over age 50 tend to be abstainers, especially women; and men under age 30 are especially likely to experience serious drinking problems (Clark & Midanik, 1982). However, a large majority of men appear to "mature out" of their problems without outside intervention. Over a 3-year period, for example, 15 percent of a representative sample either moved into or out of a problem group (Cahalan, 1970, p. 115); and among those who reported a past history of drinking problems rates of current remission approximated 50 percent (Cahalan & Room, 1974, p. 48).
5. Sociodemographic variables affect drinking behavior. Those with low economic and social status are less likely than others to drink, but more likely to get into trouble if they do drink. Residents of the South and less urbanized areas are less likely to be drinkers, but heavy drinkers in these "dryer" areas are more likely to experience negative reactions to their drinking. In general, members of minority ethnic groups and those with unstable work or family environments are more subject to drinking problems Cahalan & Room, 1974; Clark & Midanik, 1982).
6. Heavy or problem drinkers are involved more deeply than others in social networks supporting drinking. For example, they tend to report frequent drinking by parents and spouses, more drinking with coworkers, and more social activities with a drinking context (Cahalan et al. 1969; Cahalan & Room, 1974).

Perhaps more important than such specific findings is the general perspective that has grown out of the Alcohol Research Group studies. In contrast to "alcoholism," these researchers have concerned themselves with "drinking problems." They report that in their samples the alcoholism syndrome, as defined by the Jellinek theory, is simply not visible. Instead, they observe results such as these:

1. The various types of drinking problems are only loosely intercorrelated. Loss of control, withdrawal symptoms, and other danger signs associated with the Jellinek model of alcoholism do not form a coherent cluster of events (Clark, 1976).
2. Those persons who report loss of control and other symptoms of alcoholism do not behave as the model says they should. For example, a substantial proportion of those who report loss of control do not drink heavily and have not experienced the adverse consequences expected of an alcoholic group (Clark, 1976).
3. All types of drinking problems, including loss of control, tend to go into remission over time. Longitudinal studies indicate that many troubled drinkers who report one type of problem at Time 1 report the absence of that problem at Time 2 (Clark & Cahalan, 1976; Roizen et al., 1978). This does not fit the progressive, irreversible model of alcoholism.

These findings certainly indicate that the traditional model of alcoholism does not apply to the "problem drinkers" identified in general-population surveys. It would therefore be incorrect to count such problem drinkers as "alcoholics," if that means people whose alcohol-related difficulties resemble those of patients at alcoholism clinics. It would also be improper to conclude that the problem drinkers identified by surveys are "prealcoholic." Possibly some subset of them will go on to develop a disorder similar to the clinical syndrome, but longitudinal data suggest that most problem drinkers do not follow a progressive path. Unfortunately, we have very limited empirical evidence about the process by which individuals change from the status of "heavy drinker" or "problem drinker" to "alcoholic."

NIAAA Information and Attitude Surveys

When the National Institute on Alcohol Abuse and Alcoholism was founded, it began to collect a variety of data including national sample surveys. In 1971, NIAAA commissioned a baseline survey on public information and attitudes relating to alcohol (Louis Harris and Associates, 1971). It was followed by a series of additional surveys carried out to evaluate an NIAAA public education campaign. As shown in table 4, four surveys were conducted between 1972 and 1974, and two in 1975 (Harris, 1974; Rappeport et al., 1975). Most of the measures in these surveys were related to recognition and recall of campaign messages in the mass media, but some behavioral data were also collected.

Basic tabulations of the NIAAA surveys replicated most of the demographic correlations of the Alcohol Research Group studies (NIAAA, 1974). Heavier drinking, defined as a total volume of one ounce of ethanol or more per calendar day, was again found to be concentrated among men, particularly younger men. One of the few changes from previous results was that in the 1970s there were only small differences based on region of the country and on urbanization of locality (e.g., 12 percent of residents in cities and suburbs were heavier drinkers, compared with 9 percent in more rural areas).

The NIAAA surveys provided, for the first time, a set of systematic data permitting direct comparison between the national population and institutionalized alcoholics. The same measures used in the NIAAA surveys were also employed in interviews with alcoholics admitted to federally funded alcoholism treatment centers. Comparative analysis showed that problem drinkers identified in the general population were far less impaired than the alcoholics admitted to treatment (Armor et al., 1978). For example, mean total volume of ethanol consumption among the alcoholics was 8.4 ounces per day, compared with 4.4 ounces for problem drinkers in the general-population survey, and 0.9 ounces for the total survey sample. Similarly, unemployment rates were 60 percent for the alcoholics, 12 percent for the problem drinkers, and 4 percent for the total survey sample. Moreover, long-term followup of the alcoholics indicated that most of them continued to have drinking problems despite temporary remissions (Polich et al., 1981). In contrast, longitudinal surveys of comparable groups of problem drinkers have revealed that most of them experience long-lasting remissions (Clark & Cahalan, 1976; Roizen et al., 1978).

The NIAAA and Alcohol Research Group surveys have been combined to study trends in alcohol-related attitudes, knowledge, and behavior (NIAAA, 1978; Clark and Midanik, 1982). Results of these analyses documented the stability of aggregate drinking behavior over the period since the 1960s; no significant trends in alcohol consumption or problem drinking have been found either for the total population or for subgroups defined by age and sex. This is consistent with aggregate data on alcoholic beverage sales, which showed a steady increase between 1940 and 1970 but a leveling off thereafter (NIAAA, 1978, 1981). However, there have been some significant trends in attitudes toward drinking, showing an increased proportion of the population recognizing alcohol as a drug and a decreased proportion citing "moral weakness" as the cause of alcoholism.

Adolescent Drinking Surveys

Although the data are incomplete, it is probable that the proportion of adolescents who regularly drink alcoholic beverages increased between the 1940s and the 1960s and then leveled off (Blane & Hewitt, 1977; Rachal et al., 1982). Today over 60 percent of high school students drink once a month or more often. Whether rising or not, this rate has prompted concern about adolescent drinking.

Much of the research on adolescent drinking concerns college students. A review of all studies conducted between 1960 and 1975 concluded that lifetime prevalence of drinking probably rose a little, from 71 percent before 1966 to 88 percent in the 1970s (Blane and Hewitt, 1977). A study of over 7,000 New England college students in 1977 found 23 percent of men, but only 4 percent of women, reporting consumption of 6 or more cans of beer on typical occasions (Wechsler and McFadden, 1979). Samples of military personnel in the same age groups also show high rates of consumption (Cahalan et al., 1972; Cahalan & Cisin, 1975; Polich & Orvis, 1979), although rates of adverse consequences appear no higher for military personnel than for civilians of the same sex and educational level (Polich, 1979). The prevalence of drinking problems among these adolescent groups needs to be considered in national assessments, since people aged 18 to 24 drink heavily, and traditional household-based sampling frames omit many of them. However, no national study has systematically combined these special groups with the general population to obtain comprehensive national estimates.

A comprehensive assessment has been made for younger adolescents. In 1974 and 1978 representative national surveys of junior and senior high school students were conducted by the Research Triangle Institute (RTI) (Rachal et al., 1975, 1976, 1982). Uniquely among high-school surveys, these studies drew a probability sample from a national sampling frame, carried out quantitative analyses, and reported methods in detail. Among the principal findings were the following.

1. In 1978, 15 percent of high school students (21 percent of boys, 9 percent of girls) were classified as "heavier" drinkers, meaning consumption of 5 or more drinks per occasion with drinking occasions at least once a week. An additional 17 percent (19 percent of boys, 16 percent of girls) drank slightly less, but still in amounts classified as "moderate/heavy" (i.e., 2 to 4 drinks per occasion with drinking occasions at least once a week, or 5 or more drinks per occasion with drinking occasions at least 3 to 4 times a month).
2. Thirty-one percent of the students reported drunkenness 6 times or more in the preceding year ("being drunk or very, very high"). Of these, more than two-thirds reported at least one event from a list of adverse social consequences developed by RTI (trouble with teachers, difficulties with friends, criticism from a date, trouble with the police, or driving after having a "good bit to drink").
3. Few significant differences were noted between the 1974 and 1978 survey results. In particular, the amount of drinking in the RTI surveys remained virtually constant between the two time periods. There was, however, one exception: The rate of "alcohol misuse," as defined by RTI, rose from 27 percent in 1974 to 31 percent in 1978. In the authors' classification, misusers included all students who reported drunkenness 6 or more times, or at least three types of adverse consequences each occurring two or more times in a year.

4. Many demographic differences found in general-population surveys were not replicated among youth. For example, in 1974 the percentage of heavy drinkers varied between 10 and 11 percent for groups classified by parents' occupational status; between 9 and 13 percent for regional areas; and between 10 and 11 percent for metropolitan versus nonmetropolitan areas. Adolescents appear to be quite a bit more uniform in drinking practices than adults, suggesting that whatever youthful drinking problems exist are likely to be prevalent in all communities.

These data demonstrate that drinking is now the norm among American teenagers, even those of junior high school age (Rachal et al., 1975). Many adolescents regularly consume substantial amounts of alcohol (e.g., drinking once a week or more often and consuming at least 5 drinks at a time). These patterns are widespread throughout all social strata, ethnic groups, and geographic areas, despite legal prohibition and community disapproval. Moreover, alcohol is by far the most frequently used psychoactive drug among adolescents, far more popular than marijuana and other drugs that receive more attention in the press (Johnson et al., 1981).

What is less clear is the extent to which these youthful drinkers actually experience significant "problems" because of alcohol. On the one hand, in the 1978 study, only 2 percent of the students reported the criterion level of adverse consequences used in the definition of alcohol misuse. On the other hand, frequent drunkenness was widespread, and that might be a precursor of more serious disorders. Moreover, some of the concrete problems that are used as indicators for adults may not be sensitive measures among youth. Adolescents, for example, do not usually have a spouse or employer whose displeasure can be taken as a reasonable sign of a drinking problem, and the incipient health problems caused by excessive alcohol consumption are unlikely to show up in a healthy young person.

With the available data, therefore, it is difficult to evaluate adolescents' reports of alcohol-related problems. Surely, most of them are not instances of behavior that point to more serious behavioral disorders in the future. Once, again, however, the absence of longitudinal studies makes it impossible to trace the sequence by which alcohol problems develop over time.

Future Directions in Survey Research

So far, the main accomplishment of sample surveys has been to draw a broad descriptive portrait of alcohol-related problems. This outline reveals patterns of alcohol abuse that are quite distinct from those of the severely dependent or addicted alcoholic. Most surveys have found only a small proportion of the sample who report even mild indications of alcoholism, as it is seen in clinics. Nonetheless, large numbers of respondents report some significant adverse effect of drinking, such as trouble in the family, impairment of work performance, or a law enforcement incident connected with drinking. And of course still more people report regular consumption of quantities of alcohol sufficient for short-term impairment and intoxication.

Surveys have also contributed a distinct perspective to models of developmental processes in alcoholism. Based on retrospective reports of alcoholics, traditional models of alcoholism posited that dependence developed in a progressive sequence of addictive symptoms, beginning when the problem drinker reached the stage of "loss of control." Longitudinal surveys of problem drinking in the general population show a different pattern. They suggest that most drinking problems go into lasting remission, that they are not part of a tightly-knit syndrome of symptoms, and that loss of control over drinking may not be the central factor in the progression or remission of alcohol abuse. These results are consistent with the fact that heavy drinking and problem drinking are concentrated among young men, most of whom obviously "mature out" of their problems. As yet, however, no empirically-based models exist to explain which types of problem drinkers remit and which do not, or why.

As for the factors that cause excessive drinking in the first place, research evidence is meager. Drinking contexts, interpersonal patterns of association, legal regulations, and stressful life events are among the factors hypothesized as causal agents. However, the existing data on causal effects come largely from cross-sectional surveys, where it is very difficult to determine the causal order that applies to the various factors.

Thus the extent of national data on alcohol abuse and alcoholism is inadequate to answer some of the most important questions in the epidemiology of drinking problems. Although virtually every section of this research terrain needs further exploration, we will list four areas of special importance.

Alcohol Consumption

The measurement of alcohol consumption in surveys remains in a primitive state. Most investigators have been content to construct an arbitrary classification of categories of drinkers ("heavy," "moderate," etc.). What is needed instead is a set of clearly conceived variables that reflect the actual independent dimensions of drinking behavior, such as total volume and frequency of intoxication, following up on the initial work of Cahalan and Cisin (1968b). Attempts should be made to quantify these parameters and to examine their separate correlates and effects. The importance of consumption has become more widely appreciated as nonsurvey evidence on the risks of heavy drinking has accumulated. For example, a substantial body of data shows a strong relation between cirrhosis mortality and national per capita alcohol consumption, as measured by beverage sales (Schmidt, 1976). We need to specify the reasons for that relationship by examining individual consumption and its effects. Some research has been done to pursue the link between dosages of ethanol and biological toxicity (Lieber, 1979), but survey research should assist by determining the relationship between consumption levels and the psychologic and economic effects of drinking.

Alcohol Dependence

Up to now, survey research has downplayed the importance of the alcohol dependence syndrome. Partly this reflects a reaction to the overstatements made by proponents of the traditional disease conception of alcoholism (Robinson, 1972). Yet, dependence is plainly seen in clinics and it appears to be a continuously distributed variable rather than an all-or-nothing attribute (Edwards et al., 1977). Therefore, surveys ought to be able to measure mild forms of dependence. However, only the most recent (1979) national survey inquired into the frequency of alcohol dependence symptoms. As a result, we do not know much about the phenomenon of alcohol dependence in the general population. Results from a special population, the U.S. Air

Force (Polich & Orvis, 1979), suggest that dependence can be measured and that it is important, but much more intensive analysis is needed. In addition, comparisons between normal and institutionalized populations, using the same measures on both, would aid in developing a standardized measure. Obtaining a measure of dependence that would indicate different levels of severity could also help identify those individuals in a survey who are prealcoholic. Then longitudinal studies could explore the significance of mild dependence as a possible precursor of full-blown alcoholism.

The types of drinking that are associated with dependence also deserve more study. From clinical descriptions it is as yet unclear whether the most appropriate clues to dependence lie in the quantity, frequency, circumstances of drinking, or the degree of deviance manifested in the drinking (Edwards et al., 1977). Further study should also explore the significance of the "danger signs" or so-called "addictive symptoms" that many sample surveys have employed as indicators of dependence. At present, these signs are treated as valid indicators of addiction (or addiction-in-the-offing) in many treatment and casefinding activities. It would therefore be valuable to know the utility of these danger signs as stand-in measures of dependence and as predictors of future alcohol-related problems.

Survey Validity

For alcohol consumption, the validity problem is highly visible: survey data account for only one-half to two-thirds of aggregate alcoholic beverage sales. Judging by studies of alcoholics, self-reports of major adverse effects of drinking (arrest, hospitalization, etc.) appear to be quite valid. The evidence on the validity of dependence symptoms is meager, consisting of scattered confirmatory reports by collaterals.

The uncertainties about self-reports are compounded by the other factors that could reduce survey accuracy. Particularly for skewed variables such as consumption, some errors could be produced by incomplete sampling frames (e.g., excluding transients and other heavy-drinking groups from household surveys). Other errors could be introduced by nonresponse (e.g., failure of surveys to interview all heavy drinkers, who may be disproportionately represented among not-at-home cases). The degree of bias introduced by these sampling problems should be addressed. In addition, direct assessments of self-report validity are needed, using solid external criteria.

Developmental Processes

As we have noted at several points in this paper, our knowledge of the developmental processes of alcohol abuse is highly tentative. If we knew which patterns of drinking were likely to eventuate in serious problems at later times, these "risky" behavior patterns might furnish clues to the causal processes involved. Even if the etiology of alcohol abuse remains incompletely understood, knowledge of risk factors could improve diagnosis and prevention efforts. Such knowledge would also aid us in the definition of "alcohol abuse." If a behavior appears to place an individual at high risk of a later alcohol-related problem, other things being equal, there is reason to presume that the behavior is a "problem." Knowledge of such risk factors could thus reduce the arbitrariness of current definitions of alcohol abuse.

Finally, developmental studies offer the potential for resolving the current divergence between clinical perspectives about "alcoholism" and survey experience with "drinking problems." At some point in their lives, some of the problem drinkers identified in surveys undoubtedly reach a stage of severe alcohol dependence. Currently available data do not allow us to draw conclusions about that process with confidence. Yet knowledge about the process is crucial. Prospective, longitudinal cohort studies will be required if epidemioilogy is to help elucidate the causal processes that generate alcohol abuse and alcoholism.

Summary

Studies of alcohol abuse have identified three broad types of alcohol-related problems: (1) *dependence on alcohol*, a condition in which the individual's ability to limit drinking is impaired; (2) *excessive consumption*, a level of alcoholism intake regarded as unsafe or deviant; and (3) *adverse consequences of drinking*, representing any effects of alcohol that seriously harm the individual.

Survey measurement of these types of alcohol abuse is essential for epidemiologic purposes, but needs further refinement. With current measurement methods, survey data on concrete drinking problems appear valid, whereas data on alcohol consumption may be substantially understated for some individuals or population subgroups.

Various national surveys conducted from the mid-1960s to 1979 have shown no significant trends in the extent of alcohol abuse over that period. Results indicate that alcohol-related problems affect at least 9 percent of the population, with higher rates among young adults and adolescents. However, the types of problems reported in surveys are rarely as severe as those observed in alcoholism clinics. In fact, the validity of the traditional model of alcoholism, as described in retrospective studies of clinic patients, is seriously challenged by the findings of general population studies. For future research, this review concludes that the areas of greatest importance are measurement of alcohol consumption, assessment of alcohol dependence, and prospective studies of the development of alcohol abuse.

References

Armor, D.J., Polich, J.M. & Stanbul, H.B. (1978). *Alcoholism and Treatment*. New York: John Wiley & Sons.

Bailey, M.B., Haberman, P.W. & Alksne, H. (1965). The epidemiology of alcoholism in an urban residential area. *Quart. J. Stud. Alc.* 26:19–40.

Blane, H.T. & Hewitt, L. E. (1977). *Alcohol and Youth: An Analysis of the Literature, 1960–75*. Springfield, Virginia: National Technical Information Service.

Boland, B. & Roizen, R. (1973). Sales slips and survey responses: New data on the reliability of survey consumption measures. *Drink. Drug Prac. Surv.* 8:5–10.

Bowman, R. S., Stein, L. I. & Newton, J. R. (1975). Measurement and interpretation of drinking behavior. *J. Stud. Alc.* 36:1154–1172.

Bradburn, N. M. & Sudman, S. (1979). *Improving Interview Method and Questionnaire Design*. San Francisco: Jossey-Bass.

Caetano, R., Edwards, G., Oppenheim, A. N. & Taylor, C. (1978). Building a standardized alcoholism interview schedule. *Drug Alc. Depend.* 3:185–197.

Cahalan, D. (1970), *Problem Drinkers.* San Francisco: Jossey-Bass.
Cahalan, D & Cisin, I. H. (1968a). American drinking practices: Summary of findings from a national probability sample. I. Extent of drinking by population subgroups. *Quart. J. Stud. Alc.* 29:130–151.
Cahalan, D. & Cisin, I. H. (1968b). American drinking practices: Summary of findings from a national probability sample. II. Measurement of massed versus spaced drinking. *Quart. J. Stud. Alc.* 29:642–656.
Cahalan, D. & Cisin, I. (1975). *Final Report on a Service-Wide Survey of Attitudes and Behavior of Naval Personnel Concerning Alcohol and Problem Drinking.* Washington, D.C.: Bureau of Social Science Research.
Cahalan, D., Cisin, I. H. & Crossley, H. M. (1969). *American Drinking Practices.* New Brunswick, New Jersey: Rutgers Center of Alcohol Studies.
Cahalan, D., Cisin, I., Gardner, G. L. & Smith, G. C. (1972). *Drinking Practices and Problems in the U. S. Army, 1972.* Washington, D.C.: Information Concepts, Inc.
Cahalan, D. & Room, R. (1974). *Problem Drinking Among American Men.* New Brunswick, New Jersey: Rutgers Center of Alcohol Studies.
Clark, W. B. (1976). Loss of control, heavy drinking and drinking problems in a longitudinal study. *J. Stud. Alc.* 37:1256–1290.
Clark, W. B. & Cahalan, D. (1976). Changes in problem drinking over a four-year span. *Addict. Behav.* 1:251–259.
Clark, W. B. & Midanik, L. (1982). Alcohol use and alcohol problems among U.S. adults: Results of the 1979 national survey. In: *Alcohol and Health Monograph No. 1: Alcohol Consumption and Related Problems,* U.S. Department of Health and Human Services. Washington, D.C.: Government Printing Office.
Davies, D. L. (1976). Definitional issues in alcoholism. In: *Alcoholism: Interdisciplinary Approaches to an Enduring Problem,* ed. R. E. Tartar & A. A. Sugarman. Reading, Massachusetts: Addison-Wesley.
Donovan, J. E. & Jessor, R. (1978). Adolescent problem drinking: Psychosocial correlates in a national sample study. *J. Stud. Alc.* 39:1506–1524.
Edwards, G., Gross, M. M., Keller, M., Moser, J. & Room, R. (1977). *Alcohol-Related Disabilities.* Geneva: World Health Organization, Offset Publication Number 32.
Edwards, G., Hensman, C. & Petro, J. (1973). Drinking in a London suburb. Reinterview of a subsample and assessment of response consistency. *Quart. J. Stud. Alc.* 34:1244–1254.
Engs, R. C. (1977). Drinking patterns and drinking problems of college students. *J. Stud. Alc.* 38:2144–2156.
Filstead, W. J., Goby, M. J. & Bradley, N. J. (1976). Critical elements in the diagnosis of alcoholism: A national survey of physicians. *J.A.M.A.* 236:2767–2769.

Guze, S. B., Tuason, V. B., Stewart, M. A. & Picken, B. (1963). The drinking history: A comparison of reports by subjects and their relatives. *Quart. J. Stud. Alc.* 24:249–260.

Harris, L. & Associates, Inc. (1971). *American Attitudes Toward Alcohol and Alcoholics,* Study No. 2138. New York: Louis Harris and Associates.

Harris, L. & Associates, Inc. (1974). *Public Awareness of the National Institute on Alcohol Abuse and Alcoholism Public Education Campaign and Public Attitudes Toward Drinking and Alcohol Abuse, Phase Four and Overall Summary,* Study No. 2355. New York: Louis Harris and Associates, Inc.

Hochstim, J. R. (1967). A critical comparison of three strategies of collecting data from households. *J. Am. Stat. Assoc.* 62:976–989.

Jellinek, E. M. (1946). Phases in the drinking history of alcoholics. *Quart. J. Stud. Alc.* 7:1–88.

Jellinek, E. M. (1952). Phases of alcohol addiction. *Quart. J. Stud. Alc.* 13:673–684.

Jellinek, E. M. (1960). *The Disease Concept of Alcoholism.* New Brunswick, N. J.: Hillhouse Press.

Johnston, L. D., Bachman, J. G. & O'Malley, P. M. (1981). *Highlights from Student Drug Abuse in America, 1975–1981.* Washington, D.C.: National Institute on Drug Abuse.

Keller, M. (1962). The definition of alcoholism and the estimation of its prevalence. In: *Society, Culture, and Drinking Patterns,* ed. D. J. Pittman & C. R. Synder. New York: Wiley.

Keller, M. (1972). On the loss-of-control phenomenon in alcoholism. *Br. J. Addict.* 67:153–166.

Kish, L. (1967). *Survey Sampling.* New York: Wiley.

Knupfer, G. (1966). Some methodological problems in the epidemiology of alcoholic beverage usage: Definition of amount of intake. *Am. J. Public Health* 56:237–242.

Knupfer, G. (1967). The epidemiology of problem drinking. *Am. J. Public Health* 57:973–986.

Knupfer, G. (1979). The validity of survey data on drinking problems: A comparison between respondents' self-reports and outside sources of information. In: *Drinking Patterns and Problems: A Decade of Studies in the San Francisco Area,* Ed. G. Knupfer, & W. J. Clark, unpublished book manuscript. Berkeley, CA: University of California.

Lelbach, W. (1974). Organic pathology related to volume and pattern of alcohol use. In: *Reserach Advances in Alcohol and Drug Problems,* Vol. 1, ed. R. J. Gibbins, et al. New York: Wiley.

Lieber, C. S. (1979). Ethanol and the liver: A decreasing "threshold" of toxicity. *Am. J. Clin. Nutrit.* 32:1177–1180.

Lloyd, R. W. & Salzberg, H.C. (1975). Controlled social drinking: An alternative to abstinence as a treatment goal for some alcohol abusers. *Psychol. Bull.* 82:815–842.

Ludwig, A. M. & Wikler, A. (1974). "Craving" and relapse to drink. *Quart. J. Stud. Alc.* 35:108–130.

Maisto, S.A., Sobell, L. C. & Sobell, M. B. (1979). Comparison of alcoholics' self-reports of drinking behavior with reports of collateral informants. *J. Consult. Clin. Psychol.* 47:106–112.

Marquis, K. H., Duan, N., Marquis, M. S. & Polich, J. M. (1981). *Response Errors in Sensitive Topic Surveys.* Santa Monica: The Rand Corporation.

Mulford, H. A. (1964). Drinking and deviant drinking, U.S.A., 1963. *Quart. J. Stud. Alc.* 25:634–650.

Mulford, H. A. & Miller, D. E. (1960a). Drinking in Iowa. II. The extent of drinking and selected sociocultural categories. *Quart. J. Stud. Alc.* 21:26–39.

Mulford, H. A. & Miller, D. E. (1960b). Drinking in Iowa. III. A scale of definitions of alcohol related to drinking behavior. *Quart. J. Stud. Alc.* 21:267–278.

Mulford, H. A. & Miller, D. E. (1960c). Drinking in Iowa. IV. Preoccupation with alcohol and definitions of alcohol, heavy drinking, and trouble due to drinking. *Quart. J. Stud. Alc.* 21:279–291.

National Council on Alcoholism (1972). Criteria for the diagnosis of alcoholism. *Ann. Intern. Med.* 77:249–258.

National Institute on Alcohol Abuse and Alcoholism (1974). *Second Special Report to the U.S. Congress on Alcohol and Health.* Washington, D.C.: U.S. Government Printing Office.

National Institute on Alcohol Abuse and Alcoholism (1978). *Third Special Report to the U.S. Congress on Alcohol and Health.* Washington, D.C.: U.S. Government Printing Office.

National Institute on Alcohol Abuse and Alcoholism (1981). *Fourth Special Report to the U.S. Congress on Alcohol and Health.* Washington, D.C.: Government Printing Office.

Pernanen, K. (1974). Validity of survey data on alcohol use. In: *Research Advances in Alcohol and Drug Problems,* Vol. 1, ed. R. J. Gibbins et al. New York: Wiley.

Polich, J. M. (1979). Alcohol problems among civilian youth and military personnel. In: *Youth, Alcohol, and Social Policy,* ed. H. T. Blane & M. E. Chafetz. New York: Plenum Press.

Polich, J. M. (1981). Alcohol abuse in civilian and military populations. *Am. J. Public Health* 71:1125–1132.

Polich, J. M. (1982). Validity of self-reports in alcoholism research. *Addict. Behav.* 7:123–132.

Polich, J. M., Armor, D. J. & Braiker, H. B. (1981). *The Course of Alcoholism: Four Years After Treatment.* New York: Wiley.

Polich, J. M. & Orvis, B. R. (1979). *Alcohol Problems: Patterns and Prevalence in the U.S. Air Force.* Santa Monica: The Rand Corporation.

Rachal, J. V., Williams, J. R., Brehm, M. L., Cavanaugh, B., Moore, R. P. & Eckerman, W. C. (1975). *A National Study of Drinking Behavior, Attitudes, and Correlates.* Research Triangle Park, NC: Research Triangle Institute.

Rachal, J. V., Hubbard, R. L., Williams, J. R. & Tuchfeld, B. S. (1976). Drinking levels and problem drinking among junior and senior high-school students. *J. Stud. Alc.* 37:1751–1761.

Rachal, J. V., Maisto, S. A., Guess, L. L. & Hubbard, R. L. (1982). Alcohol use among youth. In: *Alcohol and Health Monograph No. 1: Alcohol Consumption and Related Problems,* U.S. Department of Health and Human Services. Washington, D.C.: Government Printing Office.

Rappeport, M., Labaw, P. & Williams, J. (1975). *The Public Evaluates the NIAAA Public Education Campaign,* Vols. 1 and 2. Princeton, New Jersey: Opinion Research Corporation.

Riley, J. W. & Marden, C. F. (1947). The social pattern of alcoholic drinking. *Quart. J. Stud. Alc.* 8:265–273.

Robinson, D. (1972). The alcohologist's addiction: Some implications of losing control over the disease concept of alcoholism. *Quart. J. Stud. Alc.* 33:1028–1042.

Roizen, R., Cahalan, D. & Shanks, P. (1978). Spontaneous remission among untreated problem drinkers. In: *Longitudinal Research in Drug Use: Empirical Findings and Methodological Issues,* ed. D. B. Kandel. New York: Wiley.

Room, R. (1971). Survey vs. sales data for the U.S. *Drink. Drug Pract. Surv.* 3:15–16.

Room, R. (1977). Measurement and distribution of drinking patterns and problems in general populations. In: *Alcohol-Related Disabilities,* ed. G. Edwards, M. Gross, M. Keller, J. Moser, R. Room. Geneva: World Health Organization, Offset Publication 32.

Schmidt, W. (1976). Cirrhosis and alcohol consumption: An epidemiological perspective. In: *Alcoholism: New Knowledge and New Responses,* ed. G. Edwards, & M. Grant. Baltimore: University Park Press.

Sobell, L. C. & Sobell, M. B. (1975). Outpatient alcoholics give valid self-reports. *J. Nerv. Ment. Dis.* 161:32–42.

Sobell, L.C. & Sobell, M. B. (1978) Validity of self-reports in three populations of alcoholics. *J. Consult. Clin. Psychol.* 46:901–907.

Sobell, M. B., Sobell, L. C. & Samuels, F. H. (1974). Validity of self-reports of alcohol-related arrests by alcoholics. *Quart. J. Stud. Alc.* 35:276–280.

Sobell, M. B., Sobell, L. C. & VanderSpek, R. (1979). Relationship among clinical judgment, self-report and breath analysis measures of intoxication in alcoholics. *J. Clin. Consult. Psychol.* 47:204–206.

Straus, R. & Bacon, S. (1953). *Drinking in College.* New Haven: Yale University Press.

Sudman, S. (1967). *Reducing the Cost of Surveys.* Chicago: Aldine.

Wechsler, H. & McFadden, M. (1976). Sex differences in adolescent alcohol and drug use: A disappearing phenomenon. *J. Stud. Alc.* 37:1291–1301.

Wechsler, H. & McFadden, M. (1979). Drinking among college students in New England. *J. Stud. Alc.* 40:969–981.

World Health Organization (1952). *Expert Committee on Mental Health, Alcoholism Subcommittee, Second Report.* Geneva: World Health Organization, Technical Report Series Number 48.

Chapter 3

Methodologic Issues in the Study of Special Populations

ELIZABETH R. MORRISSEY

Investigators concerned with the epidemiology and etiology of alcoholism or problem drinking encounter metodologic and conceptual issues similar to those confronted by epidemiologists and survey researchers in general. The study of special populations such as women and teenagers, however, present a range of methodologic problems requiring more complex and creative solutions than are generally required in epidemiologic investigations. The purpose of this chapter is to review, within the context of existing research findings, measurement and research design problems unique to the study of alcohol abuse and alcoholism in special populations. Examples are drawn primarily from the literature on alcoholic women, although a few examples are included from research on teenage problem drinking. The issues discussed, however, are relevant to research on problem drinking or alcoholism among ethnic minorities, various socioeconomic strata, and other population subgroups defined on the basis of status characteristics.

Unique measurement and research design issues arise in the study of special populations primarily because status characteristics such as age, gender, and ethnicity are indicators not only of membership in a special population, but also of appropriate role behaviors, including norms governing alcohol consumption, for members of that population (Knupfer & Room, 1964). In research on subpopulations it is therefore essential that findings be evaluated within the context of general knowledge available on the subpopulation under study. Given variations in drinking patterns and role responsibilities by status characteristics, the prevalence of specific types of alcohol-related problems will vary by population subgroup (Clark, 1966b) and the correlates of problem drinking will also vary with status characteristics. Questions arise as to whether variation in the correlates and consequences of abusive drinking across subgroups represent differences in roles adopted by members of these subgroups, variations in forms of deviant behavior unrelated to alcohol abuse that are characteristic of the subgroup under study, differences in drinking patterns characteristic of different groups, or are indicative of general factors associated with alcohol abuse and alcoholism. To the extent that certain correlates and consequences of alcohol abuse are observable across subpopulations, our understanding of the psychosocial determinants of alcoholism will be enhanced. Psychosocial factors uniformly associated with abusive drinking and alcoholism, regardless of the nature of the study population in which they are observed, can be identified as possible triggers of alcoholic drinking.

Because alcoholism is generally defined partly in terms of the social, medical, legal, and economic consequences of alcohol use (National Council on Alcoholism, 1972; Catanzaro, 1967; Woodruff, Goodwin & Guze, 1974), in estimating the prevalence of alcoholism within any population subgroup, several questions must be addressed. First, what are the social and economic roles typically pursued by members of the subgroup? Second, what constitutes deviant performance of these roles and what is the prevalence within the subgroup of specific types of deviant behaviors whether or not the behaviors are alcohol-related? Third, what specific types of legal and medical problems are generally experienced by members of the subgroup? What factors, including the status characteristics defining the boundaries of the subgroup, determine whether individuals will come to the attention of a physician, police officer, judge, or psychiatric clinic? Finally, given knowledge of variation in drinking patterns by status characteristics, how are drinking behaviors related to the probability of the manifestation of problems and to the probability of being identified as an alcoholic or problem drinker? Answers to these questions hinge on measurement procedures applied in the study of special populations and on the careful development of research designs for use in future studies.

The focus here is on general research strategies applicable in the study of special populations. In this discussion, I assume that the major goals of research efforts are (1) to accurately describe the prevalence of alcoholism or problem drinking in general and in subgroups of the population; (2) to identify, through an examination of the characteristics of individuals identified as alcoholic or problem drinkers and of the correlates of drinking problems, psychosocial factors that play a role in the onset and exacerbation of alcoholic drinking. Although, as Keller has argued (1960), the identification of alcoholism by the clinician and the identification of alcoholism by the epidemiologist involve fundamentally different processes and therefore require different definitional procedures, research definitions of problem drinking necessarily include a consideration of the ways in which medical, mental health, and law enforcement professionals recognize individuals who are alcoholic or problem drinkers. The focus here on the development of research definitions of alcoholism and problem drinking for use in the study of special populations will, therefore, identify issues that are not only relevant to investigators in the field but are also of concern to clinicians working with clients from special populations.

Measurement Issues

General Strategies

The alcohol studies literature reflects a long history of concern with items useful in identifying problem drinkers and alcoholics (Jackson, 1957; Mulford & Miller, 1960; Knupfer & Room 1966), as well as with the measurement of alcohol consumption levels and drinking patterns (Cahalan & Cisin, 1968; Little, Schultz & Mandell, 1977). Indicators of problem drinking or alcoholism can generally be broken down into three categories: items measuring preoccupation with alcohol or psychological dependence; those tapping personal and medical consequences of alcohol use; and those measuring alcohol impaired role performance or troubles due to drinking. Cahalan and Room (1974) suggest a more elaborate division of measures of problem drinking including indicators of binge drinking, psychological dependence, loss of control, symptomatic drinking, and several possible types of social consequences of drinking. The measurement of social consequences of drinking—belligerence, problems with spouse, relatives, friends, employers, co-workers, police, health and finances—present serious problems when the focus is on special populations. Problems arise because the majority of scales of problem drinking and screens for alcoholism were developed primarily in light of knowledge generated in studies of adult male samples (Cahalan & Room 1974; Zung & Charalampous, 1975; Selzer et al., 1975).

The established emphasis on the development of indicators and scales appropriate to the characterization of alcoholism among adult males has several interesting consequences. First, as Clark (1966b) has shown, there is a direct relationship between the nature of indicators of alcohol-related problems used and resulting prevalence rates. His analysis revealed that, in studies of the general population, women were more likely to be defined as problem drinkers when definitional elements such as level of alcohol consumption and the use of alcohol to reduce tension were emphasized and less likely to be identified as problem drinkers when definitional elements such as interpersonal conflicts and the occurrence of formal social control were emphasized. When problem drinking or alcoholism is defined partly in terms of the impact of alcohol abuse on the performance of social and economic roles, in subgroups of the population with roles that differ substantially from typical adult male roles, estimates of the prevalence of alcohol abuse and alcoholism will be biased.

More seriously, and as Clark demonstrated, when items used to measure drinking problems are combined into scales, not only do differing scales result in different estimates of the prevalence of problem drinking, different scales identify totally different individuals as problem drinkers. Clark illustrated his point partially through a presentation of data describing gender differences in rates of problems. The greatest gender differences in rates of alcohol-related problems occurred in the areas of employment and legal difficulties (Clark, 1966b, p. 653). Similar observations have been reported by numerous other investigators (Edwards et al., 1972). When measures of alcoholism and problem drinkling are combined into scales, estimates of the prevalence of problems among various subgroups are potentially biased to an even greater extent than are estimates based on single indicators.

Measurement of Alcoholism and Alcohol Abuse in Special Populations

Emerging Trends: The Development of New Instruments

In recognition of the problems introduced by the use of measures developed in studies of adult males, several investigators are proposing instruments to be used in the study of alcohol abuse among women (Russell & Bigler, 1978) and among youth (Mayer & Filstead, 1979). Published instruments generally focus on appropriate role behaviors in the subgroup for which the instrument is designed. For example, Mayer and Filstead (1979) propose a questionnaire for use with adolescent samples which includes items focussing on performance in school, relationships with peers and family, and self-perception of drinking behavior (cf. Babst et al., 1979). Other investigators have also proposed instruments to characterize teenage drinking problems so that, as Smart (1979, p. 130) points out, problem drinking among adolescents is measured in many different ways. In at least one instance (Rachal et al., 1976), teenagers could be classified as problem drinkers solely on the basis of frequent drunkenness.

In the case of women, Russell and Bigler have used a standard alcohol screening test but "eliminate questions about behavior that is more typical of male than female alcohol abuse" (1978, p. 5). The strategy represented by these approaches takes cognizance of age and gender variations in social and economic roles. However, these attempts to formulate scales are premature. The logic, in fact, suggests that it is appropriate to redefine the dependent variable (alcoholism or problem drinking) when the researcher focuses on a group other than adult males. If we are to further our understanding of alcoholism and alcohol abuse, observing variation in the rates of specific types of alcohol-related problems across population segments will provide insights into the psychosocial factors that trigger alcohol abuse. If the definition of alcoholism used is changed from one group to another, it is impossible to establish whether or not the same dependent variable is being examined. It is therefore impossible to assess the impact of status characteristics and of the differential response of agents of social control to various subgroups on the probability of the development of alcoholism or problem drinking.

Alternative Measurement Strategies: Restricting the Denominator

Several general strategies can be applied in developing scales to characterize problem drinking in special populations. For example, differences in the types of alcohol-related problems experienced by men and women have been discussed in several reports (Glatt, 1961; Rimmer et al., 1971). Clearly, and as we have pointed out in other work (Schuckit & Morrissey, 1976), if women are less likely than men to be in the labor force, they are certainly less likely to experience occupational problems related to alcohol use. This illustration, which is limited to a single set of indicators of alcohol-related problems and a single element of gender role variation, is relatively simple. With a focus on a single indicator of alcohol-related problems, the necessary adjustments can be made through a careful definition of the population at risk by, in this example, restricting the analysis to employed persons, so that comparisons between males and females are adjusted for gender differences in labor force participation. Recent evidence based on comparisons of employed males and females indicates, in fact, that rates of alcohol-related problems among working women and men are quite similar (Liban & Smart, 1979).

More complex issues arise, however, when one begins to consider the differential probability of deviant occupational performance among males and females. Among women who are employed, there are higher rates of both acute and disabling conditions resulting in time lost from work than among employed males (National Center for Health Statistics, 1978a; 1978b). Thus, in comparing male and female rates of alcohol-related absenteeism from work, indicators should be weighted in consideration not only for the lower probability of female participation in the labor force but also of the greater probability of female absenteeism. It may well be, for example, that among workers with comparable rates of absenteeism, gender differences in the probability of experiencing employment-related alcohol problems are insignificant. This strategy corresponds, very simply, to the introduction of statistical controls for factors that may influence the relationship between gender and the probability of experiencing alcohol-related problems. This illustration, however, identifies the major problem. Definitional elements in most conceptions of alcoholism are highly correlated with culturally defined age and gender differences in role behaviors.

The Development of Scales

More serious problems arise, as discussed above, when items used to measure drinking problems are combined into scales. The solution to such problems requires the development of weights for various indicators of alcoholism or problem drinking, so that the combination of items into scale scores does not result in the type of distortion described in Clark's analysis. For any given indicator of alcohol-related problems, the relative risk of occurrence of the problem in a criterion group and in a particular subpopulation could be established so that it would be possible to develop appropriate weights. For example, because women are less likely than men to be employed outside the home, items measuring alcohol-related employment problems among women would be weighted by a factor greater than one. However, because the sex ratio associated with absenteeism from work is less than one, an item measuring alcohol-related absenteeism among women would be weighted by a factor less than one. Were these weights available, so that indicators of employment-related alcohol problems were adjusted both for gender differences in labor force participation and in lost time from work, scale scores would be less likely to reflect distortions resulting from differences in population subgroups attributable to factors other than alcohol abuse.

An alternative strategy useful in developing scales of problem drinking is suggested by Clark's (1966b) finding that women are most likely to be identified as problem drinkers when the definition of problem drinking includes items measuring level of intake and the use of alcohol to reduce tension, as well as by Harford's (1979) suggestion that the study of alcohol problems among adolescents would benefit from an analytic separation of internal and external reasons for drinking. As noted earlier, almost all scales of problem drinking or screens for alcoholism include questions regarding psychological dependence on alcohol or preoccupation with alcohol (NCA Criteria Committee, 1972; Catanzaro, 1967, p. 31). To the extent that researchers in the field can agree that psychological dependence or preoccupation are acceptable as core definitional elements in the study of alcholism or problem drinking, behavioral indicators of drinking problems could be developed for use in different subpopulations through an investigation of the strength of the relationship between items measuring the core definitional elements and specific behavioral consequences.

An example from our previously published work (Schuckit & Morrissey, 1978) illustrates this strategy quite well. Given that alcohol-related police contacts are commonly used indicators of drinking problems, instruments developed for use in studies of teenagers have incorporated items questioning respondents about police contacts involving drinking (Rachal et al., 1976; Mayer & Filstead, 1979). Because alcohol use by adolescents is prohibited by law in all jurisdictions in the United States, the receipt of an alcohol-related citation by an adolescent may well represent nothing more than an instance of alcohol *use*. Because of these differences in laws applying to adults and teenagers, drinking-related police contact has a very different meaning in the two populations. For example, in 1974, of 48,727 juveniles arrested in the United States for alcohol-related violations, nearly two-thirds were arrested for nonspecific offenses described as "violation of liquor laws" including possession of alcohol. Among persons over 18, only 6 percent were arrested for liquor law violations, with the remainder arrested for driving while intoxicated or public drunkenness (Gottfredson, Hindelang & Parisi; 1977, p. 527). Our own work (Schuckit & Morrissey, 1978) indicates that a single liquor law violation committed by a teenager is not necessarily indicative of a drinking problem. Adolescents with a history of multiple liquor law violations, however, and those who receive citations for driving while intoxicated or public drunkenness evidence fairly serious problems related to alcohol. Examining the relationship between items measuring alcohol intake, preoccupation, and dependence and items tapping various behavioral consequences of alcohol abuse would more completely describe differences between population subgroups and provide the basis for developing weights useful in combining items into scales so that meaningful comparisons between subgroups could be made.

Two general methodologic strategies are appropriate for solving measurement problems in the study of alcohol abuse. The first involves weighting indicators of alcohol-related problems based on the prevalence of a given problem in specific groups or on the correlates of preoccupation and dependence, as discussed above. A second approach, which suggests careful attention to research design, would involve the study of alcoholic women as compared to nonalcoholic women and of teenage problem drinkers as compared to teenagers who do not experience alcohol-related problems. This strategy would allow for an assessment of differences between problem and nonproblem drinkers within a population subgroup and begin to isolate factors which are correlates of alcohol abuse rather than of gender roles or of the maturational process.

Research Design Issues

Research designs employed in previously reported studies of alcoholic women illustrate three problems in the study of special populations. First, age and gender differences in rates and in the nature of drinking problems provide better insight into differences between males and females and between young and old than into alcoholism or problem drinking. Second, studies of treated alcoholics or problem drinkers provide evidence which better describes the nature of the process of social control than the psychosocial nature of the disease alcoholism. Third, factors identified in the study of alcoholic women are remarkably similar to factors identified in the study of other types of female deviant behavior. As will be discussed more completely below, the design of research, and especially the nature of the control group selected, limits the nature of the questions that can be addressed in studies of special populations.

The Nature of the Control Group

For example, in the literature on alcoholic women, the dominant research approach has involved comparisons of male and female problem drinkers. The earliest studies tended to focus primarily on clinical populations of exclusively female patients (Curran, 1937; Wall, 1937; Van Amberg, 1942) without benefit of a comparison group of male clients or females who had not entered treatment. With the pioneering work of Lisansky (1957), in which she compared females to male patients, the emphasis in the literature shifted to studies of the differences between problem-drinking men and women. Most recently, in recognition of the fact that gender differences in clinical populations may be a reflection of gender differences in general, investigators have begun to emphasize comparisons of women treated for alcoholism to "normal" female controls. Nevertheless, as is summarized in table 1, of empirical works most often referred to in reviews of the literature on alcohol abusing women, 41 percent include no comparison group, 45 percent compare males to females, and a minority use control groups of normal females.

The dominant research strategy represented in the literature on alcoholic women has had two major consequences. First, when studies of gender differences in drinking patterns identified in community surveys are compared to differences between the drinking habits of males and females studied in treatment settings, it becomes clear that research on alcoholic women has progressed little. Second, reported differences in the types of alcohol-related problems experienced by males and females are primarily a consequence of differences in gender roles and in the response of agents of social control to males and females. Examples from the literature on alcoholic women illustrate the deficiencies evident in existing research.

Research on Gender Differences in the Prevalence of Alcohol Use

Females, in general, have consistently been found to be less likely to drink than males, to drink less frequently, and to drink smaller amounts of alcohol when they do drink. Despite the consistency of this finding, which has been verified in cross-cultural studies (Child et al., 1965), gender differences in alcohol use in this country vary by age, social class, and decade. Among younger age groups and populations studied in the 1970s, there is increasing evidence of diminishing differences between the sexes in the prevalence of alcohol use. Abelson and Atkinson

TABLE 1
Research Designs of Studies
of Problem Drinking and Alcoholic Women

		Comparison or Control Groups	
Year reported	***Absent***	***Present***	
		Comparison group of alcoholic or problem drinking males:	***Comparison group of "normal" females:***
1937	Curran Wall		
1942	Van Amberg		
1955		Levine	
1957		Lisansky	
1958	Rosenbaum		
1959	Myerson		
1961	Fort & Porterfield Woodside	Glatt	
1963	Cramer & Blacker Podolsky		Karp et al.
1964	de Lint, 1964b	de Lint, 1964a	
1966	Cramer & Blacker Johnson et al. Myerson Senseman Wood & Duffy	Zelen, et al.	
1967		Winokur & Clayton Pemberton	
1968	Kinsey	Winokur & Clayton	
1969	Schuckit et al.	Curlee Wilkinson et al. Schmidt & de Lint	
1970		Curlee Mogar et al. Sclare Wanberg & Knapp Wanberg & Horn	

TABLE 1 (*continued*)

Year reported	*Absent*	*Present*	
1971	Jacob & Lavoie	Bateman & Peterson Blane et al. Curlee Garrett Rathod & Thompson Rimmer et al.	Belfer et al. Jones
1972	Schuckit & Winokur	Bateman & Petersen	Parker
1973	Bahr	Garrett & Bahr	Busch et al. Wislnack
1974	Clarke		Hart
1975	James		
1976			Obitz
1977		Mulford	
1978	Morrissey & Schuckit		
1979	Hatsukami & Owen		

(1975) found the prevalence of alcohol use to be increasing nationally between 1972 and 1974, with rates of use among males and teenagers increasing more quickly than rates among females and adults. Both Hanson (1974), in a study of college students, and Johnston et al. (1977), in a panel study of high school students, report increases in the proportion of students who use alcohol and note a convergence in the male and female rates of use among these younger samples. A study done by the Michigan Department of Public Health (1975) concludes that gender differences in the prevalence of alcohol use are smallest among those between the ages of 13 and 34. Eighty-two percent of the females in that age group and 91 percent of the males reported ever having used alcohol.

Research on Gender Differences in Patterns of Alcohol Use

Diminishing gender differences in the prevalence of alcohol use are not necessarily evidence for changes in female drinking patterns. Despite the fact that Cahalan and Treiman (1976b) found that nearly equal proportions of teenage males and females report being intoxicated at least once a month (13% and 12% respectively), the best evidence continues to point to differences in the amount of alcohol use by men and women. It is undoubtedly still the case, as Knupfer found in 1964, that women drink less than their male associates. She reported that, although 12 percent of the women usually drank more than male drinking companions, the greatest majority (67%) drank less. Room and Beck (1974), in a review of findings from national population surveys completed between 1964 and 1971, conclude that although the prevalence of alcohol use among women is increasing, the increase is accounted for primarily by females who become light or moderate drinkers. The greatest increase in drinking among adult women seems to be occurring among urban residents who are members of the upper social classes (Cahalan et al., 1969). Among these women, rates of heavy drinking are reported to increase with increasing age while among lower class women, rates of heavy drinking decrease with age (Room, 1972). The bulk of existing evidence indicates that, even though the prevalence of alcohol use among women in the United States may be increasing, age and gender differences in the frequency and quantity of alcohol consumption persist (Knupfer & Room 1964). Given that women in general drink smaller amounts of alcohol than men, it is not surprising that, among the predominantly heavy drinkers studied in treatment settings, males are found to drink greater quantities of alcohol than females (Rimmer et al., 1971; Garrett & Bahr, 1973; Wanberg & Horn, 1973).

Research on Gender Differences in the Circumstances of Alcohol Use

Gender differences in the circumstances and patterning of alcohol use are also remarkably consistent regardless of whether study subjects are drawn from the general population or contacted in treatment settings. In an early investigation of gender differences in the first drinking experience, Ullman (1957) analyzed data from a study of college undergraduates to find that the circumstances surrounding students' first drinking experiences described differences between male and female drinking patterns in general. Specifically, males were more likely to have their first drink in the company of friends, to drink to intoxication, and to begin drinking regularly thereafter. Female students, by contrast, were more likely to remember their first drinking experience, to have first used alcohol at home with family members, and to wait a longer period of time before another drinking occasion. Women in treatment are found to begin drinking at an older age, on the average, than the males to which they are compared (Rimmer et al., 1971; Glatt, 1961). Glatt reports that female patients not only begin drinking at a later average age than males, a longer period of time elapses between the time they take their first drink and the time when they first become intoxicated. This result parallels Ullman's (1957) finding indicating that young women do not become regular drinkers following their first experience with alcohol, but delay the second drinking occasion for a longer period of time than young men. Johnson et al. (1966) found similarities between the first drinking experience of patients they studied and that of the college students studied by Ullman. They wrote, "Most of the women had their initial exposure to alcohol at social gatherings or in their own homes" (1966, p. 343).

The tendency for females to begin drinking at home and with family members persists beyond the first drinking experience. Women are consistently less likely to drink in taverns (Clark, 1966a; Cahalan & Treiman, 1976a; Harford, 1977), and when they do frequent taverns they are most likely to be with a spouse or male companion. Among heavy drinking women, however, patterns of alcohol intake more nearly approximate typically male habits. Female heavy drinkers, while they more often drink at home alone than female moderate or light drinkers, also drink more often in taverns with friends. They evidence a tendency to drink socially in the home less often in favor of solitary drinking at home and to engage increasingly in gregarious drinking in public places (Blane et al., 1979).

As is true of drinking women in general, the circumstances of the first drinking experiences of female alcohol abusers characterize later patterns as well. Alcohol-dependent women are more likely than alcoholic males to drink at home (Wood & Duffy, 1966; Johnson et al., 1966; Senseman, 1966) with a spouse (Wanberg & Horn, 1970) or with family and friends (Johnson et al., 1966). Although reviews of the literature often convey the impression that solitary drinking at home is the modal pattern among female alcohol abusers (Schuckit & Morrissey, 1976; Beckman, 1975), solitary drinking and drinking in the home do not necessarily covary. Heavy-drinking women seem to be slightly more likely than males with comparable levels of alcohol intake to drink alone, but women in general are more likely to drink at home. Furthermore, among treatment populations the tendency to drink alone varies by age and social class, with younger women preferring to drink in taverns and bars alone, and older, higher status women preferring solitary drinking at home or drinking at parties (Cramer & Blacker, 1963; Wood & Duffy, 1966). Solitary drinking among females increases directly as a function of the quantity of alcohol consumed (Blane et al., 1979; Garrett & Bahr, 1973) even among homeless women who, by definition, do not drink at home. As Blane's recent analysis suggests, women who drink more often are certainly going to drink alone more often than other women.

That women are more likely than men to drink at home with a spouse or other family members, or to drink in restaurants (Becker & Kronus, 1977; Harford, 1977) is consistent with the observation that females prefer drinking with meals (Edwards et al., 1973). The pattern of drinking with meals in evidence among female samples is one possible explanation for Knupfer's (1964) finding that males and females who report an equivalent average weekly volume of alcohol consumption are likely to space drinking episodes differently. Females drink small amounts every day, while males are more likely to concentrate relatively heavy drinking on weekends. In the same vein, Calahan and Cisin (1968, p. 649) report that, based on studies of probability samples, males are consistently more likely than females to evidence a high maximum volume of alcohol intake, even when the average quantity of alcohol use is held constant.

Similar drinking patterns are reported in the literature on alcoholic women. Among the female patients studied by Fort and Porterfield (1961), the majority reported steady, daily drinking, while less than one-fifth described their alcohol consumption as periodic. Lisansky (1957) speculatively agrees that females are more likely to be plateau drinkers, drinking smaller quantities per occasion than heavy drinking males but drinking every day. Cramer and Blacker's (1963) analysis suggests variation in female heavy drinking patterns by age. Their evidence indicates that while younger women may be heavy, steady drinkers, older women are more likely to use alcohol heavily on a periodic basis. Because subjects included in Cramer and Blacker's investigation were reformatory inmates and therefore predominantly from the lower and lower-middle classes, their findings are congruent with Cahalan and Cisin's (1968) analysis of the spacing of drinking episodes among heavy drinkers from the general population. Among women consuming a medium or high volume of alcohol, young, middle and lower class females were more likely to evidence a pattern that included a variable high maximum of alcohol intake, while higher status and older women drinking similar amounts of alcohol overall were more likely to space drinking episodes so the maximum volume consumed on any one occasion was relatively constant.

Evidence for gender differences in drinking styles is available from other studies done in treatment settings in which males are more often found to be binge drinkers than are females (Rimmer et al., 1971). Johnson et al. (1966) note that all of the women included in their study simultaneously became heavy drinkers and daily drinkers. Unfortunately these women were not compared to male alcohol abusers. Research reported by Wanberg and Horn (1973) takes issue with the characterization of heavy drinking females as more likely than males to be plateau or maintenance drinkers. Their finding that males score higher on a factor including items tapping what the authors refer to as sustained drinking and contrast to periodic drinking is, however, partially due to the fact that the majority of items included in the factor are more clearly indicative of loss of control over alcohol intake and/or addiction to alcohol than of the quantity of alcohol used or of the spacing of drinking episodes. They also found that controlled, daily, heavy drinking was equally characteristic of males and females in their study population. It would therefore seem that there is at least some question about the extent to which gender differences in drinking patterns in the general population adequately characterize differences between the alcohol use patterns of males and females in treatment.

Research on Gender Differences in Motivations for Alcohol Use

Differences in the patterning and circumstances of use are also related to gender variation in motivations for alcohol use. Clark

(1966b) found females to be more likely to refer to social reasons for drinking, while males more often admitted drinking to change their mood or to reduce tension. More recent evidence is consistent with Clark's findings. Becker and Kronus (1977, p. 488) note that females' predominantly social reasons for alcohol use are congruent with the settings in which women are most likely to drink and with their preference for wine. This latter preference is in contrast to the male preference for beer (Cahalan et al., 1969, p. 67). There is, however, some evidence that the preferred type of beverage alcohol varies with the quantity consumed. Blane et al. (1979) recently reported that heavy-drinking women were more likely to prefer liquor and less likely to prefer wine than female moderate drinkers. Blane's study also suggests that women who drink heavily may be less strongly motivated to drink by social considerations than are women who drink less.

Edward's analysis of motivations for drinking among respondents who used alcohol at least monthly revealed few gender differences and indicated that males and females are nearly equally likely to use alcohol to reduce tension (1973, p. 578). Males were significantly more likely than females, however, to drink alcohol to quench thirst, to relieve boredom, because of the pressure of occupational demands, or out of habit. Following a factor analysis of the items regarding motivations for drinking, Edwards et al. (1973) concluded that male and female motivations for alcohol use are roughly similar, although males may be more likely to develop abusive drinking patterns as a result of using alcohol to relieve unpleasant feelings.

Even though alcohol-abusing women are just as likely as women in general to refer to social reasons for drinking (Mulford, 1977, p. 1632), they are also as likely or more likely than alcohol-abusing males to cite individual reasons for drinking. In Mulford's (1977) study of clients in outpatient Communilty Alcoholism Programs in Iowa, women were more likely than men to report using alcohol to settle nerves, forget pressure, get to sleep or overcome loneliness. A substantial proportion of both sexes, over three-fourths, used alcohol to relieve tension, and this pattern was even more apparent among married clients.

This brief review of the literature on alcoholic women illustrates that gender differences in the quantity of alcohol consumed, the type of beverage preferred, the patterning of alcohol intake, and the circumstances surrounding the first and later episodes of alcohol use are consistently found regardless of whether studies are conducted in treatment settings or in the community. Many of the "unique" characteristics of alcoholic women reported in the literature are a restatement of differences between male and female drinking behaviors and contribute little to our understanding of the psychosocial correlates to alcohol abuse. If more of the studies reported in the literature had focussed on control groups of normal women or even on control groups of women treated for disorders other than alcoholism, more information would be available on the truly unique properties of female alcoholism.

Studies of Treatment Populations

If females are less likely to be heavy drinkers and less likely to drink outside of social contexts, it should be no surprise that they are also less likely than males to experience alcohol-related problems and to be identified as problem drinkers. Results obtained in national surveys of the United States population indicate that only 3 percent of adults report being treated for alcohol-related problems. Even among subjects who admitted experiencing interpersonal or health-related problems because of alcohol, only 19 percent of the males and 10 percent of the females had been treated (Calahan & Treiman, 1976b). The relatively small proportion of alcohol-dependent and problem-drinking females found in studies of the general population accounts for the fact that most studies of problem-drinking women are conducted in treatment settings. The conduct of research on alcoholic women primarily in treatment settings accounts for the fact that the literature on gender differences among alcoholics provides little insight into the psychosocial etiology of alcoholism. As discussed above, gender differences in drinking patterns, circumstances of drinking, and motivations for alcohol use are remarkably similar in treated and untreated populations. Likewise, gender differences in the types of alcohol-related problems typically experienced by patients admitted to alcoholism treatment reflect general differences between the male and female roles. This has been noted repeatedly in reviews of the literature on alcoholic women (Gomberg, 1979; Schuckit & Morrissey, 1976).

Gomberg (1977), in a recent summary of findings resulting from studies of alcohol abusers in treatment, notes the following contrasts between males and females:

1. Because women begin to drink and experience their first intoxication at a later age, they have a later onset of alcohol-related problems and come to treatment after a shorter period of alcohol abuse (Curlee, 1970; Rathod & Thomson, 1971; Winokur & Clayton, 1968; Mulford, 1977).
2. Women are less likely than alcohol-abusing men to drink every day, and men are more likely to report binge drinking (Rimmer et al., 1971). When women do drink sporadically, their drinking bouts are shorter (Wanberg & Horn, 1973).
3. With respect to alcohol-related social problems, women are less likely than men to: (*a*) be arrested (Linsansky, 1957; Rimmer et al., 1971; Mulford, 1977) or (*b*) be dismissed from a job (Wanberg & Horn, 1973); but more likely to experience marital disruptions because of alcohol use (Mulford, 1977).
4. Alcohol-abusing women have also been reported to be more likely than males to evidence a history of depression and suicide attempts (Rimmer et al., 1971) and to be characterized by higher rates of psychiatric treatment prior to the treatment of alcoholism (Curlee, 1970; Rathod & Thomson, 1971).

Differences in the types of problems experienced by males and females as a result of alcohol use are not surprising in view of the differential visibility of alcohol-related problems typically experienced by males and females. Results indicating that alcohol-abusing women consume less alcohol, begin drinking at a later age, are less likely to drink sporadically, are more likely to prefer wine over beer, and more likely to drink at home alone or with family members than are alcohol abusing men parallel differences observed in studies of samples from the general population of drinkers. That women are more likely than men to have experienced alcohol-related marital problems (Mulford, 1977) reflects traditional expectations regarding the importance of the wife/mother role relative to the husband/father role in the family. Similarly, that women are less likely than males to experience alcohol-related employment problems (Wanberg & Horn, 1973) reflects traditional expectations regarding the male role as breadwinner. Differences in numbers of alcohol-related arrests reported by alcoholic men and women in treatment (Lisansky, 1957; Rimmer et al., 1971; Mulford 1977) parallel gender differences in arrest rates for all types of offenses. Even when women do come to the attention of the police for problem drinking, they are less likely than males to be formally processed for drunken behavior (Pastor, 1979; Angeriou & Paulino, 1976). Higher rates of suicide attempts, neuroses, and depression noted among alcoholic women when compared to men (Rimmer et al., 1971; Curlee, 1970) parallel gender differences in the incidence of psychiatric disorder and rates of use of psychiatric services in the general population (Gove & Tudor, 1973; Becker, 1974). Medical complications resulting from alcohol addiction are least likely to differentiate between males and females in treatment, although women generally tend to be less likely to report experiencing serious symptoms such as hallucinations and withdrawal sickness.

Although some investigators claim that women in treatment are more likely than men to have experienced familial problems as a result of alcohol abuse (Wall, 1937; Glatt, 1961; Winokur & Clayton, 1968), evidence on this point is partly inferred from the fact that female patients are sometimes found to be more likely to be divorced than male patients. However, when Lisansky (1957) compared divorce rates among the patients she studied to those of the populations from which the patients were drawn, rates of marital disruption for both males and females were similarly inflated. More recently, Mulford (1977, p. 1628) found that rates of multiple marriages among outpatient clients were double the rates in the general population for males and triple the rates in the general population for females. Married women, however, were reportedly more dissatisfied with their current marriages than were married males. Women in treatment settings may also be more likely than males to be divorced or separated because they are more likely than married women to be formally processed by police (Angeriou & Paulino, 1976) and therefore to be referred to treatment. There are generally few gender differences in the proportions of treatment populations married at the time of treatment (Wanberg & Horn, 1973; Rimmer et al., 1971; Mulford, 1977), although males are more likely to have never married.

The Impact of Selection Factors on Research Results

Given the reluctance of agents of legal social control to react to intoxicated women (Pastor, 1979), it may require more serious, persistent, and visible deviant behavior on the part of female alcohol abusers for referral to treatment to be initiated. Angeriou and Paulino (1976) report that in order for women to be cited for driving while intoxicated it is nearly essential that they be involved in an auto accident resulting in property damage. In the absence of property damage, verbal abuse of an officer will elicit the issuance of a citation. Similar reasoning accounts for the higher rates of suicide attempts and psychiatric hospitalizations observed in populations of alcohol-abusing females as compared to alcohol-abusing males. Those women who do not engage in repeated and visible deviant behavior in conjunction with alcohol abuse are less likely to be subjected to social control.

Apart from the primarily social consequences of drinking, slight gender differences are also apparent in the physiological consequences of alcohol use. Males are found to be more likely to experience blackouts, shakes, and hallucinations as a result of alcohol use. This result can quite simply be attributed to their heavier alcohol intake which generally persists for a longer period of time prior to treatment and is characterized by binge drinking.

It seems reasonable to assume that women who are subjected to social control for alcohol abuse, while they are characterized by drinking histories and alcohol use patterns somewhat similar to nonabusing females, adopt predominantly male styles of drinking as they become heavier drinkers. While males are generally more likely to drink to relax to reduce tension, among treatment populations this result is reversed. It may be that, to the extent that women begin to emphasize the depressant effects of alcohol as desirable, the probability of their becoming alcohol dependent increases. There is some evidence that the adoption of traditionally male roles affects the probability of women's use of alcohol as a depressant. Wanberg and Knapp

(1970) report that women are more likely to feel that drinking helps you work better and Wanberg and Horn (1973) later report this item to be part of a factor including a measure of the use of alcohol to reduce tension. The factor constructed by Wanberg and Horn, however, did not differentiate between males and females in a treatment setting.

The emphasis in the literature, while providing interesting insights into gender differences in drinking patterns and drinking problems, does not provide an understanding of why certain psychosocial factors trigger alcoholism in some women, while other women who may also be affected by the same factors do not become alcoholic. If may well be that some of the characteristics of alcoholic women identified by investigators in studies of treated alcoholics represent conditions under which women are *identified* as alcohol abusers rather than unique properties describing female alcoholics. For example, women who repeatedly attempt suicide, use psychiatric services, or drive under the influence of alcohol are more likely to enter alcoholism treatment than women who abuse alcohol without engaging in other forms of deviant behavior. To assess the extent to which factors thought to be associated with alcoholism in women actually are psychosocial correlates of alcohol abuse and not merely correlates of help-seeking behavior or of female deviant behavior in general, future comparisons must be made between treated and untreated alcoholic women and between alcoholic women and women who engage in other types of deviant behavior.

Implications for the Identification of Etiologic Factors

The collection of data from treated women has yet a more serious consequence. It is impossible to determine, from studies completed to date, whether phenomena such as sex role confusion, life change, and affective disorder are determinants of alcohol abuse among females or determinants of help-seeking behavior. For example, the tendency for women to begin drinking alcoholically in response to discrete life change events was first noted by James Wall (1937) and has been reported by numerous investigators since that time (Curlee, 1969; Lisansky, 1957; Fort & Porterfield, 1961; Morrissey & Schuckit, 1978). While these studies have focused on the impact of discrete life change events on the development of problem drinking among females, others have argued that minor, continuing stresses have a greater impact on the development of female alcoholism (Johnson et al., 1966; Kinsey, 1968; Wood & Duffy, 1966) than major life change does. Given findings that the experience of major life change increases the chances of using psychiatric services (Hudgens, 1974), the fact that studies of the role of life change in the development of problem drinking have been completed in treatment settings is a serious limitation. It may be true that the experience of stressful events is more closely related to entering alcoholism treatment than to the onset of alcoholism (Mulford, 1977). The resolution of this question will require the comparison of women treated for alcoholism to women treated for other types of disorders.

The need to compare alcoholic women to females identified as deviant in other respects is also suggested by parallel findings in the literature on psychopathologies among women in general and in studies of alcoholic women. For example, Riess and Safer (1979) in reviewing two studies of lesbian women write:

> Mother domination was true in each research. High frequency of parental discord and death or absense of one parent were seen by the two sets of authors (1979, p. 283).

Gomberg (1979, p. 220) notes similar problems in the backgrounds of alcoholic women and writes that "early history of family disruption is also true of women who manifest other forms of deviant behavior. . . ."

Similarly, in our earlier review of the literature on alcoholic women (Schuckit & Morrissey, 1976), etiologic factors effecting alcoholism in women were classified as related to hormonal differences between males and females, gender identity differences, and variations in sex role behaviors. A similar classification of the differences between males and females is made by Seiden (1979, pp. 434–435) in her discussion of psychophysiological illnesses. Factors influencing the results of comparisons of males and females, she argues, are anatomical, hormonal differences; hereditary differences; and differences related to social gender roles. Gender roles can influence the exposure to risk factors, the nature of symptom manifestation and the diagnostic process. When a disease is defined partly in terms of social behaviors, as is true of alcoholism, variation in the manifestation of symptoms in different subgroups must be partitioned into components so differences determined by age and/or gender roles may be identified.

Research on Adolescent Problem Drinking

The literature on adolescent problem drinking focuses on issues similar to those found in the literature on adult alcoholics. The impact of early familial disorganization on the development of teenage drinking problems has been repeatedly observed (Wechsler & Thum, 1973). As is true of studies of alcoholic women, familial factors identified as correlates of youthful alcohol abuse are also correlates of other types of deviant behaviors engaged in by teenagers. In the cases of both adolescent alcohol and drug abuse, frequent, heavy intake is associated with deliquent behavior and less than optimal social functioning. Jessor and Jessor (1975), in a report of the results of a cohort study, indicate that the age of onset of drinking and extent of drinking problems are correlated with manifestations of other forms of deviant behavior. The earlier the first drinking experience and the more serious alcohol-related problems, the greater the probability there will be manifestations of other forms of deviant behavior. This is consistent with findings from cross-sectional studies of the drinking practices of delinquent youth which generally report more serious alcohol involvement in these populations (MacKay, et al., 1963, 1967; MacKay, 1963, 1965; Pearce & Garrett, 1970; Schonfield, 1966/67; Stenmark, et al., 1974; Gibbens, 1972; Backhouse & James, 1969; Blacker, Demone & Freeman, 1965). The same correlation has been reported between use of drugs other than alcohol and self-reported delinquent behavior and between drug use and official delinquency (Johnston,1974; Stenmark et al., 1974).

The consistency of the relationship between adolescent problem drinking and other forms of deviant behavior has led to a recent explicit proposal (Zucker, 1979) of a "delinquency theory" of teenage problem drinking. In describing a development perspective for use in the study of problem drinking, Zucker (1979, p.118) presents data which "showed that a harsher, more negative familial environment and a more impulsive behavioral style were characteristic of antisocial behavior more than of problem drinking and were more characteristic of problem drinking than of heavy drinking." Zucker's approach emphasizes two essential priniciples in the study of drinking problems and alcoholism. First, findings of research on adolescents must be evaluated in the context of general knowledge regarding teenage behavior and development. Secondly, alcohol abuse and problem drinking must be analyzed in relationship to the occurrence of other forms of deviant behavior among teenagers.

Conclusion

Several problems arise in the study of alcohol abuse and alcoholism when the focus is on special populations. As illustrated here with examples from the literature on alcoholic women and teenaged problem drinkers, when alcoholism is defined partly in terms of the social consquences of alchol abuse, age and gender variations in acceptable role behaviors influence estimates of the prevalence of alcohol problems. It is argued that the strategy of developing special screens for alcoholism in women or in teenagers is not a productive research strategy if our goal is ultimately to identify psychosocial factors that may trigger alcoholic drinking. It is suggested that, instead of modifying existing instruments used to characterize alcoholic drinking by deleting, adding, or developing completely new items, efforts should focus on establishing weights for indicators of alcoholic drinking and behavior. Weighting procedures could be designed to make a single scale applicable across subpopulations. This would allow for meaningful comparisons between males and females and between young and old.

It is also argued that a number of questions must be addressed in the study of special populations. Differences in social roles typical of members of various subgroups contribute to the need for complicated scaling procedures. Variations in role components also present design problems in the study of subpopulations. To the extent that gender comparisons, for example, can be put into the context of what we know about differences between males and females in our culture, the invariant properties of alcoholism can be identified. As is clear from the earlier discussion, the bulk of the literature on alcoholic women provides information that simply describes known differences between male and female drinking practices and between male and female gender roles.

Furthermore, as seen in studies of female alcoholism and of teenage problem drinking, factors emphasized in the explanation of pathologic drinking behavior are the same factors used to explain female psychopathology and adolescent deviant behavior in general. Were studies of abusive drinking formulated within the context of what is known about both "normal" and deviant behavior in special populations, not only would our understanding of alcoholism be enhanced, but general theories of deviant behavior in subpopulations would begin to emerge.

The understanding of the course of alcoholism in special populations can best be achieved through studies comparing problem and nonproblem drinkers within the same population. The result of comparisons of females to males, for example, may be confounded by differences between the sexes unrelated to alcohol abuse. More seriously, when comparisons are made between males and females in treatment settings, differences in the response of the legal or medical system to males and females affect results. Women are, of course, more likely to use medical and psychiatric services than males, and men are more likely to be arrested than females. To assess the manner in which variation in the identification of individuals as alcoholic may bias research results, comparisons between treated and untreated members of special populations are necessary. These types of comparisons are especially important in the study of teenage problem drinking, as it has been repeately reported in the literature that young people who get in trouble with the police for any reason are much more likely to use psychoactive drugs, including alcohol, than youth who have no contact with police. Comparisons of problem and nonproblem drinkers within special populations and of treated and untreated alcoholics are essential if we are to begin to understand the impact of psychosocial factors on the course of alcoholism or problem drinking in special populations.

References

Abelson, H.I. & Atkinson, R.B. (1975). *Public Experience With Psychoactive Substances.* Part I: Main Findings. Princeton, New Jersey: Response Analysis Corporation.

Argeriou, M. & Paulino, D. (1976). Women arrested for drunken driving in Boston. *J. Stud. Alc.* 37:648–658.

Babst, D.V., Dembo, R. & Burgos W. (1979). Measuring consequences of drug and alcohol abuse among junior high school students. *J. Alc. Drug Educ.* 25:11–19.

Backhouse, C.I. & James, I.P. (1969). The relationship and prevalence of smoking, drinking and drug taking in (delinquent) adolescent boys. *Br. J. Addict.* 64:75–79.

Bahr, H.M. (1973). Homeless women. In: *Skid Row: An Introduction to Disaffiliation*, ed. H. Bahr. New York: Oxford University Press, pp. 175–221.

Bateman, N.I. & Peterson, D.M. (1971). Variables related to outcome of treatment for hospitalized alcoholics. *Int. J. Addict.* 6:215–224.

Bateman, N.I. & Peterson, D.M. (1972). Factors related to outcome of treatment for hospitalized white male and female alcoholics. *J. Drug Issues* 2:66–74.

Becker, C. & Kronus, S. (1977). Sex and drinking patterns: An old relationship revisited in a new way. *Soc. Prob.* 24:482–497.

Becker, J. (1974). *Depression: Theory and Research.* Washington, D.C.: V.H. Winston.

Beckman, L.J. (1975). Women alcoholics: A review of social and psychological studies. *J. Stud. Alc.* 36:797–824.

Belfer, M.L., Shader, R.I., Carroll, M. & Harmatz, J.S. (1971). Alcoholism and Women. *Arch. Gen. Psychiat.* 25:540–544.

Blacker, E., Demone, H.W. & Freeman, H.E. (1965). Drinking behavior of delinquent boys. *Quart. J. Stud. Alc.* 26:223– 237.

Blane, H.T., Ritchey, D. & Connor, B.C. (1979). Heavy-drinking Irish American women: A psychosocial profile. Paper presented at the National Council on Alcoholism Forum. Washington D.C.: April 27–May 2.

Busch, H., Kormendy, E. & Feuerlein, W. (1973). Partners of female alcoholics. *Brit. J. Addict.* 68:179–184.

Cahalan, D. & Cisin, I.H. (1968). American drinking practices: Summary of findings from a national probability sample. II. Measurement of massed versus spaced drinking. *Quart. J. Stud. Alc.* 29:642–656.

Cahalan, D., Cisin, I.H. & Crossley, H.M. (1969). *American Drinking Practices.* New Brunswick, N.J.: Rutgers Center of Alcohol Studies.

Cahalan, D. & Room, R. (1974). *Problem Drinking Among American Men.* New Brunswick, N.J.: Rutgers Center of Alcohol Studies.

Cahalan, D., Roizen, R. & Room, R. (1976). Alcohol problems and their prevention: Public attitudes in California. In: *The Prevention of Alcohol Problems*, ed. R. Room & S. Sheffield. Sacramento, Calif.: California Office of Alcoholism, pp. 354–403.

Cahalan, D. & Treiman, B. (1976a). Drinking behavior, attitudes, and problems in Marin County, California. Berkeley, Calif.: Social Research Group, School of Public Health, University of California.

Cahalan, D. & Treiman, B. (1976b). Drinking behavior, attitudes, and problems in San Francisco. Berkeley, Calif.: Social Research Group, School of Public Health, University of California.

Carver, V. (1977). The female alcoholic in treatment. *Can. Psychol. Rev.* 18:96–103.

Catanzaro, R.J. (1967). Psychiatric aspects of alcoholism In: *Alcoholism*, ed. D.J. Pittman. New York: Harper and Row, pp. 31–45.

Child, S.L., Barry, H. & Bacon, M. (1965). Sex Differences: A cross cultural study of drinking. *Quart. J. Stud. Alc.* (Supplement) 3:49–61.

Clark, W. (1966a). Demographic characteristics of tavern patrons in San Francisco. *Quart. J. Stud. Alc.* 27:316–327.

Clark, W. (1966b). Operational definitions of drinking problems and associated prevalence rates. *Quart. J. Stud. Alc.* 27:648–668.

Clarke, S.K. (1974). Self esteem in men and women alcoholics. *Quart. J. Stud. Alc.* 35:1380–1381.

Cramer, M.J. & Blacker, E. (1963). 'Early' and 'late' problem drinkers among female prisoners. *J. Health Human Behav.* 4:282–290.

Cramer, M.J. & Blacker, E. (1966). Social class and drinking experience of female drunkenness offenders. *J. Health Human Behav.* 7:276–283.

Curlee, J. (1969). "Alcoholism and the 'Empty Nest'." *Bulletin of the Menninger Clinic* 33:165–171.

Curlee, J. (1970). A comparison of male and female patients at an alcoholism treatment center. *J. Psychol.* 74:239–247.

Curlee, J. (1971). Sex differences in patient attitudes toward alcoholism treatment. *Quart. J. Stud. Alc.* 32:643–650.

Curran, F.J. (1937). Personality studies in alcoholic women. *J. Nerv. Ment. Dis.* 86:645–667.

deLint, J. (1964a) Alcholism, birth rank and parental deprivation. *Am. J. Psychiat.* 120:1062–1065.

deLint, J. (1964b). Alcoholism, birth order, and socializing agents. *J. Abnorm. Soc. Psychol.* 69:457–458.

Demone, H.W. & Wechsler, H. (1976). Changing drinking patterns of adolescents during the last decade. In: *Alcoholism Problems in Women and Children*, ed. M. Greenblatt & M. Schuckit. New York: Grune and Stratton.

Edwards, G., Hensman, C. & Peto, J. (1972). Drinking in a London suburb. III. Comparisons of drinking troubles among men and women. *Quart. J. Stud. Alc.* (Supplement) 6:120–128.

Edwards, G., Hensman, C. & Peto, J. (1973). A comparison of female and male motivation for drinking. *Int. J. Addict.* 8:577–587.

Fort, T. & Porterfield, A.G. (1961). Some backgrounds and types of alcoholism among women. *J. Health Human Behav.* 2:283–292.

Garrett, G.R. & Bahr, H.M. (1973). Women on Skid Row. *Quart. J. Stud. Alc.* 34:1228–1243.

Gibbens, T.C. (1972). Drink, drugs and delinquency. *Med. Sci. Law* 12: 257–261.

Glatt, M.M. (1961). Drinking habits of English (middle-class) alcoholics. *Acta Psychiat. Scand.* 37:88–113.

Gomberg, E.S. (1974). Women and alcoholism. In: *Women in Therapy*, ed. V. Franks & V. Burtle. New York: Brunner/Mazel, pp. 167–170.

Gomberg, E.S. (1977). Women with alcohol problems. In: *Alcoholism, Development, Consequences and Interventions*, ed. N. Estes & E. Heineman. St. Louis: C.V. Mosby, pp. 174–185.

Gomberg, E.S. (1979). Problems with alcohol and other drugs. In: *Gender and Disordered Behavior*, ed. E.S. Gomberg & V. Franks. New York: Brunner/Mazel, pp. 204–240.

Gottfredson, M.R., Hindelang, M.J. & Parisi, N. (1977). *Sourcebook of Criminal Justice Statistics, 1976*. U.S. Department of Justice.

Gove, W.R. & Tudor, J.F. (1973). Adult sex roles and mental illness. *Am. J. Sociol.* 78:812–835.

Hanson, D.J. (1974). Drinking attitudes and behaviors among college students. *J. Alc. Drug Educ.* 19:6–14.

Harford, T.C. (1977). Contextual drinking patterns among men and women. Paper presented at the National Council on Alcoholism Forum Meetings, San Diego.

Harford, T.C. (1979). Ecological factors in drinking. In: *Youth, Alcohol, and Social Policy*, ed. H.T. Blane & M.E. Chafetz. New York: Plenum Press, pp. 147–182.

Hatsukami, D. & Owen, P.L. (1979). Treatment outcome in female alcoholics: A new perspective. Paper presented at the Annual Medical Scientific Meetings of the National Council on Alcholism, Washington, D.C.

Hudgens, R.W. (1974). Personal catastrophe and depression: A consideration of the subject with respect to medically ill adolescents, and a requiem for retrospective life event studies. In: *Stressful Life Events: Their Nature and Effects*, ed. B.S. Dohrenwend & B.P. Dohrenwend. New York: John Wiley and Sons, pp. 119–134.

Jackson, J.K. (1957), The definition and measurement of alcoholism. H-technique scales of preoccupation with alcohol and psychological involvement. *Quart. J. Stud. Alc.* 2:240–262.

James, J.E. (1975). Symptoms of alcoholism in women: A preliminary survey of A.A. members. *J. Stud. Alc.* 36:1564–1569.

Johnson, M.W. (1965). Physicians' views on alcoholism: with special reference to alcoholism in women. *Nebraska State Med. J.* 50:378–384.

Johnson, M.W., DeVries, J.C. & Houghton, M.I. (1966). The female alcoholic. *Nurs. Res.* 15:343–347.

Johnson, S. & Garzon, S.R. (1978). Alcoholism and women. *Am. J. Drug Alc. Abuse* 5:107–122.

Johnston, L. (1974). Drug use during and after high school: Results of a national longitudinal study. *Am. J. Public Health* 64(Supplement): 29–37.

Johnston, L.D., Bachman, J.G. & O'Malley, P.M. (1977). *Drug Use Among American High School Students 1975–1977*. Rockville, Maryland: National Institute on Drug Abuse.

Jones, M.C. (1971). Personality antecedents and correlates of drinking patterns in women. *J. Consult. Clin. Psychol.* 36:61–69.

Karp, S.A., Poster, D.C. & Goodman, A. (1963). Differentiation in alcoholic women. *J. Personality* 31:386–393.

Keller, M. (1960). Definition of alcoholism. *Quart. J. Stud. Alc.* 21:125–134.

Kinsey, B.A. (1968). Psychological factors in alcoholic women from a state hospital sample. *Am. J. Psychiat.* 124:1463–1466.

Knupfer, G. (1964). Female drinking patterns. In: North American Association of Alcoholism Programs, Selected papers presented at the 15th Annual Meeting. Washington, D.C.: NAAAP, pp. 140–160.

Knupfer, G. & Room, R. (1964). Age, sex and social class as factors in amount of drinking in a metropolitan community. *Soc. Prob.* 12: 224–240.

Knupfer, G. & Room, R (1966). Some methodological problems in the epidemiology of alcoholic beverage usage: The definition of amount of intake. *Am. J. Public Health* 56:237–242.

Levine, J. (1955). Sexual adjustment of alcoholics. A clinical study of a selected sample. *Quart. J. Stud. Alc.* 16:675–678.

Liban, C. & Smart, R.G. (1979). Generational and other differences between males and females in problem drinking and its treatment. Paper presented at the Annual Medical Scientific Meetings of the National Council on Alcoholism, Washington, D.C.

Lindbeck, V.L. (1972). The woman alcoholic: A review of the literature. *Int. J. Addict.* 7:567–580.

Lisansky, E.S. (1957). Alcoholism in women: Social and psychological concomitants. I. Social history data. *Quart. J. Stud. Alc.* 18:588–623.

Little, R.E., Schultz, F.A. & Mandell, W. (1977). Describing alcohol consumption: A comparison of three methods and a new approach. *J. Stud. Alc.* 38:554–562.

Lolli, G. (1953). Alcoholism in women. *Conn. Rev. Alc.* 5:9–11.

MacKay, J. (1963). Problem drinking among juvenile delinquents. *Crime Deliq.* 9:29–38.

MacKay, J. (1965). Alcohol, alcoholism, and youth. *Social Work* 10:75–80.

MacKay, J., Murray, A.E. & Haggerty, T.J. (1963). Juvenile delinquency and drinking behavior. *J. Health Human Behav.* 4:276–282.

MacKay, J.R., Phillips, D.L. & Bryce, F.O. (1967). Drinking behavior among teenagers: A comparison of institutionalized and non-institutionalized youth. *J. Hlth. Soc. Behav.* 18:46–54.

Mayer, J. & Filstead, W.J. (1979). The Adolescent Alcohol Involvement Scale: An instrument for measuring adolescents' use and misuse of alcohol. *J. Stud. Alc.* 40:291–299.

Michigan Department of Public Health (1975). *Alcohol and Other Drug Use and Abuse in the State of Michigan.* Detroit: Office of Substance Abuse Services.

Morrissey, E.R. & Schuckit, M.A. (1978). Stressful life events and alcohol problems among women seen at a detoxification center. *J. Stud. Alc.* 39:1559–1576.

Mulford, H.A. (1977). Women and men problem drinkers: Sex differences in patients served by Iowa's Community Alcoholism Services. *J. Stud. Alc.* 38:1624–1639.

Mulford, H.A. & Miller, D.E. (1960). Drinking in Iowa. IV. Preoccupation with alcohol and definitions of alcohol, heavy drinking and trouble due to drinking. *Quart. J. Stud. Alc.* 2:279–291.

Myerson, D.J. (1959). Clinical observations on a group of alcoholic prisoners with special reference to women. *Quart. J. Stud. Alc.* 20:555–572.

Myerson, D.J. (1966). A therapeutic appraisal of certain married alcoholic women. *Int. Psychiat. Clin.* 3:143–157.

National Center for Health Statistics (1978a). *Acute Conditions—Incidence and Associated Disability.* DHEW Publication No. (PHS) 78-1548. Hyattsville, Maryland: U.S. Department of Health, Education, and Welfare.

National Center for Health Statistics (1978b). *Current Estimates for Health Interview Survey.* DHEW Publication No. (PHS) 78-1554. Hyattsville, Maryland: U.S. Department of Health, Education, and Welfare.

National Council on Alcoholism Criteria Committee. (1972). Criteria for the diagnosis of alcholism. *Am. J. Psychiat.* 119:127–135.

Pastor, P. (1979). Policing drunken women: Routine police encounters with female public inebriates. Paper presented at the Annual Meetings of the Society for the Study of Social Problems. Boston, Massachusetts.

Pearce, J. & Garrett, J.D. (1970). A comparison of drinking behavior of delinquent youth vs. nondelinquent youth in the State of Idaho and Utah. *J. School Health* 40:131–135.

Pemberton, D.A. (1967). A comparison of the outcome of treatment in female and male alcoholics. *Brit. J. Psychiat.* 113:367–373.

Podolsky, E. (1963). The woman alcoholic and premenstrual tension. *J. Am. Med. Women's Assoc.* 18:816–818.

Rachal, J.V., Hubbard, R.L., Williams, J.R. & Tuchfold, B.S. (1976). Drinking levels and problem drinking among junior and senior high school students. *J. Stud. Alc.* 37:1751–1761.

Rathod, N.H. & Thomson, I.G. (1971). Women alcoholics: A clinical study *Quart. J. Stud. Alc.* 32:45–52.

Riess, B.F. & Safer, J.M. (1979). Homosexuality in females and males. In: *Gender and Disordered Behavior*, ed. E.S. Gomberg & V. Franks. New York: Brunner/Mazel, pp. 257–286.

Rimmer, J., Pitts, F.N. Jr., Reich T. & Winokur, G. (1971). Alcoholism. II. Sex, socioeconomic status and race in two hospitalized samples. *Quart. J. Stud. Alc.* 32:942–952.

Room, R. (1972). Drinking patterns in large U.S. cities: A comparison of San Francisco and national samples in the U.S.A. *Quart. J. Stud. Alc.* (Supplement) 6:28–57.

Room, R. & Beck, K. (1974). Survey data on trends in U.S. consumption. *Drink. Drug Pract. Surv.* 9:3–7.

Rosenbaum, B. (1958). Married women alcoholics at the Washingtonian Hospital. *Quart. J. Stud. Alc.* 19:79–89.

Russell, M. & Bigler L. (1979). Screening for alcohol-related problems in an outpatient obstetric gynecologic clinic. *Am. J. Obstet. Gynecol.* 134: 4–12.

Schmidt, W. & de Lint, J. (1969). Mortality experiences of male and female alcoholic patients. *Quart. J. Stud. Alc.* 30:112–118.

Schonfield, J. (1966/67). Differences in smoking, drinking and social behavior by race and delinquency status in adolescent males. *Adolescence* 1:367–380.

Schuckit, M.A., Pitts, F.N., Reich T. & Winokur, G. (1969). Alcoholism. I. Two types of alcoholism in women. *Arch. Gen. Psychiat.* 20:301–306.

Schuckit, M.A. & Morrissey, E.R. (1976). Alcoholism in women: Some clinical and social perspectives with an emphasis on possible subtypes. In: *Alcoholism Problems in Women and Children*, ed. M. Greenblatt & M.A. Schuckit. New York: Grune and Stratton, pp. 5–35.

Schuckit, M.A. & Morrissey, E.R. (1978). Minor in possession of alcohol: What does it mean? In: *Currents in Alcoholism*, Vol. IV, ed. F. Seixas. New York: Grune and Stratton, pp. 339–355.

Schuckit, M.A. & Winokur, G. (1972). A short-term follow-up of women alcoholics. *Dis. Nerv. Sys.* 33:672–678.

Sclare, A.B. (1970). The female alcoholic. *Brit. J. Addict.* 65:99–107.

Seiden, A.M. (1979). Gender differences in psychophysiological illness. In: *Gender and Disordered Behavior*, ed. E.S. Gomberg & V. Franks. New York: Brunner/Mazel, pp. 426–449.

Selzer, M.L., Vinokur, A. & vanRooijen, L. (1975). A self administered short Michigan alcoholism screening test. *J. Stud. Alc.* 36:117–126.

Senseman, L.A. (1966). The housewife's secret illness. *Rhode Island Med. J.* 13:40–42.

Smart, R.G. (1979). Priorities in minimizing alcohol problems among young people. In: *Youth, Alcohol and Social Policy*, ed. H.T. Blane & M.E. Chafetz. New York: Plenum Press.

Stenmark, D.E., Wackwitz, J.H., Pelfrey, M.C. & Dougherty, F. (1974). Substance use among juvenile offenders: Relationships to parental substance use and demographic characteristics. *Addict. Dis.* 1:43–54.

Ullman, A.D. (1957). Sex differences in the first drinking experience. *Quart. J. Stud. Alc.* 18:229–239.

Van Amberg, R.J. (1942). A study of 50 women patients hospitalized for alcohol addiction. *Dis. Nerv. Sys.* 3:246–251.

Wall, J.H. (1937). A study of alcoholism in women. *Am. J. Psychiat.* 93:943–952.

Wanberg, K.W. & Horn, J.L. (1970). Alcoholism symptom patterns of men and women. *Quart. J. Stud. Alc.* 31:40–61.

Wanberg, K.W. & Horn, J.L. (1973). Alcoholism syndromes related to sociological classifications. *Int. J. Addict.* 8:9–120.

Wanberg, K.W. & Knapp, J. (1970). Differences in drinking symptoms and behavior of men and women alcoholics. *Brit. J. Addict.* 64:347–355.

Wechsler, H. & Thum, D. (1973). Alcohol and drug use among teenagers: A questionnaire study. In: *Proceedings of the 2nd Annual Alcoholism Conference of the NIAAA.* Washington, D.C.: U.S. Government Printing Office, pp. 34–36.

Wilkinson, P., Santamaria, J.N., Rankin, J.G. & Martin, D. (1969). Epidemiology of alcoholism: Social data and drinking patterns of a sample of Australian alcoholics. *Med. J. Australia* 1:1020–1025.

Winokur, G. & Clayton, P. (1967). Family history studies. II. Sex differences and alcoholism in primary affective illness. *Brit. J. Psychiat.* 115:973–979.

Winokur, G. & Clayton, P. (1968). Family history studies. IV. Comparison of male and female alcoholics. *Quart. J. Stud. Alc.* 29(3):885–891.

Wood, H.P. & Duffy, E.L. (1966). Psychological factors in alcoholic women. *Am. J. Psychiat.* 123:341–345.

Woodruff, R.A., Goodwin, D.W. & Guze, S.B. (1974). *Psychiatric Diagnosis.* New York: Oxford University Press.

Woodside, M. (1961). Women drinkers admitted to Holloway Prison during February 1960. *Br. J. Criminol.* 1:221–235.

Zelen, S.L., Gould J.F. & Olson, R.W. (1966). Sex-contingent differences between male and female alcoholics. *J. Clin. Psychol.* 22:160–165.

Zucker, R.A. (1979) Developmental aspects of drinking through the young adult years. In: *Youth, Alcohol and Social Policy*, ed. H.T. Blane & M.E. Chafetz. New York: Plenum Press, pp. 91–146.

Zung, B.J. & Charalampous, K.D. (1975). Item analysis of the Michigan Alcholism Screening Test. *J. Stud. Alc.* 36:127–132.

Chapter 4

Alcohol-Related Morbidity and Mortality in Offspring of Drinking Women: Methodologic Issues and a Review of Pertinent Studies

ANN PYTKOWICZ STREISSGUTH
RUTH E. LITTLE

When clinical studies indicated that there was a syndrome of offspring malformation, growth deficiency, and mental retardation associated with chronic maternal alcoholism many important questions were raised:

What are the manifestations of the disorder? (How is a case defined?)
What is the frequency of occurrence? (What is the prevalence of the syndrome?)
What are the associated risk factors?
What effects are related to lower levels of consumption? (Is there a dose-response curve?)
What are the mechanisms of causation?

All but the last question can be addressed by epidemiologic studies. However, the studies are long and cumbersome to conduct, and often involve an interdisciplinary team of investigators that is difficult to coordinate. Methodologic issues are complex and the logistics of the study design often require elaborate and expensive procedures. Furthermore, the conclusions derived from the results are open to variable interpretation. Controversy continues over the public health implications of the findings and the extent to which they should influence public policy.

This chapter addresses four main topics: (1) the clinical findings that set the stage for the epidemiologic studies; (2) methodologic issues in the assessment of offspring effects related to maternal alcohol use; (3) review of the outcome studies that have been carried out; and (4) methodologic problems of interpretation.

Clinical Studies of Fetal Alcohol Syndrome

Astute clinicians in several countries independently observed that some offspring of alcoholic mothers were particularly at risk and that some of the adverse effects resulted from intrauterine alcohol exposure.

In 1899 Sullivan, a physician at the Liverpool jail, observed that the mortality rate was over twice as high among offspring of female alcoholics compared to their nonalcholic female relatives.

In France in the 1950s and 1960s several clinical studies appeared describing developmental problems and growth deficiency in children of alcoholic parents. A medical thesis filed in Paris in 1957 by Rouquette described morphologic abnormalities in offspring of alcoholic mothers but apparently was never published. In 1968 Lemoine published an article describing 120 children born to alcoholic parents, primarily mothers, and noted characteristic facial appearance, growth deficiency, and mental retardation. Unfortunately, this work was published in a small medical journal and did not receive much attention. Scientific interest in the teratogenic effects of alcohol was stimulated by the work of Jones and Smith (1973) who published a small number of cases in *Lancet*. These findings were heralded as a new syndrome (fetal alcohol syndrome) with a known etiology (maternal alcoholism). Worldwide interest was kindled as fetal alcohol syndrome came to be called a preventable form of mental retardation and maternal alcoholism came to be recognized as a major cause of birth defects.

These clinical studies have been a rich source of hypotheses for the epidemiologic studies, perhaps responsible for the vast amount of new data generated on this topic in a relatively brief period of time.

The early case reports of fetal alcohol syndrome (FAS) have now been confirmed by hundreds of case studies in the world medical literature (e.g., Clarren & Smith, 1978; Majewski et al., 1976; Dehaene et al., 1977a, 1977b; Olegård et al., 1979; Pierog et al., 1979; DeBeukelaer et al., 1977; Root et al., 1975; Obe & Majewski, 1978; Tze et al., 1976; Spiegal et al., 1979). Affected children have three main characteristics: growth deficiency, morphologic abnormality (including a characteristic facies), and central nervous system abnormalities.

The growth deficiency is of prenatal onset, so infants with FAS are usually below the 3rd percentile for length, weight, and head circumference at birth. These growth disturbances reflect the inadequacy of the intrauterine environment. Children with FAS continue to manifest growth retardation as they mature and often remain below the third percentile in these dimensions. Many infants with FAS fail to thrive, and this is often unameliorated even after provision of an adequate environment.

The morphologic aberrations include a set of characteristic facial features, including short palpebral fissures, flat nasal bridge, short upturned nose, maxillary hypoplasia, indistinct philtrum, and narrow upper lip. Other features are also often present, such as eye abnormalities (ptosis, strabismus), ear abnormalities, and epicanthic folds. Minor joint and limb anomalies (including altered palmar creases) are often present. Heart defects have been noted in about 35% of cases.

The central nervous system abnormalities have included jitteriness and tremulousness in infancy, weak sucking, slow mental and motor development, hyperactivity, and mental retardation.

Clinical studies have also reported a variety of associated characteristics that are not part of the usual diagnostic picture. These include irritability and increased frequency of seizures, low Apgar scores and respiratory distress at birth, and renal abnormalities (Jones et al., 1973; Jones & Smith, 1973; Pierog et al., 1979; DeBeukelaer et al., 1977). Chromosome studies on dozens of clinical cases have been normal, and clinical biochemical studies also are generally within normal limits (e.g., Root et al., 1975; Obe & Majewski, 1978; Tze et al., 1976; Spiegal et al., 1979). However, several studies have shown EEG abnormalities in some infants of alcoholic mothers even without growth deficiency or fetal alcohol syndrome (Olegård et al., 1979; Havlicek et al., 1977).

After the first series of FAS cases were described, it became apparent that affected children could be ranked on a continuum of severity of affect (Majewski et al., 1976; Olegård et al., 1979, Streissguth et al., 1978b). Some children possessed all of the characteristics while others had only some of the diagnostic features. These latter children have been described as "fetal alcohol effects." The prognostic implications of a partial diagnosis are less clear than for the full syndrome. Furthermore, the diagnosis of "fetal alcohol effects" may be less reliable, although these possibilities have not been evaluated.

Studies of intellectual development in FAS children have been reported from several countries. In Germany (Majewski et al., 1976), France (DeHaene et al., 1977a) Sweden (Olegård et al., 1979) and the United States (Streissguth et al., 1978a; Streissguth et al., 1978b), IQ studies are in general agreement: (*a*) average IQ of children with an FAS diagnosis is in the mildly retarded range (around IQ 65–68); (*b*) the range of IQ scores among affected children is very broad (from profoundly retarded to normal IQ); (*c*) the severity of IQ deficit is related to the severity of physical characteristics; and (*d*) the IQ deficit does not appear to be substantially ameliorated by an improved environment, although long-term studies are continuing.

A broad range of measurable infant outcomes related to maternal alcohol use has been noted by clinicians and there remains little doubt that the fetal alcohol syndrome exists. Unfortunately, the clinical descriptions of maternal alcoholism are much less definitive. Clinical observations that describe the affected child in great detail often describe the mother summarily as an "alcoholic." Important descriptive information on the mothers that would help establish hypotheses to test related risk factors is usually absent in clinical accounts. Maternal age is the most frequently reported characteristic, while smoking, use of other drugs, socioeconomic status, and maternal education and occupation are rarely mentioned. More importantly, descriptive details on maternal drinking are often totally absent. The reason for this paucity of information probably derives partly from the difficulty of producing valid information on this topic. Alcoholics' self-reports of actual consumption may be inaccurate for a number of reasons. Furthermore, many of the children described in the case studies are no longer with their natural mothers, so retrospective documentation of consumption habits is often impossible to obtain. Nevertheless, more detailed descriptions of the extent of maternal alcoholism are certainly important for untangling the important questions about why some alcoholic mothers have affected children while others do not. From the clinical studies, we know far more about the characteristics of the affected children than about the mothers who produced them.

Methodologic Issues in Epidemiologic Studies

Experimental Design

Three main types of study designs have been used to examine the offspring effects of maternal alcohol use: the general prospective study, the retrospective cohort study, and the case-control study.

Case Control Studies

The case control study begins with the identification of actual cases of a given outcome or disease. Control patients are then selected from the same population, either randomly, successively, or according to certain matching criteria to control for confounding factors. Retrospective (or recall) data on the independent variables are then obtained.

The primary advantage of case-control studies is that they are easily conducted at reasonable cost. Case-control studies are particularly appropriate if the outcome (or disease) under study is rare. In FAS, the outcome or disease has already occurred and cases can readily be identified. One of the primary disadvantages of case-control studies is that information about the independent variables may be collected long after the fact and this information is subject to an unknown degree of imprecision due to memory error, distortion, and the influence of subsequent events; there may also be substantial bias unless interviewers are blind to disease status. Another disadvantage is that certain unknown factors may contribute to sample selection bias, and these are often difficult to isolate and examine. Finally, the prevalence of the outcome or disease cannot generally be calculated from a case-control study, nor can the relative risks (or odds ratio) of the outcome be determined, unless certain conditions are met.

There are very few true case-control studies of pregnancy outcome and its relation to maternal alcohol use. An example of a pertinent study using the case-control method is that conducted by Stein, Susser, Warburton and Kline at three New York City hospitals (Warburton et al., 1979). Every woman who had a spontaneous abortion during a certain period was enrolled in the study as a case. Controls were women obtaining prenatal care at the same hospitals whose pregnancy lasted more than 28 weeks. Cases and controls were matched for payment status, maternal age, and date of last menstrual period. Patients were interviewed about a variety of environmental factors that could effect spontaneous abortion, including amount of alcohol consumed during pregnancy. Another case-control study involves an examination of risk factors in preterm delivery, conducted by Berkowitz (1981) in New Haven, Connecticut. Women at one hospital who delivered single live children before 37 weeks of gestation during 1977 were the cases; controls were a 10% random sample of all live births having gestational age equal to or greater than 37 weeks. Gestational age was determined by the Dubowitz method. Information on sociodemographic, medical-obstetrical, biological, environmental, and psychosocial factors was obtained from hospital records and from a standard, structured questionnaire that was administered to both cases and controls during their postpartum hospital stay. These independent variables were then evaluated for the relationship to preterm delivery.

The case-control method is efficient for studying the variety of factors that may influence a given event, but it necessarily restricts the analysis to one dependent variable. It is not suitable for examination of a spectrum of effects that may derive from exposure to an agent. Nor is it suitable if clusters or partial clusters of effects have special significance, as in FAS.

Retrospective Cohort Studies

The retrospective cohort study is characterized by selection of two or more groups according to the presence or absence of a given factor (or the existence or nonexistence of an independent variable). The outcome, which may already have occurred, is then measured. These studies are less costly than the prospective studies described below, and they permit examination of a broad spectrum of outcomes. Cohort studies that gather information retrospectively may have all the problems noted above for case-control studies. However, prevalence and relative risk may be obtained under appropriate conditions.

In one retrospective cohort study of the effects of maternal drinking on offspring, Russell (1977) addressed the question of infant birth weight in offspring of alcoholic mothers. All subjects were female patients in an alcoholism outpatient facility seen during a 6-year period. From the medical records, it was determined which patients had an alcohol-related diagnosis, and these constituted the experimental group. The control group were all comparable patients in the same period without an alcohol-related diagnosis. The dependent variable was infant birth weight data obtained from official birth records. Outcome rates in the two groups were compared to each other and to those expected in the general population. Although the study also attempted to examine rates of congenital malformations in the two groups, extensive underreporting of birth defects on birth certificates precluded this.

In another retrospective cohort study, Little et al. (1980), compared birth weights of infants born to two groups of recovered alcoholic women. One group of women were alcoholic and drinking during an index pregnancy, and the other group were alcoholic prior to conception but had abstained during the index pregnancy. These two groups were compared to each other and to a control group of women who had never been alcoholic and were not drinking heavily during the pregnancy. Subjects in all three groups were women who heard about the study and volunteered to participate. They were screened and interviewed retrospectively regarding their history of alcoholism and their drinking during the index pregnancy. A group match on maternal education, smoking during pregnancy, race of offspring, and age of offspring at time of interview was effected. Outcome data on infant birthweight were obtained by maternal report (Little et al., 1980), and data on offspring IQ was obtained by conducting blind standardized IQ tests of the children (Streissguth et al., 1979).

A retrospective cohort study of this type combines many of the advantages of the general prospective study with the low cost of the case-control study. The investigation can be conducted in 1 or 2 years. A comparable prospective study would take 15 years or more to carry out. However, there are two major disadvantages:

1. *Potential sampling bias.*—It is possible that an intervening event (such as the birth of a defective child) might cause some mothers to avoid participation, thereby biasing the experimental group. This can be a serious problem in studies where outcome could influence sample selection. Furthermore, if the children most heavily affected by maternal alcohol use during pregnancy die in infancy, there will be a systematic deletion of subjects from one end of the continuum of maternal alcohol usage.
2. *Inaccurate reporting of the independent variable.*—It is possible that recovered alcoholic women could not recall the details of their alcohol use during the index pregnancy, particularly in cases where the children were already grown. Recall can be facilitated in a variety of ways, including obtaining substantiating data when possible. In the above study (Little et al., 1980), 85% of the alcoholic women in the sample belonged to Alcoholics Anonymous and appeared highly cognizant of the years during which they were and were not drinking. A group of nonrecovered alcoholics interviewed in a similar context might present many more problems with reliability and validity.

Furthermore, knowledge of outcome could distort maternal reporting of the independent variable. For example, a mother who felt her 10-year-old child was normal might report only light drinking because she concluded that she was not drinking enough during the pregnancy to alter development. On the other hand, knowledge of an affected child could produce the opposite effect and result in a woman "remembering" drinking more than she really had.

General Prospective Studies

The most frequently used type of study for examining the offspring effects of maternal alcohol use during pregnancy has been the general prospective study. Here, a sample thought to be representative of a population is selected, and the independent and dependent variables are assessed as they occur. Thus maternal alcohol use is assessed during pregnancy, and the offspring effects are assessed after delivery, or as they occur later in life. The advantage of this type of design is that it eliminates several potential sources of bias inherent in both the case-control and the retrospective cohort study. Recall as a potential source of error in assessment of the independent variable is reduced, and any bias in reporting the independent variable that might result from knowledge of the pregnancy outcome is eliminated. Prospective studies also permit estimates of the incidence and prevalence of the disease or condition under study. Clearly, the disease or condition being examined must be relatively frequent to use this type of study design.

The main disadvantage of prospective studies is that they can be long and cumbersome, depending on the nature of the outcome variable studied. They are usually quite expensive, with the cost proportional to the duration of the followup. Prospective studies examining birthweight or other dependent variables that can be obtained from hospital records are the least expensive, because no actual followup contact with the offspring is needed.

A special kind of prospective study is the longitudinal prospective study. Here the independent variable is assessed as it occurs (i.e., during pregnancy), and offspring are examined at various times to measure the dependent or outcome variables. Longitudinal prospective studies are the most expensive and cumbersome because the sample must be maintained for long periods in order to evaluate the dependent measures. However, longitudinal prospective studies provide definitive estimates of disease rates, or outcomes related to the independent variable, and the change in these rates over time.

Several prospective studies of alcohol use during pregnancy have examined outcomes ranging from spontaneous abortion to behavioral changes in the newborn and infant. In California in 1980 Harlap and Shiono examined the medical records of 32,019 pregnant women who had been interviewed during pregnancy regarding drinking, smoking, and other factors that might influence pregnancy outcome. Self-reports of average drinks per day had been obtained during pregnancy, and these were compared to the risk of abortion in both the first and the second trimester. Statistical adjustment was made for maternal age, parity, race, marital status, smoking, and the number of previous spontaneous or induced abortions. Smoking and maternal weight were also studied as confounding variables.

A similar general prospective study with a different method of defining the independent variable was conducted by Sokol, Miller, and Reed (1980) on data from 12,127 medical records of prenatal patients at Cleveland General Hospital. Rather than systematically assessing alcohol use, Sokol et al. compared the outcomes of women who had an entry of alcohol abuse in their chart with the balance of their sample. Maternal age, race, educational level, parity, time of first prenatal visit, smoking, and several other variables were considered as potentially confounding. Outcome variables studied were sex, neonatal condition and mortality, perinatal mortality, congenital malformations, and infant growth. A new prospective study underway at Cleveland General Hospital is using several criteria for assessing the independent variable, including alcohol use and alcohol problems by self-report, (Sokal et al., 1981).

A third general prospective study was done by Ouellette, Rosett, and colleagues (1976) at Boston City Hospital (the Boston Pilot Study). The investigators studied a consecutive sample of 633 women who were interviewed at their first prenatal visit. Nutritional status, smoking, and drug use were determined; alcohol use was estimated using a measure of present consumption. Three hundred twenty-two infants of these women were examined by a pediatric neurologist for congenital anomalies, growth abnormalities, and neurologic irregularities. This inner-city sample was primarily nonwhite and unmarried and represented an extremely high-risk group. Two additional longitudinal studies of drinking during pregnancy are underway, one in Boston (Alpert et al., 1981) and one in Loma Linda, California, (Kuzma et al., 1981).

Little (1977) conducted a prospective study of a very different population in Seattle, Washington. Using a consecutive sample of 801 patients of a health maintenance organization, interviews were conducted in the 4th month of pregnancy and the 8th month of pregnancy. Maternal height, age, parity, smoking, gestational age, and sex of child were all considered as possible confounding variables in the relationship between alcohol use and infant birthweight. Alcohol consumption was estimated in terms of the average ounces of ethanol consumed per day at three distinct but contiguous periods both before and during the pregnancy. Birthweight information was obtained from the medical records after delivery.

In France, Kaminski et al., (1978) studied over 9,000 pregnant women from 12 maternity hospitals in Paris. Subjects were interviewed during pregnancy about their age, marital status, tobacco use, parity, socioprofessional class, and pregnancy and fertility history. Again, alcohol use was measured by estimating average daily consumption of ethanol during pregnancy. Dependent variables under study were stillbirth and neonatal mortality, birthweight, intrauterine growth, placental weight, congenital malformations, and prematurity. All information on dependent variables was taken from the medical records.

A large longitudinal prospective study of alcohol and pregnancy (The Pregnancy and Health Study) is also being conducted in Seattle on a population similar to Little's but involving a second hospital to obtain a more diverse sample. Streissguth et al. (1981) studied 1,529 consecutive women receiving prenatal care at two Seattle hospitals by the 5th month of pregnancy. This sample was primarily white, middle-class, and well-educated. Information on maternal age, parity, socioeconomic status, smoking, drug use, and many other related variables was obtained in a personal interview in the fifth month of pregnancy. A wide variety of pregnancy outcomes have been studied, including growth deficiency, morphologic aberrations, and CNS abnormalities. The offspring are being examined at 8 months, 18 months, and 4 years to determine the long-term effects of exposure to alcohol in utero. A school-age assessment at 7 years of age is planned.

Assessment of the Dependent Variable

Traditional outcome variables for epidemiologic studies include fetal wastage (spontaneous abortions and stillbirths), perinatal and neonatal deaths, congenital malformations, growth deficiency (primarily weight), and occasionally IQ. However, a wide variety of outcome or dependent variables are possible in assessing the teratogenic effects of maternal alcohol use during pregnancy. Since a large body of clinical studies is available in the literature, many hypotheses regarding potential dependent variables can be derived by extrapolating from case studies of children with FAS. The three main areas of defect demonstrated in children with an FAS diagnosis are (1) growth deficiency, (2) morphological aberration, and (3) central nervous system damage. If these are the areas of deficit most strongly effected by intrauterine exposure to high levels of alcohol, it seems logical to look in these same areas for milder deficits related to lower levels of intrauterine alcohol exposure.

One important methodologic factor that should be considered in evaluating outcome data is whether or not the data were gathered "blind," or without knowledge of maternal drinking characteristics. Without blind assessments, the possibility of inadvertent bias in assessing or recording the outcomes cannot be ruled out.

Growth Deficiency

The neonatal outcomes of birth weight, birth length, and head circumference have been of particular interest because of their obvious reflection of the adequacy of the intrauterine environment. However, as clinical studies have shown continued growth deficiency in children with an FAS diagnosis, even in the presence of an adequate environment, followup growth parameters are also of potential interest. These are the easiest outcome variables to assess because they appear quite reliably in hospital records and thus can be easily obtained on large numbers of subjects.

Morphologic Aberrations

Two approaches to assessing deviant morphology have been used. In the Boston Pilot Study (Rosett et al., 1976; Ouellette & Rosett, 1976) individual infants were examined by a pediatric neurologist who rated them according to the number of major and minor malformations that were present in each infant. This method produced quantifiable differences in offspring that were related to amount of maternal alcohol use reported during pregnancy, but could not produce data relevant to the number of newborns with characteristics of FAS, possibly because the pattern of malformations was not considered.

The Pregnancy and Health Study in Seattle (Streissguth et al.,

1981) used a different approach with different goals. Here a dysmorphologist examined a sample of infants and rated them acording to a variety of morphologic characteristics that have been found clinically in infants with the fetal alcohol syndrome (Hanson, et al., 1978). The hypothesis was that infants born to heavier social drinkers might have some of these characteristics even in the absence of the full syndrome. The characteristics evaluated included short palpebral fissures, long or indistinct philtrum, thin upper vermillion, midface hypoplasia, short upturned nose, flat nasal bridge, altered palmar creases, and hemangiomas. Hypotheses derived from clinical cases were particularly important in determining this list because many of these characteristics are not generally listed as major or minor malformations. Their significance lies not in their presence as individual signs, but for their part in the cluster of characteristics that together define the fetal alcohol syndrome. Certain clusters of these morphologic characteristics, in combination with intrauterine growth deficiency, were used to define global outcomes termed FAS or partial effects of alcohol exposure in utero.

Questions regarding the birth prevalence of FAS can only be answered by studies such as the latter. The prevalence of FAS in a given population cannot be determined from studies that assess only the standard major and minor malformations as outcome variables. Clearly, the type of data gathered and the way it is used to define a case will determine the type of conclusions that can be drawn.

Central Nervous System Abnormalities

Outcome variables reflecting deficits in central nervous system functioning are more difficult to assess at birth, particularly in milder cases. At least two factors are responsible for this. First, proper use of behavioral outcome data often requires a variety of empirical controls that are difficult to implement in the newborn nursery, particularly within the framework of a longitudinal design. (See Streissguth et al., 1981, for a full description of how these issues were dealt with for the Pregnancy and Health Study.) Second, it is difficult to determine which types of behaviors to assess in the newborn. The mental retardation that characterizes many FAS children as they mature is usually not apparent in the newborn period. Nevertheless, some clinical case studies of FAS infants do describe deviant newborn behaviors such as tremulousness, weak sucking, hyperacusis, irritability, opisthotonos, and seizures (Pierog et al., 1979). Two of the prospective studies have attempted to assess specific newborn behaviors that might be related to maternal alcohol use during pregnancy. The Boston Pilot Study used clinical ratings of jitteriness (Rosett et al., 1976; Ouellette et al., 1977) and an automated bassinet (Sander et al., 1977; Rosett et al., 1979) for recording patterns of sleep/wakefulness. The Seattle Pregnancy and Health Study (Streissguth et al., 1981) used a variety of newborn behavioral assessments, each requiring a different methodology. These included operant learning techniques (Martin et al., 1977), automated assessment of sucking pressure (Martin et al., 1979), monitoring of naturally occurring behaviors (Landesman-Dwyer et al., 1978) and standardized clinical assessments with the Brazelton Neonatal Behavior Rating Scale (Streissguth et al., 1977). Data from each of these behavioral procedures were analyzed separately in relation to maternal use of alcohol during pregnancy.

Additional data on newborn status can be obtained from the hospital charts, although incomplete data may be a problem in some settings. The Cleveland Prospective study (Sokol et al., 1981), through use of an automatically computerized data base already available in the obstetrical service, has been able to use data from hospital charts very effectively. Apgar scores, routinely rated at 1 and 5 minutes after delivery have been used in two studies (Sokol et al., 1980; Streissguth et al., 1982) as well as need for ventilatory resuscitation, heart rate abnormality, and gross variables reflecting general health, such as number of days in intensive care, in hospital, etc. (Streissguth et al., 1982).

Fetal Wastage and Infant Mortality

Traditional outcome variables for epidemiologic studies have included spontaneous abortions, stillborns, and perinatal deaths. These variables are easy to measure, are binary (yes/no), and are readily obtainable from hospital records by personnel needing little specialized training. Furthermore, such outcomes are relatively inexpensive to assess. The low frequency of occurrence requires a large sample size when these outcomes are used in a prospective design; the case-control design provides a way of decreasing the sample size, but puts certain restrictions on the analyses and usually necessitates a retrospective account of the independent variable (i.e., maternal drinking).

Assessment of the Independent Variables

Perhaps the thorniest problem in such studies is how to assess maternal alcohol intake, the primary independent variable. Two main techniques have been used: (1) attempts to quantify actual consumption of alcohol, and (2) attempts to quantify problems with alcohol. Each method is fraught with its own set of problems. Both ultimately rely on self-reports, making them subject to whatever bias is introduced by the willingness or unwillingness of women to reveal this aspect of their behavior.

Quantification of Alcohol Use

If we assume that alcohol is teratogenic then we might also assume that the more alcohol to which the fetus is exposed, the more adverse would be the impact. Accurate assessment of actual intake would therefore seem important. Studies using this approach have generally explored alcohol-use scales already developed by the alcohol field, such as the quantity-frequency interview developed by Mulford and Miller (1960) and expanded by Jessor et al. (1968) and Cahalan et al. (1969) to include questions about variability. With this procedure, a woman is asked about the amount that she consumes and the variability of her consumption. Various techniques are then used to reduce this data to a quantifiable score. Jessor et al. (1968) devised a measure of average ounces of absolute alcohol per day which has been termed an "AA" score. This is a convenient continuous variable to use in analysis. Cahalan et al. (1969) devised two categorical rank scores, the QFV (quantity-frequency-variability) index and the VV (volume-variability) score. Other studies have used just one or two alcohol-use questions within a large prenatal questionnaire. Number of drinks per day or week is the most usual alcohol question used in this context.

Several methodological problems remain unsolved in terms of assessing alcohol use during pregnancy:

1. The time frame across which a woman is asked to average her use patterns seems to be an important variable. Several studies now indicate that women cut down their alcohol

use during pregnancy and that this is true for social drinkers as well as alcoholics (Little et al., 1976; Streissguth et al., 1977).

Intrauterine alcohol exposure may have different effects depending on the time during gestation that heavy exposure occurs. Attempts to average across discrepant drinking periods may make the independent variable too imprecise to show an effect even when there is one. Therefore, some studies have several estimates, one for the period prior to pregnancy or its recognition, and another for "during" pregnancy (Little et al., 1976; Streissguth et al., 1977, 1981).

2. Another problem involves binge drinking versus regular drinking.

   With most alcohol-use scales, individual differences in drinking patterns get averaged out to average drinks per day. Although convenient for statistical analyses, it seems unlikely that seven drinks on Saturday night would have the same impact on the fetus as one drink a night for seven nights. Cahalan's VV score does categorize drinkers according to a two-way schema of maximum drinks × average consumption. Theoretically, with a large enough sample size, one should be able to separate out subjects with a high maximum score (5 or more drinks per occasion) from those with more frequent lower-level consumption. To date, this has not been a particularly productive method of examining the effects of different patterns of alcohol use. The difficulties of assessing alcohol use accurately over the 9 months of pregnancy may make it impossible to determine the precise amount of alcohol associated with a given effect in human studies.

3. Type of alcoholic beverages consumed has been the topic of some interest, but small sample size has usually precluded attempts to study the impact of specific types of beverages. Most of the studies assessing self-reported intake have used a summary score averaging across all types of beverages consumed (with the formula: 1 bottle of beer = 1 glass of wine = 1 cocktail or ounce of spirits). Kaminski's study in France (1978) has a large enough sample size to separate out types of beverages, and beer and cider are implicated as most related to adverse pregnancy

outcomes. However, as beer and cider drinkers may have different consumption patterns compared to wine drinkers, further work seems needed on the extent to which the outcomes are related to beer and cider as such and not to the pattern of consumption.

4. Validity of self-reported alcohol use data continues to be a problem. There is no reasonable way to validate what women say about their drinking practices. While some women may underrepresent their drinking, others may overrepresent, particularly with respect to binges.
5. The reliability of self-reported alcohol use during pregnancy has been examined and found to be quite good (Streissguth et al., 1976; Little et al., 1977). One study evaluated the test-retest reliability of the AA, QFV, and VV scores over a 1-week interval. Pearson's correlations were r = 0.90 for the AA scores during pregnancy (Streissguth et al., 1976). Furthermore, there was little systematic drift in one particular direction for the scores that did change. However, as might be anticipated, women reporting the heaviest drinking showed the greatest change on retest. As this is the end of the drinking continuum where the greatest effects would be expected, the poorer test-retest reliability at this end indicates the caution with which specific "cut-offs" of safe or harmful drinking levels should be viewed. Another study (Little et al., 1977) assessing the reliablity of retrospective recall of drinking over a 4-month retrest, obtained an r of 0.61. This latter figure could be thought of as an estimate of the amount of "forgetting" that occurs during a 4-month period of pregnancy.
6. The timing of the interview is probably also an important source of variability in estimating drinking during pregnancy. Klemetti and Saxen (1967) found serious recall problems in postpartum drug use interviews. The primary advantage of the postpartum interview is that data can theoretically be obtained on the whole interview at one time. However, the data obtained in the postpartum interview may be less reliable because of forgetting and because of the impact of the infant on the mother's recall of her drinking during pregnancy. More reliable data can probably be obtained by conducting the interview during pregnancy even if several interviews are necessary.

7. Format and setting. The relative merits of an interview compared to a self-administered questionnaire have not been reported in samples of pregnant women, although pilot studies in our laboratory suggest that a personal interview (without husband or children present) conducted by an "outside" interviewer (not part of the health-care delivery system) provides the best data.

For all its shortcomings, the alcohol-use interview, conducted during pregnancy and under the above conditions, is probably the best single determinant of the independent variable in studies of social drinking.

Assessment of Alcohol-Related Problems

The second method of assessing the independent variable is to measure it indirectly. The rationale for this is that it is difficult to obtain good data on actual consumption levels and it is better to measure secondary characteristics of heavy alcohol use. Such studies can be considered to be addressing the question of offspring effects of maternal alcohol abuse rather than the effects of social drinking.

Several approaches have been used to assess alcohol-related problems in pregnant women. One study (Sokol et al., 1981) is using standardized scales such as the Michigan Alcohol Screening Test (MAST) for assessing problems related to drinking. One problem with this method is that some of these scales, such as the MAST, were standardized on men and may therefore be relatively insensitive to drinking problems in women. Other studies (Russell & Bigler, 1979) have just listed possible alcohol-related problems and asked women to indicate which they have experienced. Others have relied on clinical assessments by hospital personnel or data reported on medical records (Russell 1977; Jones et al., 1974).

Studies using alcohol-related problems to identify the experimental group are clearly studying a different and more deviant group of women than studies that use a moderate level of alcohol consumption as the independent variable on which the groups are selected. Thus the findings or lack of findings from each study need to be evaluated in terms of the method used for defining the independent variable.

Several problems arise with using alcohol-related problems to define the independent variable:

1. The time-frame presents a problem. Should women be selected only if they are experiencing alcohol-related problems during the pregnancy, or should history of alcohol-related problems qualify a woman as a subject? If the latter is used, such a study would presumably be evaluating an indirect effect of earlier alcohol abuse on a later pregnancy. While there may be some rationale for this idea (Streissguth, 1980; Little et al., 1980), such a study would not technically be evaluating the teratogenic effects of alcohol.
2. Validity of self-report may be as much of a problem with this type of question as with self-reports of level of consumption. Evidence from two studies indicates that women may be less willing to confide about alcohol-related problems to medical personnel than to outside interviewers (Russell & Bigler, 1979; Little; 1976).
3. Obtaining such data from hospital records would appear to be a particularly poor strategy because of the well-recognized difficulty that medical personnel have with identifying alcohol-related problems. Although one could be fairly certain about the subjects identified as "alcohol problems" the real concern is the number of women with actual alcohol-related problems who are not identified as experimentals. The rate of false positives should be minimal but the rate of false negatives may be sizable, depending on the precision of the techniques for identifying the independent variable.
4. Because women drink less during pregnancy and probably have fewer alcohol-related problems, the use of "problems" to measure the independent variable may result in a very small sample size of experimental subjects. One recent study queried women about both alcohol use and alcohol-related problems (Streissguth et al., 1977). Not only was there little congruence between subjects identified by each type of question, but less than 1% of the pregnant women interviewed stated that they had experienced at least one of the four following alcohol-related problems: family break-up, loss of job, hospitalization, or nontraffic-related arrest. By comparison, 6% of the subjects

specified at least five "personal effects" reasons for drinking (a scale developed by Jessor et al., 1968).

5. One further difficulty with using "alcohol problems" as the independent variable is that it may have little relationship to the level of intrauterine alcohol exposure experienced by the fetus. Many other factors may relate to the number of alcohol-related problems experienced by a given woman. For example, some problems such as arrests or loss of job may be particularly related to low socioeconomic status. If other possibly related factors are not adjusted for in the design, effects could be attributed to alcohol that are more directly related to other factors.
6. Another related problem that affects both methods of defining the independent variable is the individual woman's metabolism of alcohol. A given amount of alcohol, ingested by various women, may have quite a different impact on the fetus. To date, there have been no studies that have adjusted for this factor in the assessment of alcohol-related offspring effects, although Chernoff (1977) has reported that this is a significant factor in rodent studies. Furthermore, there have been no reported studies in pregnant women that have used grams of alcohol per kilogram body weight in defining the independent variable. Several studies (Little, 1977; Streissguth et al., 1981) have, however, used a measure of maternal size (height or weight) in regression analyses.

Assessment of Potentially-confounding Variables

Alcohol use and alcohol-related problems are significantly correlated with other factors such as smoking, caffeine use, and use of other drugs and medications (Little, 1977; Streissguth et al., 1981). Some of these other factors also have known fetal effects related to use during pregnancy. This is particularly true for smoking where many of the offspring effects that have been reported are the same type of effects reported for alcohol use (Landesman-Dwyer & Emanuel, 1979). Clearly, great caution must be used in an experimental design that does not permit some separation of these factors. Most of the smoking studies were carried out before the time when alcohol was thought to be teratogenic, so they failed to adjust for or even assess alcohol use. However, given the body of data that already exists regarding the adverse offspring effects of smoking during pregnancy, it would be unfortunate to design a drinking study today that failed to adjust for smoking. Although the teratogenic properties of caffeine are not well established in humans, the presence of some positive findings associated with maternal caffeine use (Weathersbee & Lodge, 1977; Borlee, et al., 1978) would suggest to the cautious investigator that caffeine should also be a control variable.

Simultaneous adjustment for other drug use is also important even though offspring effects may not be as clearly delineated (Wilson, 1973). Without such control of potentially confounding factors, effects might be attributed to alcohol that should be attributed to other drugs or to an alcohol-drug interaction.

Unfortunately, the simultaneous consideration of these factors makes studies complex and expensive. Even though large-scale, well-controlled, epidemiologic studies will be needed to answer some of the questions raised here, we should not lose sight of the importance of thoughtful clinical studies, which were, after all, the type of investigation from which the adverse effects of heavy alcohol use during pregnancy were first evident.

Analysis

The classic methods of epidemiology were devised for binary outcomes: presence or absence of disease. Several types of pregnancy outcomes permit binary classification, for example, stillbirth, spontaneous abortion, perinatal or neonatal mortality, gestational age below (or above) a certain number of weeks, birthweight below a certain fixed figure, and congenital malformations. For these outcomes, relative risk (or an odds ratio) can be calculated where study design permits. The relative risk (RR) of an outcome, given a suspected causative factor, is the rate of disease in persons exposed to the factor divided by the rate of disease in persons not exposed to the factor. For alcohol use, the ratio can be the rates of outcome in offspring of drinkers versus nondrinkers or in abusers versus nonabusers, or in persons drinking a certain minimum amount versus those drinking less. General prospective studies permit estimates of relative risk. So do retrospective cohort studies if the cohorts are representative of a defined population. Relative risk can be obtained from case-control studies if the probability of the outcome is low (less than 10%) in both exposed and unexposed persons, and if both cases and controls have the same probability of exposure as the population from which they are drawn.

Binary outcomes such as stillbirth and spontaneous abortion are ideally suited to the methods of epidemiology such as the 2 × 2 table. Other pregnancy outcomes (like birthweight) can be analyzed by using either continuous data or by bisecting the continuum at some specific point, such as "low birthweight" (commonly defined as < 2500 gm). IQ scores are another example of data that can be analyzed either as a continuous variable or as a binary variable, bisecting the continuum at < 70 IQ points for example, (often considered a cutoff for "mental retardation"). However, the analysis of any continuous pregnancy outcome variable is more powerful if techniques that take advantage of the spectrum of values (such as regression analysis) are used. Regression models are particularly suited to these analyses because of their capability of statistically adjusting for a variety of potentially confounding variables.

Patterns or clusters of outcomes are generally unsuitable for analysis by traditional epidemiologic methods if variation within the cluster is of interest. Fetal alcohol syndrome is an example. If only diagnosed cases of the full-blown syndrome are studied, information on children having partial FAS will be missed. These children may provide valuable insights into the role of maternal alcohol use in disturbance of fetal growth and development. The studies of alcohol use and pregnancy outcome that do not lend themselves to the classic binary outcome model are generally more difficult to interpret than those that do, but they provide a rich fund of information that compensates for the complexity of their analysis.

Review of Outcome Studies

The following section briefly reviews some of the outcome studies addressing the issue of the offspring effects of maternal alcohol use during pregnancy. Methodologic issues are addressed as relevant to understanding discrepancies between studies. The studies cited in this review are illustrative rather than exhaustive.

Relative risks have been calculated for those outcomes that are suitable for this method and that come from studies where the proper conditions were met and sufficient data were reported. As table 1 indicates, the relative risk associated with intrauterine alcohol exposure is substantial for each of the following outcomes: spontaneous abortion, stillbirth, and small-for-dates infants. Disparate findings are reported for gestational age. Discrepancies among studies can probably be explained in terms of differences in study design and population.

Fetal Wastage and Infant Mortality

The first epidemiologic investigation in the field of drinking and pregnancy was conducted by Sullivan in 1899. Using a retrospective cohort design, this physician studied children of 120 female alcoholics in the Liverpool prison and compared them with children born to 28 of their nondrinking female relatives. The rate of infant mortality and stillbirth was 2-1/2 times higher in children of the alcoholics, compared to children of their sober relatives. Not until 1974 was this topic again addressed. In that year, Mau and Netter (1974) reported on a prospective study of 5,200 pregnancies in Germany and estimated a relative risk of 1.68 for spontaneous abortion. Their findings are based on a binary classification of drinking (drinking/no drinking) and gross underreporting probably occurred since only 0.1% of all subjects reported drinking "frequently." Unfortunately, no control for smoking or other relevant variables was employed.

In 1974, using a retrospective cohort design, Jones et al., (1974) reported on children of a subgroup of women in the Collaborative Perinatal Study who had mention of alcoholism in their chart. This subgroup consisted of only 69 women—0.001 percent of the total group—and they probably represent the most extreme manifestation of alcohol abuse. Of these 69, alcoholism was verified in 23, and two controls were selected for each of these cases, matched on socioeconomic status, education, race, age, parity, marital status, and study institution. Drinking in the alcoholic cohort probably represents such an extreme degree of exposure that no inference of relative risk should be drawn.

Three recent prospective studies have estimated the relative risk of various forms of fetal wastage. Kaminski et al. (1978) reported a significantly increased relative risk of stillbirth

TABLE 1
Relative Risks of Fetal Wastage, Pre-term Delivery, and Intrauterine Growth Retardation by Differing Levels of Maternal Alcohol Use During Pregnancy

	Any alcohol use	*1–2 Drinks daily*	*More than 2 or 3 drinks daily*	*Alcohol abuse*
Spontaneous abortion				
Mau, Germany (1974)	1.7			
Harlap, USA (1980) (versus nondrinkers)		2.0	3.5	
Stillbirth				
Kaminski, France (1978) (> 40 cl vs. ≤ 40 cl)			2.6	
Sokol, USA (1980)				0.5
Pre-term delivery				
Mau, Germany (1974)	1.5			
Berkowitz, USA (1981)[a] (7 drinks/wk vs. less)		1.7		
Ouellette, USA (1978)[b] ("heavy" vs. not "heavy")			4.2	
Kaminski, France (1978) (> 40 cl vs. ≤ 40 cl)			0.9	
Sokol, USA (1980) (pediatric estimate)				0.8
Small-for-dates infants				
Ouellette, USA (1978) ("heavy" vs. not "heavy")			3.6	
Kaminski, France (1978) (> 40 cl vs. ≤ 40 cl)			1.4	
Sokol, USA (1980)				2.7

Note: This table contains data on relative risks that were either presented in the individual papers or relatively easy to calculate from data presented.
[a]Adjusted odds ratio used for ≥ 7 drinks/week vs. less.
[b]"Heavy" drinking is at least 45 drinks monthly and at least 5 drinks on occasion. Here denominator rate is for drinkers of less than this amount.

(RR = 2.6) among women who consumed the equivalent of at least 40 cl of wine daily during pregnancy (approximately 1.6 ounces of ethanol), compared to women who drank less than this. The risk was dose-related, and independent of smoking, maternal age, parity, socioeconomic status, and previous pregnancy history. For women drinking 41–60 cl wine, RR = 2.26; above this amount, RR = 3.78. The risk of stillbirth was increased for both smokers and nonsmokers who drank at least 40 cl wine daily (RR = 2.45 and 2.32 respectively). The excess risk of stillbirth was due primarily to abruptio placenta (which was also independent of smoking). Women consuming only beer and cider were at particularly high risk. Kaminski also found that the rate of neonatal mortality for infants of drinkers of at least 40 cl wine was elevated (10.2 v. 8.1), but the increase was not statistically significant.

Only one other study has investigated the relationship of stillbirths to maternal drinking habits. Sokol et al. (1980) reported no significant relationship between maternal alcohol abuse and rate of stillbirth. However, several methodologic factors may account for this discrepancy with Kaminski's findings. Sokol's cases were identified as alcohol abusers in the hospital record. As Sokol notes, the sensitivity of this method of case definition is low and many abusers may have been misclassified. Furthermore, as no consumption data were obtained, it is possible that some of the cases were actually not drinking during the index pregnancy. Sokol et al. (1980) did report a significant increase in risk of mild abruptio placenta, (RR = 3.4), which supports the finding by Kaminski et al. (1978). Risk of neonatal death and perinatal mortality were also increased (RR = 1.8 and 1.3, respectively), though these increases were not statistically significant.

Two studies corroborate the early Mau and Netter (1974) finding of increased risk of spontaneous abortion. Harlap and Shiono (1980) reported a dose-related increase in risk of spontaneous abortion in the second trimester. If an average of 1–2 drinks per day are consumed during pregnancy, RR = 1.98 (compared to nondrinkers). The relative risk increases to 3.52 for more than two drinks daily. Both relative risks are highly statistically significant and are not explained by age, parity, race, marital status, smoking, or the number of previous spontaneous or induced abortions. Risk for first trimester abortion was not elevated. Warburton et al. (1979) has also reported a relationship between drinking and spontaneous abortion. Nearly five times as many cases as controls were daily drinkers during pregnancy, and nearly three times as many (2.7) drank at least weekly. Drinking by trimester in which the abortion occurred was not specified. A further report from this study (Kline et al., 1980) adjusted for a variety of other variables including smoking, marijuana, caffeine, and maternal age, race, and weight. They concluded that drinking twice a week or more was still associated with a significantly increased risk of spontaneous abortions (adjusted odds ratio of 2.62).

Gestational Age

The relationship between alcohol use and length of gestation remains controversial. A case-control study by Berkowitz (1981) reveals that first and second trimester alcohol consumption was significantly related to preterm delivery (< 37 weeks by the Dubowitz method). The analysis adjusted for socioeconomic and marital status, maternal weight gain, prepregnancy weight, and smoking through multivariate techniques. An adjusted odds ratio of 1.66 (for seven drinks/weeks vs none) was calculated. Russell (1977) found twice as many premature deliveries among her alcoholic cohort as would be expected from population estimates, although smoking was uncontrolled. Mau and Netter (1974) also found premature deliveries significantly increased (RR = 1.53), though again no control or adjustment for other factors was made.

In the prospective study of Ouellette et al. (1977) both pre- and postterm deliveries were significantly more frequent in a heavy-drinking cohort. "Heavy" drinking was defined as at least 45 drinks a month and at least 5 drinks at a time on some occasions (Cahalan's VV = high volume, high maximum). Seventeen percent of this cohort delivered prematurely (Dubowitz assessment, criteria for prematurity unspecified) compared to 5 percent of the cohort of infrequent drinkers (RR = 3.4). Postmature infants were born in 20% and 8% of the cohorts, respectively (RR = 2.5). Again, smoking was not controlled in this investigation.

The prospective studies by Kaminski et al. (1978), Sokol et al. (1980), and Streissguth et al. (1981) found that gestational age was not associated with alcohol use. In fact, Kaminski reported a higher rate of deliveries at 36 weeks or less among women drinking less than 40 cl wine than among heavier drinkers. There was also no difference in mean gestational age. The findings of Sokol are congruent: alcohol abusers had a lower rate of both preterm (< 38 weeks) and postterm (42 weeks) deliveries than nonabusers when obstetric methods were used to determine gestational age. However, when determining gestational age through the use of pediatric methods, there was a slight excess of postterm deliveries (not statistically significant) in the alcohol cohort.

Intrauterine Growth

The studies that explore the relationship between intrauterine growth and alcohol dosage give primarily positive results.

In 1976, Kaminski and colleagues published the results of a large prospective study showing a significant reduction in birthweight associated with maternal alcohol use during pregnancy, even after adjusting for other relevant variables including smoking. At maternal consumption of 3 or more drinks/day, the birth weight decrement was 58 grams.

In 1977, Russell reported a threefold increase in intrauterine growth retardation for children of her alcohol cohort compared to population-based estimates, although smoking was not taken into account. In 1977, Little published a study documenting a significant decrement in birthweight that was related to self-reported alcohol intake after adjusting for smoking. Using regression analysis on a stratified subsample of a prospective study sample, an AA score of one ounce of absolute alcohol per day in late pregnancy was associated with a 160-gram decrement in birthweight. Drinking the same quantity in the 6 months prior to pregnancy was associated with a decrease of 91 gm in birthweight. These significant decreases were obtained after adjustment for not only smoking, but also for gestational age, maternal age, height, parity, and sex of child. A similar birthweight decrement (52 gm) has been reported by the Seattle prospective longitudinal study (Streissguth et al., 1981). This latter study also found a significant alcohol-related decrease in birth length and head circumference, after adjusting for smoking, caffeine, and other relevant variables. Van den Berg (1977) reported a

34-gram decrease in birthweight of offspring of women drinking at least one drink a day. Sokol et al. (1980) reported an average decrease in birthweight of 187 grams in infants of alcohol abusers. Two studies have reported no birthweight effects related to maternal drinking, Mau and Netter (1974) and Pettersson and Melander (1975), but both examined only a binary alcohol variable (drinking vs. no drinking) which would not be expected to detect subtle variations in offspring birthweight. An additional study (Tennes & Blackard, 1980) also reported no significant alcohol-related effects on birthweight, but the sample size was quite small (n = 278) and the number of heavier drinkers in the sample was particularly small.

Some studies have considered "small-for-dates" infants (generally defined as below the 10th percentile of expected weight for gestational age). Ouellette et al. (1977) found an increased risk of small-for-dates infants (RR = 3.38 for heavy vs. infrequent drinking); birthweight, length, and head circumference were all affected, but smoking was not adjusted for. The relative risk of small-for-dates infants reported by Sokol et al. (1980) is 2.7; for nonsmokers only, the relative risk reported is 2.4. The figure reported by Kaminski is less: 1.25 for women ingesting 41–60 cl wine and 1.73 for women drinking over 60 cl (both vs. women drinking ≤ cl). When both heavier drinking groups are combined, the elevated risk is highly significant (RR = 1.43 for ≤ 40 cl). Silva et al. (1981) also found significantly more small-for-dates infants, with microcephally and short palpebral fissures born to heavier drinking mothers. In this population of poor mothers in Brazil, poor nutrition characterized all the mothers and was not differentially related to maternal alcohol use.

Little and Streissguth et al. (1980) compared mean birthweights of infants born to their drinking alcoholic cohort with birthweights of infants born to nonalcoholics; the difference was 493 gm. This is substantially greater than the difference reported by Sokol et al. (1980) and may reflect the misclassification of alcohol abusers into the nonalcoholic cohort in the Sokol study. The major finding of the Little and Streissguth study, however, was that mean birthweight of infants born to women with a history of alcoholism was 258 gm lower than mean birthweight of the infants born to nonalcoholics, even when the alcoholic women were totally abstinent during pregnancy. Differences in mean birthweights persisted regardless of maternal age, height, parity, and smoking status, or gestational age or sex of the child. This finding suggests that a history of maternal alcohol abuse may pose a significant risk to fetal growth independent of alcohol use in the pregnancy.

Morphology, Malformations and the Birth Prevalence of Fetal Alcohol Syndrome

Three prospective studies have evaluated congenital malformations in relation to maternal alcohol variables. Ouellette et al. (1977) reported a significantly higher percent of both minor and major malformations among infants born to heavier drinking mothers. Congenital anomalies were found in 9% of the offspring of the lightest drinking mothers, in 14% of offspring of the moderate drinking group, and in 32% of the offspring of the heavy drinking mothers.

Kaminski and colleagues (1978) did not report any difference in major anomalies for infants of women drinking over 40 cl wine/day on the average, and data on minor malformations were not given. Neither of these studies reported identification of any newborns with FAS, although it is not clear whether the pattern of anomalies that characterizes the syndrome was sought in these studies, or whether only single malformations were considered. Furthermore, the Kaminski data were gathered prior to the identification of FAS and some characteristics of the syndrome (such as short palpebral fissures, maxillary hypoplasia, indistinct philtrum, etc.) are not commonly evaluated as malformations.

Sokol et al. (1980) reported data from neonatal examinations conducted on 42 liveborn offspring of alcohol-abusing women. Of these, 16 (38%) had at least one major or minor anomaly. This was significantly more than the 10% "expected" rate of malformations, but they did not use a control group from their own population.

In addition to reporting the frequency of major and minor anomalies, three studies have reported a combined rate of malformations and/or growth deficiency. These data are summarized in table 2. The two studies conducted on high-risk inner city populations (Sokol et al., 1980; Ouellette et al., 1977) report 50%–70% of the offspring of very heavy drinking women have either growth deficiency *or* major *or* minor malformations. For

TABLE 2

Maternal Alcohol Use and Proportion of Infants at Risk for Growth Deficiency and/or Malformations

Study	*Maternal alcohol use*	*Abnormal infants*
Hanson, et al., 1978 (low-risk population)	I. 0–2 Drinks/day	2%
	II. 2–4 Drinks/day	11%
	III. ≥ 4 Drinks/day (1.7% of 1,529 gravidas)[a]	19%
Ouellette et al., 1977	I. Drank 0–1/month	35%
	II. >1. and < 111	36%
	III. ≥ 1½ drinks/day + sometimes 5 drinks/occasion (9% of 633 gravidas)[a]	71%
Sokol et al., 1980	Alcohol abuse (1.7% of 12,127 gravidas)[a]	50%

Note: Criteria for abnormality differed across studies. Hanson et al. used growth deficiency *and* physical anomalies associated with FAS; Ouellette et al. and Sokol et al. used growth deficiency, major *or* minor malformations, or neurologic abnormality.

[a] This is the percent of women drinking at the stated risk level in the total sample.

the Boston study (Ouellette et al., 1977) this is twice the percentage found in the lighter drinking groups; however, the confounding effect of maternal smoking is not examined in the Boston study. The Seattle study (Hanson et al., 1978) used more stringent criteria in that a newborn had to have growth deficiency *plus* certain morphologic characteristics of FAS in order to be counted as "abnormal". As table 2 indicates, the rate of "abnormality" is lower in all drinking categories for the Seattle study, probably due to the stringent criteria as well as the population characteristics (primarily married, middle-class, white women). However, a dose-response effect is suggested: women reporting 2–4 drinks/day had five times more "abnormal" infants while women drinking 4 or more drinks/day had nine times more "abnormal" infants than the controls. Drinks/day should be viewed as only a rough estimate rather than a clear cutoff point, due to the methodologic problems involved in assessing alcohol use during pregnancy, as discussed earlier.

Birth prevalence of FAS has been addressed by three studies (see table 3). The first published data were from Dehaene and colleagues (1977a) who conducted a series of studies in hospitals in an industrialized area of northern France. A birth prevalence of 1/1,000 was reported by Dehaene when only full FAS cases were counted. The rate when milder manifestations of the syndrome were counted was 1/350. A more recent report (Dehaene et al., 1981) presents data from years 1977–1979, showing a birth prevalence of 1/690 births for the full syndrome.

Olegård and colleagues (1979) reported a birth prevalence of 1/600 births for full FAS cases and 1/300 births for milder manifestations in a study of deliveries in Göteberg, Sweden.

Both of these studies appear to have identified alcoholic mothers and then examined their offspring born during a certain period. The number of FAS infants born during this period was then compared to the number of deliveries in the study area during the same period.

In the Seattle study (Streissguth et al., 1981; Hanson et al., 1978) two newborns were diagnosed with the full fetal alcohol syndrome. Assessment of the condition was made without knowledge of the mother's alcohol use. This rate of 1/750 births should be considered a minimal estimate because only a sample of the newborns were examined (82 born to the heavier drinkers and 81 controls). Some other infants born to equally heavy

TABLE 3
Birth Prevalence of Fetal Alcohol Syndrome

Country	*Author*	*Cases/births*	*Birth prevalence*		*Characteristics*
			Partial FAS	***Full FAS***	
France (Roubaix)	Dehaene et al., 1977a	9/3487 11/3440	1/350	1/1000	Sample: many lower class Cases: children of severe, chronic alcoholic mothers
	Dehaene et al., 1981	12/8284	1/212	1/690	
U.S. (Seattle)	Hanson et al., 1978	2/1500		1/750	Sample: primarily white, middle-class Cases: children of non-white, welfare, chronic alcoholic mothers
Sweden (Göteborg)	Olegård et al., 1979	24/7600	1/300	1/600	Cases: children of alcoholic mothers

drinking women were inadvertently not examined at birth due to such factors as name changes, early discharges, conflicts with hospital routines or delivery at nonstudy hospitals.

Many factors can influence the rate of occurrence reported by various studies. These include population characteristics, sampling procedures, criteria for identifying a case, procedures for assessing the independent variable, etc. The general congruence of the figures reported by these three studies lends greater credence to the findings and leads to the conclusion that the birth prevalence of FAS is high enough to make the condition an important health problem.

Intelligence, Behavior, and Other Offspring Outcomes

Studies of intellectual development in children diagnosed as having FAS have generally been clinical or descriptive in that they had no control or comparison group. These studies have been important in that they have suggested hypotheses for further investigation. The finding that many FAS children are mentally retarded (e.g., Lemoine et al., 1968; Jones et al., 1973; and Streissguth et al., 1978b) as well as the finding that there is a relationship between severity of diagnosis and level of IQ (Majewski et al., 1976; Streissguth et al., 1978b) suggests that alcohol is an important drug in terms of behavioral teratogenesis. Furthermore, the clinical reports of hyperactivity, poor perceptual-motor function, and hypo- and hypertonicity in infants and children with FAS indicate important behavioral parameters to investigate in controlled studies.

Questions regarding intellectual deficits in children of alcoholic mothers have been addressed by several studies. In the Jones et al. study (1974) 7-year-old outcome was reported for children whose mothers had been enrolled in the study during pregnancy. Children whose mothers were identified during pregnancy as chronic alcoholics had significantly lower IQ scores on the Wechsler Intelligence Scale for Children compared to a (presumably) nonalcoholic control group. Furthermore, 44% of the children born to these mothers fell in the borderline to retarded range compared to 17% of controls. The strength of this study is that the cohorts were matched carefully on a large group of variables that might affect the dependent variable (IQ).

Furthermore, as is so important in behavioral studies, all data were gathered "blind" (without knowledge of maternal drinking status). The major weakness of the study (and one which was beyond the control of the authors) was that women in the Perinatal Collaborative Study had not been systematically questioned about their use or abuse of alcoholic beverages. Therefore, as noted earlier, only children of the most extreme abusers were included in the alcohol-exposed cohort. Studies such as this may produce more dramatic findings because only children of the most severe and obvious alcoholics are examined. However, one important result of this study was the finding that some children of alcoholic mothers had intellectual deficits even in the absence of FAS characteristics.

Several interesting neonatal behavioral variables have been investigated through laboratory studies conducted within the framework of the prospective studies of the effects of maternal alcohol use during pregnancy. In the Seattle prospective study, subsets of neonates were given a variety of behavioral assessments, which were suggested by clinical observation of infants with FAS. All examinations were conducted under standardized conditions, without knowledge of maternal alcohol use during pregnancy and without knowledge of outcome on other measures. The following results have been reported:

1. Newborn sucking pressure was significantly related to maternal alcohol use, even in a sample of women drinking less than five drinks a day on the average, and after adjustment for smoking effects (Martin et al., 1979). This finding is particularly interesting because poor sucking and failure to thrive have been reported clinically in some infants with fetal alcohol syndrome.
2. Significantly poorer operant conditioning (compared to controls) was reported in newborns whose mothers were both heavy smokers and moderate drinkers (Martin et al., 1977).
3. A study of the naturally-occurring behaviors of newborns (Landesman-Dwyer et al., 1978) reported a significant relationship between maternal alcohol use and infant tremulousness, head-turns to left, hand-to-mouth behavior, and decreased bodily vigor, even after adjusting for smoking, parity, and sex of infant.

4. Maternal alcohol use has also been significantly related to decreased habituation in newborns (Streissguth et al., 1983) after adjusting for other relevant variables (a finding perhaps related to the hyperacusis that has been reported clinically in newborns with fetal alcohol syndrome, (Pierog et al., 1979).

The Boston Pilot Study has also investigated two types of neonatal behavioral variables. A significant relationship between maternal alcohol use and newborn jitteriness and hypotonia, was reported (Oullette et al., 1977), using data from neurologic assessments and with a sample that was very different from the Seattle study in terms of racial and demographic characteristics (Rosett et al., 1976). Poor state regulation (absence of a predictable sleep-waking pattern) in infants of heavier-drinking mothers compared to controls was also reported (Sander et al., 1977; Rosett et al., 1979) from data obtained from automated bassinets.

The majority of behavioral studies on alcohol effects have dealt with newborns, but in one recent followup of the Seattle longitudinal study (1981), infant mental and motor development at 8 months of age had a significant inverse relationship to maternal alcohol use during pregnancy, even after adjustment for other relevant variables including smoking. Two separate studies involving different samples have reported that children born to moderately drinking mothers had significantly poorer attending behavior at 4 years of age (Landesman-Dwyer et al., 1981; Streissguth et al., 1984).

A few other variables have been evaluated in relation to maternal alcohol use, using data from hospital records. Decreased 1-minute Apgar scores have been reported in two studies (Sokol et al., 1980; Streissguth et al., 1982) in which the effects did not appear to be related to smoking. In one of these (Streissguth et al., 1982) almost twice as many "risk level" drinkers had infants with 1-minute Apgar scores of three or below, compared to non-risk level drinkers. "Risk level" drinking was defined generally as either two or more drinks a day, and/or sometimes taking five drinks per occasion, and/or getting drunk at least once during pregnancy. Sokol and colleagues (1980) found the following intrapartum factors were significantly increased in women clinically classified as alcohol abusers compared to controls: uterine tetany, mild abruptio placenta, precipitous delivery, and heavy meconium staining. Increasing amnionitis and fever during labor have been reported in two studies (Sokol et al., 1980; Streissguth et al., 1982).

Methodologic Implications

A large body of evidence is now available regarding alcohol-related morbidity and mortality in offspring of drinking women. Although the overall relationship is clear, several methodologic factors make interpretation of the data complicated:

1. *The variety of outcomes.*—In traditional epidemiologic studies the outcome is usually clear and it's usually bad, e.g., cancer of the esophagus. The design problem, then, is to study what factors are related to this outcome.

   With alcohol and pregnancy studies the outcomes are varied. In fact, one can visualize a multidimensional *continuum* of outcomes, ranging in severity from death, down through fetal alcohol syndrome, behavioral aberrations, and finally to mean deviations in growth and development that may have little relevance in the individual case. Thus the principles of teratology may be more suitable in looking at the total picture than the principles of epidemiology. Furthermore, the absence of an effect on a particular outcome is of interest in understanding the breadth of outcomes, but does not negate the positive results obtained on other outcomes.
2. *Ambiguity in the independent variable.*—In many epidemiologic studies, the independent variable is categorically and definitively defined, i.e., presence or absence of prenatal exposure to x-irradiation. In studies of alcohol use we have a multidimensional independent variable with each dimension existing along a continuum. Moreover, one end of the continuum may be complicated by other variables that are difficult to isolate (such as chronicity of alcoholism and alcohol-related diseases). Furthermore, the independent variable may not be constant over the period of time (9 months) that an effect could occur. When the complexity of the independent variable is coupled with the unknown

validity of its measurement, misclassification of persons in the cohort may well result. Even if this does not occur, caution must be used in interpreting the levels of alcohol use that appear to be related to an effect, even though the overall relationship of alcohol use to adverse outcomes is clear.

3. *Wide variety of study samples.*—The studies reviewed above have based their findings on very diverse groups of women. For example, the samples of low-risk women used by Seattle investigators (Little, 1977; Streissguth et al., 1981) have little in common with the high-risk sample of Ouellette et al. (1977). Drinking patterns as well as demographics are different. A wide variety of study samples is desirable in order to verify that a given result is not specific to a single group, but rather represents a universal relationship between alcohol use and the outcome under study. The danger lies in generalizing the findings of one study to a population very unlike that from which the study sample was drawn. For example, the rate of perinatal mortality for infants of mothers designated as "alcoholic" in the Perinatal Collaborative Study was over eight times that of the matched "nonalcoholic" cohort. The severity of the condition in the "alcoholic" cohort precludes generalization of the findings to all alcoholic women; as noted earlier, inference of relative risk in a population requires that the cases and controls under study are indeed drawn from that population.
4. *Inadequate or inappropriate control of confounding variables.*—One general rule-of-thumb is that potentially confounding variables in epidemiologic studies should be controlled if they are related to both the independent and the dependent variable in the sample under study. Disregard of this maxim may lead to including a large number of irrelevant factors in the analysis, thus possibly obscuring the relationship under study. On the other hand, failure to include correlated variables in the analysis can result in reporting spurious relationships between the primary independent and dependent variables. The second type of mistake—ignoring important confounding variables—has occurred far too frequently in studies of drinking and pregnancy. The danger of omitting smoking data from analysis has been noted earlier. The fallacy of ignoring

factors such as maternal age, education, parity, and socioeconomic status is also clear. Nutrition is another variable that should no longer be ignored. While FAS cannot be ascribed to poor diet, inadequate nutrition may increase the risk of fetal effects related to heavy drinking. Finally, these related variables should be examined not just individually, but in multiple regression analysis in order to detect synergistic effects and to adjust for confounding variables.

Summary

Evidence to date clearly indicates that maternal alcohol use increases the risk of fetal and infant morbidity and mortality. A broad spectrum of outcomes has been demonstrated, with many ranging along a continuum of effect. A dose-response curve is apparent for some of these outcomes. Yet caution must be used in interpretation of the findings. The number of potentially confounding variables that must be considered and the diverse populations from which study samples have been drawn preclude sweeping generalizations. Furthermore, the significance of the risk in the individual case is not clear for some of the outcomes assessed, particularly the neonatal behavioral variables. In addition, the difficulty of quantifying exposure to the agent—alcohol—requires that caution be exercised in assuming that a specific effect is related to a precise dose. Estimates of both consumption and severity of effect should be regarded as approximate. The overall conclusions are strengthened, however, because they derive from multiple corroborative studies rather than from a single unreplicated investigation. In summary, alcohol use clearly raises the risk of poor pregnancy outcome.

Acknowledgments

This work was partially supported by a grant from the U.S. Department of Health, Education, and Welfare, National Institute on Alcohol Abuse and Alcoholism (AA01455); a grant from the National Institute of Child Health and Human Development (5-P01-HD0227); and by the Alcoholism and Drug Abuse Institute, University of Washington. We are grateful to Ms. Pauline

Michela and Ms. Lori Easton Laughlin for secretarial assistance. Reprint requests to Dr. A.P. Streissguth, Department of Psychiatry & Behavioral Sciences, University of Washington, GI-80, Seattle, WA 98195.

References

Alpert, J.J., Day, N., Dooling, E., Hingson, R., Ottenheimer, E., Rosett, H.L., Weiner, L. & Zuckerman, B. (1981). Maternal Alcohol Consumption and Newborn Assessment: Methodology of the Boston City Hospital Prospective Study. *Neurobehav. Toxicol. Teratol.* 3:195–201.

Berkowitz G. (1981). An epidemiologic study of preterm delivery. *Am. J. Epidemiol.* 113:81–92.

Borlee, I., Lechat, M.F., Bouckaert, A. & Mission, C. (1978). Coffee: risk factor during pregnancy? (English translation). *Louvain Med.* 97:279–284.

Cahalan, D., Cisin, I. & Crossley, H. (1969). *American Drinking Practices: A National Study of Drinking Behavior and Attitudes*, Monograph No. 6. New Brunswick, N.J.: Rutgers Center of Alcohol Studies.

Chernoff, G.F. (1977). The fetal alcohol syndrome in mice: an animal model. *Teratology* 13:223–229.

Clarren, S.K. & Smith, D.W. (1978). The fetal alcohol syndrome. *New Engl. J. Med.* 298:1063–1067.

DeBeukelaer, M.M., Randall, C.L. & Stroud, D.R. (1977). Renal anomalies in the fetal alcohol syndrome. *J. Ped.* 91:759–760.

Dehaene, P., Samaille-Villette, C., Samaille, P., Crepin, G., Wałbaum, R., Deroubaix, P. & Blanc-Garin, A.P. (1977a). Le syndrome d'alcoolisme foetal dans le nord de la France. *Rev. Alcool.* 23:145–158.

Dehaene, P., Walbaum, R., Titran, M., Samaille-Villette, C., Samaille, R.P., Crepin, G., Delahousse, G., Decocq, J., Delcroix, M., Caquant, F. & Querleu, D. (1977b). La descendance des mères alcooliques chroniques, à propos de 16 d'alcoolisme foetal. *Rev. Fr. Gynecol. Obstet.* 72:492–498.

Dehaene, P., Crepin, G., Delahousse, G., Querleu, D., Walbaum, R., Titran, M. & Samaille-Villette, C. (1981). Aspects Epidemiologiques du syndrome d'alcoolisme foetal. *Nouv. Presse Med.* 32:2639–2643.

Hanson, J.W., Streissguth, A.P. & Smith, D.W. (1978). The effects of moderate alcohol consumption during pregnancy on fetal growth and morphogenesis. *J. Ped.* 92:457–460.

Harlap, S. & Shiono, P.H. (1980). Alcohol, smoking and incidence of spontaneous abortions in the first and second trimester. *Lancet* 2: 173–176.

Havlicek, V., Childiaeva, R. & Chernick, V. (1977). EEG frequency spectrum characteristics of sleep states in infants of alcoholic mothers. *Neuropaediatrie* 8:360–373.

Jessor, R., Graves, T.D., Hanson, R.C., & Jessor, S.L. (1968). *Society, Personality and Deviant Behavior: A Study of a Tri-ethnic Community.* New York: Holt, Rinehart and Winston.

Jones, K.L., Smith, D.W., Ulleland, N. & Streissguth, A.P. (1973). Pattern of malformation in offspring of chronic alcoholic mothers. *Lancet* 1:1267–1271.

Jones, K.L. & Smith, D.W. (1973). Recognition of the fetal alcohol syndrome in early infancy. *Lancet* 2:999–1001.

Jones, K.L., Smith, D.W., Streissguth, A.P. & Myrianthopoulous, N.C. (1974). Outcome in offspring of chronic alcoholic women. *Lancet* 1: 1076–1078.

Kaminski, M., Rumeau-Rouquette, C. & Schwartz, D. (1976). Consommation d'alcool chez les femmes enceintes et issue de la grossesse. *Revue d'Epidemiologie et de Sante Publique* 24:27–40. English translation by R.E. Little and A. Schinzel (1978): Alcohol consumption in pregnant women and the outcome of pregnancy. *Alc. Clin. Exp. Res.* 2:155–163.

Klemetti, A. & Saxen, L. (1967). Prospective vs. retrospective approach in the search for environmental causes of malformations. *Am. J. Pub. Health* 57:2071–2075.

Kline, J., Shrout, P., Stein, Z., Susser, M. & Warburton, D. (1980). Drinking during pregnancy and spontaneous abortion. *Lancet* 176–180.

Kuzma, M.W. & Kissinger, D.G. (1981). Patterns of alcohol and cigarette use in pregnancy. *Neurobehav. Toxicol. Teratol.* 3:211–221.

Landesman-Dwyer, S., Keller, L.S. & Streissguth, A.P. (1978). Naturalistic observations of newborns: Effects of maternal alcohol intake. *Alc. Clin. Exper. Res.* 2:171–177.

Landesman-Dwyer, S. & Emanuel, I. (1979). Smoking during pregnancy. *Teratology* 19:119–126.

Landesman-Dwyer, S., Ragozin, A.S. & Little, R.E. (1981). Behavioral correlates of prenatal alcohol exposure: A four-year follow-up study. *Neurobehav. Toxicol. Teratol.* 3:187–193.

Lemoine, P., Harousseau, H., Borteyru, J.P. & Menuet, J.C. (1968). Les enfants de parents alcooliques. Anomalies observées: À propos de 127 cas. *Quest Med.* 21:476–482.

Little, R.E., Schultz, F.A. & Mandell, W.A. (1976). Drinking during pregnancy. *J. Stud. Alc.* 37:375–379.

Little, R.E. (1976). Alcohol consumption as reported to the physician and to an independent interviewer. In: *Work in Progress in Alcoholism,* ed. F.A. Seixas & Eggleston, S. *Ann. N.Y. Acad. Sci.* 273:588–592.

Little, R.E. (1977). Moderate alcohol use during pregnancy and decreased infant birth weight. *Am. J. Pub. Health* 67:1154–1155.

Little, R.E., Mandell, W. & Schultz, F.A. (1977). Consequences of retrospective measurement of alcohol consumption. *J. Stud. Alc.* 38: 1777–1780.

Little, R.E. & Streissguth, A.P. (1978). Drinking during pregnancy in alcoholic women. *Alcoholism: Clin. Exp. Res.* 2:179–183.

Little, R.E., Streissguth, A.P., Barr, H.M. & Herman, C.S. (1980). Decreased birth weight in infants of alcoholic women who abstained during pregnancy. *J. Ped.* 96:974–976.

Majewski, F., Bierich, J.R., Loser, H., Michaelis, R., Leiber, B. & Bettecker, F. (1976). Zur Klinik und Pathogenese der Alkohol-Embryopathie. Bericht über 68 Fälle. *Muench. Medizin. Wochenschr.* 118: 1635–1642.

Martin, J.C., Martin, D.C., Lund, C.A. & Streissguth, A.P. (1977). Maternal alcohol ingestion and cigarette smoking and their effects upon newborn conditioning. *Alc. Clin. Exp. Res.* 1:243–247.

Martin, D.C., Martin, J.C., Streissguth, A.P. & Lund, C.A. (1979). Sucking frequency and amplitude in newborns as a function of maternal drinking and smoking. In: *Currents in Alcoholism* Vol. 5, ed. M. Galanter. New York: Grune & Stratton, pp. 359–366.

Martin, D.C., Barr, H.M. & Streissguth, A.P. (1980). Birth weight, birth length, and head circumference related to maternal alcohol, nicotine and caffeine use during pregnancy. *Teratology* 21:54A.

Mau, G. & Netter, P. (1974). Kaffee und alkoholkonsum-risikofaktoren in der Schwangerschaft? *Geburtsh. Frauenheilk.* 34:1018–1022.

Mulford, H.A. & Miller, D.E. (1960). Drinking in Iowa: II. The extent of drinking and selecting sociocultural categories. *Quart. J. Stud. Alc.* 21:26–39.

Obe, G. & Majewski, F. (1978). No elevation of exchange type aberrations in lymphocytes of children with alcohol embryopathy. *Hum. Gen.* 43:31–36.

Olegård, R., Sabel, K.G., Aronsson, M., Sandin, B., Johansson, P.R., Carlsson, C., Kyllerman, M., Iverson, K. & Hrbek, A. (1979). Effects on the child of alcohol abuse during pregnancy. *Acta Paediatr. Scand.* (Suppl.) 275:112–121.

Ouellette, E.M. & Rosett, H.L. (1976). A pilot prospective study of the fetal alcohol syndrome at the Boston City Hospital. Part II: The infants. *Ann. N.Y. Acad. Sci.* 273:123–129.

Ouellette, E.M., Rosett, H.L., Rosman, N.P. & Weiner, L. (1977). Adverse effects on offspring of maternal alcohol abuse during pregnancy. *New Engl. J. Med.* 297:528–530.

Pettersson, F. & Melander, S. (1975). Prediction of birth weight. Results of a multiple regression analysis. *Upsala J. Med. Sci.* 80:135–140.

Pierog, S., Chandavasu, O. & Wexler, I. (1979). The fetal alcohol syndrome: Some maternal characteristics. *Int. J. Gynaecol. Obstet.* 16: 412–415.

Root, A.W., Reiter, E.O., Andriola, M. & Duckett, G. (1975). Hypothalmic-pituitary function in the fetal alcohol syndrome. *J. Ped.* 87:585–588.

Rosett, H.L., Ouellette, E.M. & Weiner, L. (1976). A pilot prospective study of the fetal alcohol syndrome at the Boston City Hospital. Part I: Maternal drinking. *Ann. N.Y. Acad. Sci.* 273:118–122.

Rosett, H.L., Snyder, P., Sander, L.W., Lee, A., Cook, P. Weiner, L. & Gould, J. (1979). Effects of maternal drinking on neonatal state regulations. *Dev. Med. Child. Neurol.* 21:464–473.

Rouquette, J. (1957). Influence de l'intoxication alcoolique parentéle sur le développement physique et psychique des jeunes enfants. Paris: Thése.

Russell, M. (1977). Intrauterine growth in infants born to women with alcohol-related psychiatric disorders. *Alc. Clin. Exp. Res.* 1:225–231.

Russell, M. & Bigler, L. (1979). Screening for alcohol-related problems in an outpatient obstetric-gynecologic clinic. *Am. J. Obstet. Gynecol.* 134:4–12.

Sander, L.W., Snyder, P., Rosett, H.L., Lee, A., Gould, J.B. & Ouellette, E. (1977). Effects of alcohol intake during pregnancy on newborn state regulation: A progress report. *Alc. Clin. Exp. Res.* 1: 233–241.

Silva, V.A., Laranjeira, R.R., Dolnikoff, H., Grinfeld, A. & Masur, J. (1981). Alcohol consumption during pregnancy and newborn outcome: A study in Brazil. *Neurobehav. Toxicol. Teratol.* 3:169–172.

Sokol, R.J., Miller, S.I. & Reed, G. (1980). Alcohol abuse during pregnancy: An epidemiological model. *Alc. Clin. Exp. Res.* 4:135–145.

Sokol, R.J., Miller, S.I., Debanne, S., Golden, N., Collins, G., Kaplan, J. & Martier, S. (1981). The Cleveland NIAAA Prospective Alcohol-in-Pregnancy Study: The first year. *Neurobehav. Toxicol. Teratol.* 3:203.

Spiegal, P.G., Pekman, W.M., Rich, B.H., Versteeg, C.N., Nelson, V. & Dudnikov, M. (1979). The orthopedic aspects of the fetal alcohol syndrome. *Clin. Orthop.* 139:58–63.

Streissguth, A.P., Martin, D.C. & Buffington, V.E. (1976). Test-retest reliability of three scales derived from a quantity-frequency-variability assessment of self-reported alcohol consumption. In: *Work in Progress in Alcoholism,* ed. F.A. Seixas & S. Eggleston. *Ann. N.Y. Acad. Sci.* 273:458–466.

Streissguth, A.P., Martin, D.C. & Buffington, V.E. (1977). Identifying heavy drinkers: A comparison of eight alcohol scores obtained on the same sample. In: *Currents in Alcoholism* Vol. II, ed. F.A. Seixas. New York: Grune and Stratton, pp. 395–420.

Streissguth, A.P., Herman, C.S. & Smith, D.W. (1978a). Stability of intelligence in the fetal alcohol syndrome: A preliminary report. *Alc. Clin. Exp. Res.* 2:165–170.

Streissguth, A.P., Herman, C.S. & Smith, D.W. (1978b). Intelligence, behavior, and dysmorphogenesis in the fetal alcohol syndrome: A report on 20 patients. *J. Ped.* 92:363–367.

Streissguth, A.P., Little, R.E., Herman, C.S. & Woodell, S. (1979). IQ in children of recovered alcoholic mothers compared to matched controls. *Alc. Clin. Exp. Res.* 3:197.

Streissguth, A.P., Barr, H.M., Martin, D.C. & Herman, S.C. (1980). Effects of maternal alcohol, nicotine and caffeine use during pregnancy on infant mental and motor development at 8 months. *Alc. Clin. Exp. Res.* 4:152–164.

Streissguth, A.P. (1980). Female alcoholism: Impacts on women and children. *Curr. Alc.* 7:429–434.

Streissguth, A.P., Martin, D.C., Martin, J.C. & Barr, H.M. (1981). The Seattle Longitudinal Prospective Study on Alcohol and Pregnancy. *Neurobehav. Toxicol. Teratol.* 3:223–233.

Streissguth, A.P., Barr, H.M. & Martin, D.C. (1983). Maternal alcohol use and neonatal habituation assessed with the Brazelton scale. *Child Dev.* 54:1109–1118.

Streissguth, A.P., Barr, H.M., & Martin, D.C. (1982). Offspring effects and pregnancy complications related to self-reported alcohol use. *Dev. Pharmacol. Ther.* 5:21–32.

Streissguth, A.P., Martin, D.C., Barr, H.M. & MacGregor Sandman, B. (1984). Intrauterine alcohol and nicotine exposure: Attention and reaction time in 4-year-old children. *Dev. Psych.* 20:533–541.

Sullivan, W.C. (1899). A note on the influence of maternal inebriety on the offspring. *J. Mental Sci.* 45:489–503.

Tennes, K. & Blackard, C. (1980). Maternal alcohol consumption, birth weight, and minor physical anomalies. *Am. J. Obstet. Gynecol.* 138: 774–780.

Tze, W.J., Friesen, H.G. & MacLeod, P.M. (1976). Growth hormone response in fetal alcohol syndrome. *Arch. Dis. Child.* 51:703–706.

van den Berg, B.J. (1977). Epidemiologic observations of prematurity: Effects of tobacco, coffee, and alcohol. In: *Epidemiology of Prematurity.* ed. D.M. Reed & F.J. Stanley. Baltimore: Urban and Schwarzenberg.

Warburton, D., Susser, M., Stein, Z. & Kline, J. (1979). Genetic and epidemiologic investigation of spontaneous abortion: Revelance to clinical practice. *Birth Defects: Original Article Series,* 15 No. 5A:127–136, National Foundation.

Weathersbee, P.S. & Lodge, J.R. (1973). Caffeine: Its direct and indirect influence on reproduction. *J. Reprod. Med.* 19:55–63.

Wilson, J.G. (1973). Present status of drugs as teratogens in man. *Teratology* 7:3–16.

Chapter 5

Research on Alcohol Abuse and Rehabilitation in the U. S. Navy

DOUGLAS KOLB
E. K. ERIC GUNDERSON

Alcohol consumption, particularly for recreation or celebration, has long been an accepted part of military life. At the same time, military personnel are expected to control their drinking behavior so it does not interfere with readiness to perform their duties. Until 1970 individuals who were unable to control their drinking, incurred disciplinary problems because of alcohol, or required hospitalization ran the risk of punitive actions including discharge from the service. Because of the serious potential consequences, both the alcohol abusers and supervisory personnel were likely to deny difficulties and cover up excessive drinking. Special treatment programs did not exist, and medical treatment provided during hospitalization was routine and short-term. It was suspected that diagnoses other than alcoholism, for example, transient situational disturbance, were often applied to acute cases. Research efforts during this period were negligible.

Following the dramatic rise in illicit drug use among Armed Forces personnel during the late 1960s, national and military leaders recognized that substance abuse, including alcohol abuse, was a serious public health problem.

This chapter describes alcohol rehabilitation services of the U.S. Navy and discusses the value of research on naval populations in the field of alcohol abuse. Methodology used by the Naval Health Research Center (NHRC), San Diego, and by independent research contractors is reviewed, and the extensive data bases available at NHRC for the study of alcohol abuse and rehabilitation program effectiveness are described in detail.

Finally, studies completed at this laboratory on the epidemiology of alcohol abuse in the U.S. Navy are summarized and evaluated.

Background

History

Problems of alcoholism and alcohol abuse in the U.S. Navy have been the focus of considerable attention during the past decade. This has been the direct result of two pieces of federal legislation. The first of these was Public Law 91-616, The Comprehensive Alcohol Abuse and Alcohol Prevention, Treatment, and Rehabilitation Act of 1970, which initiated a national campaign to fight alcoholism. The second was Public Law 92-129, The Armed Forces Drug and Drug Dependence Prevention, Treatment, and Rehabilitation Act of 1971, which required that control programs for alchol abuse be established for military personnel.

The Navy's immediate response was to establish five alcohol rehabilitation centers at key locations throughout the United States to provide residential treatment. Further, alcohol rehabilition units (later designated services) were soon established at numerous Navy hospitals world-wide to provide similar types of programs. Finally, alcohol rehabilitation "drydocks," which provide outpatient treatment, were established over a period of years at all principal naval commands. Drydocks have been absorbed into Counseling and Assistance Centers (CAACs) which screen and provide treatment for all types of substance abuse problems.

Almost from the beginning of these rehabilitation programs biographical data, social and family background, drinking history, and related information have been collected systematically from the participants and forwarded to a central office for machine processing. Over the years the content of the data collection instruments has changed as well as the specific office or agency responsible for collecting and processing the information. Nevertheless, relatively complete records for Navy personnel (numbering in excess of 15,000) admitted to alcohol rehabilitation facilities from 1972 through 1979 are on file at the Naval Health Research Center.

The most recent additions to data on alcohol abuse and rehabilitation among navy personnel are the records of individuals referred to the Navy Alcohol Safety Action Program (NASAP) which began in late 1975. NASAP is an educational program conducted after working hours over a period of weeks. Many of the individuals referred have been arrested for drunk driving, but individuals experiencing other kinds of problems (for example, fighting) because of alcohol also can be assigned to the program. NASAP is considered an early intervention program for incipient alcohol abusers, and its aim is to encourage individuals to think about their drinking behavior and to assume more responsibility for their actions. This extensive data base permits a variety of large-scale studies of alcohol abuse and alcoholism among Navy men and women. Examples of studies completed, in process, and planned are presented below as well as limitations of the data and the methodologic problems encountered.

Importance of Alcohol Research in Military Populations

Studies of alcoholism and alcohol abuse among Navy personnel can contribute in important ways to the understanding and treatment of alcohol problems in the larger society. They afford an opportunity to assess the nature, extent, and outcome of alcohol abuse in a large population of healthy young men and women that is a fairly representative cross-section of American youth. These men and women are from all parts of the nation and from all socioeconomic levels. It would be difficult, if not impossible, to find a comparable group for study outside of the Armed Forces, and it would be costly indeed to survey alcohol abuse problems in a large and representative youthful population and to follow the course of rehabilitation and postrehabilitation life adjustment.

In addition, approximately 15%–20% of Navy personnel who complete their first enlistments reenlist and form the cadre of career personnel who complete 20 years or more of service before retirement. Thus, besides contributing to the understanding of early alcohol abuse and alcoholism in a young population, the military makes it possible to study the long-term effects of alcohol abuse on the health and performance of men and women during the entire productive span of their lives. These studies are facilitated by the existence of relatively complete and standardized medical and service history records that are maintained in centralized computer files for the entire Navy population. These record systems and their uses will be described in some detail below.

Data bases available on alcohol abuse and rehabilitation for naval populations expanded greatly during the early 1970s when special rehabilitation programs for alcoholics and alcohol abusers were initiated. These rehabilitation services have broadened over the past several years to encompass not only treatment for alcohol-dependent individuals but educational programs for incipient alcohol abusers as well. Thus, the Navy now offers an unprecedented range and diversity of services for individuals with alcohol-related problems, and a record system that provides unparalleled opportunities for systematic analysis of the characteristics of alcohol abusers in relation to treatment modalities and outcomes.

Methodologies—Assets and Liabilities

Survey Method

Specific methods employed to study alcohol problems in the Armed Forces have depended on the goals of the investigations as well as resources available. Cahalan and associates, in a study of alcohol use and abuse patterns in Army personnel completed in the early 1970s, used a lengthy questionnaire that guaranteed anonymity to participants. It was administered by trained field teams to groups of randomly selected respondents at numerous locations also randomly selected. A similar survey was completed for Navy personnel (Cahalan et al., 1973). The presence of trained survey personnel affords the opportunity to clarify any questions respondents have about the questionnaire and thus increases the likelihood that complete data will be obtained. Furthermore, greater accuracy and completeness occur when data are collected by members of the research staff. A guarantee of anonymity to service personnel encourages their sharing information they might otherwise withhold lest it come to the attention of their superior officers and adversely affect their careers.

In a study to evaluate alcohol abuse control programs servicewide for the Department of Defense, interview teams were dispatched to strategic locations worldwide. Various questionnaires and other survey instruments were completed by patient and nonpatient groups as well as supervisory and treatment personnel. In addition, many participants and key informants (e.g., base commanders) were personally interviewed and records of treatment facilities and other pertinent organizational subunits were reviewed (Systems Development Corporation, 1975). These studies represented major research efforts requiring substantial financial and personnel resources.

Since the inauguration of special alcohol rehabilitation programs for Navy personnel in the early 1970s, extensive information has been gathered from rehabilitees by questionnaire at all types of treatment facilities worldwide. In addition, selected items of information have been obtained from key informants (treatment staff). These data have been collected centrally and loaded on computer tapes. The data provide a rich source of information about alcohol abuse problems from the abusers themselves, but there is always a question concerning the accuracy of this information. Particularly among military personnel, there may be reluctance to give information that may be considered personally damaging. Secondly, many individuals entering treatment may have been drinking heavily and therefore were not in good physical and mental condition to recall the information requested. A third possible factor affecting the accuracy of data provided by alcohol abusers is the tendency to deny problems. In the study to evaluate alcohol abuse control programs referred to earlier, ex-patients were much more likely to acknowledge such reasons as excessive drinking and problems on the job for their voluntarily entering treatment than were patients questioned during treatment. Presumably, the treatment and posttreatment experiences caused these individuals to change their perceptions of why they had been in treatment, and they could more fully acknowledge how much difficulty drinking had caused them. Of necessity the individual is the principal source of most of the information about his own experiences with alcohol. At the same time it is often desirable or preferable to use the key informant method, particularly early in the treatment process when it is important to know the nature and severity of problems related to the job, the marital relationship, and other social obligations. Thus, evaluations by Navy counselors made during the rehabilitation program have proven valid indicators of problem severity and prognosis.

Rate under Treatment

The study method used during the early investigations of alcoholism at the Naval Health Research Center was the *rate hospitalized*, based upon archival records. An important advantage of this method is that data are available on all naval personnel. While the amount of information on individuals is quite limited, the data are uniform throughout the naval population, complete for all important medical and service history events, and easily linked to other data bases by Social Security number. With the chronologically ordered personnel data files, selected populations, treated and non-treated, can be followed for specific time intervals, including post-treatment periods or comparable time periods for controls, to determine outcome criteria in terms of discharge status and recommendation for reenlistment. Longitudinal outcome studies using such criteria have been completed for entire populations of Navy personnel who have completed alcohol rehabilitation programs.

Prospective Cohort Studies Using Experimental and Archival Data

A methodology particularly suited to Navy populations is the longitudinal analysis of computer files of medical and service histories for entire cohorts of personnel who enter the service during a specified interval, for example, during a given calendar year or a series of calendar years. In one study, health and service histories covering a 10-year period from the beginning of the second enlistment were compared for men hospitalized with diagnoses of alcoholism and men never hospitalized with these diagnoses. The two groups were matched on occupation and age at enlistment. Comparisons were made on hospitalizations for any medical condition (except alcoholism) and on disciplinary occurrences over the 10 years (Kolb & Gunderson, 1977).

Special chronologic files have now been created containing the most significant medical and service history data for all enlisted Navy personnel, and these files can be easily expanded to include data pertaining to alcohol treatment. Studies are currently underway to determine causes and patterns of hospitalization before and after receiving a diagnosis of alcoholism. These analyses are being conducted on cohorts of men who entered the Navy during several different time periods in order to study the effects of alcoholism on health during early, middle, and later phases of a naval career. In each cohort, medical histories for controls will be compared with those for alcoholics.

Prospective cohort analysis of this type is actually the epidemiologic method of choice for establishing etiologic or causal relationships, identifying risk factors for alcoholism and alcohol abuse incidence, and evaluating rehabilitation program effectiveness. The essential characteristics of prospective cohort analysis are that the cohort group or groups are defined before the occurrence of disease and the groups are observed over a specific period in order to determine disease incidence. This cohort method provides direct estimates of rates of disease (alcoholism) in a population, the impact of various risk factors on incidence and outcome, and the consequences of various intervention programs. Use of the Navy Medical History Data System, combined with experimental data collected for specific purposes and for testing specific hypotheses, will provide a powerful methodology for analyzing the epidemiology, etiology, and course of alcoholism and alcohol abuse among all segments of the naval population.

The Naval Career History Data System

The Naval Health Research Center has developed an epidemiologic approach to analyzing the distribution of alcohol problems and evaluating rehabilitation programs in the Navy. Such epidemiologic studies depend on inpatient data from the Navy Medical History Data System created at NHRC during the past several years. This system contains records of all hospitalizations, medical board actions, and deaths for Navy and Marine Corps active duty personnel since 1965. These records, first collected at the Navy Medical Data Services Center in Bethesda, Maryland, are further edited and processed to construct individual medical histories that reflect morbidity and mortality over entire naval careers. Each hospitalization record contains demographic and identifying information, admitting facility, dates of admission and discharge, primary and other diagnoses, whether the condition existed prior to enlistment, occupational speciality and pay grade, marital status, hospital disposition, and medical board action (to determine fitness for duty and/or compensation for disability). Medical histories now exist for approximately 800,000 Navy men and women representing more than one million hospitalizations.

In addition, computer files containing service history information have been compiled for all active duty enlisted Navy personnel since 1965 to complement the medical history file. The service history file includes such personnel data as sex, race, birth date, marital status, schooling completed, and aptitude scores as well as a chronological history of significant changes in personnel status, for example, promotions, demotions, unauthorized absences, desertions, discharges, and reenlistments. In the near future, all changes in duty station will be added to this file so that it will be possible to track any sailor's location and type of assignment throughout his naval career. With these data bases, medical histories and alcohol treatment histories of naval personnel can be studied in the context of military service history and occupational and social information over more than a decade.

The archival data contained in the Navy Medical History Data System and the parallel service history system represent a unique and valuable health information resource. These inpatient records are especially useful because of the completeness, uniformity, and accuracy of the diagnostic data, the linkage to personnel records, and the ease of following service members throughout entire careers and into retirement. Record linkage is made possible by routine assignment of a unique number, the Social Security number, to all pertinent records. The limitations of such data for general epidemiologic purposes are restrictions as to age and sex distributions and population biases resulting from induction screening standards, early discharges for diseases and injuries that interfere with military performance, and early attrition of noncareer personnel.

The integration of the medical and personnel files has resulted in the Navy Career History Data System, which consolidates into one file the most significant items from both the medical and service histories as well as other available data that may be of interest, for example, records for alcohol rehabilitation programs. Additional data from any source can quickly and easily be incorporated into the Naval Career History Data System as either permanent segments or as temporary auxiliary data required for the duration of a particular inquiry.

These integrated files make possible comparative studies of incidence, work days lost, disposition, recurrence of illness or injury, disability, and death for all disease and accident categories. Risks of morbidity and mortality can be determined for any naval occupation, work environment, or segment of the naval population, such as those treated for alcohol problems. The file permits longitudinal analyses of disease and injury rates by sex, race, occupational speciality, job experience, pay grade, aptitude level, education, and duty assignment or geographic location. The relationships of dynamic etiologic factors such as change in occupation, promotions, demotions, disciplinary problems, marriage and children, isolated or unusual duty assignments, training failure, and hospitalization or treatment for alcohol abuse can be evaluated by means of cohort analyses conducted over a decade or longer of naval service. The Naval Health Research Center is the only military laboratory that has the capability of conducting longitudinal health studies of this kind.

Major Studies at the Naval Health Research Center

Indicators of Incidence and Prevalence

A number of studies of naval personnel treated for alcohol abuse and alcoholism have been conducted during the past several years using the medical and personnel data files described above. Among the first of these was a study that determined rates of hospitalization for major naval subgroups, that is, male enlisted, male officers, and females. For the 4-year period 1966–1969 a hospital admission rate for all categories of alcoholism of 80 per 100,000 per year was reported for Navy enlisted men, which was higher than rates generally reported for male civilian populations (Gunderson & Schuckit, 1975). More recent computations of hospitalization rates by 2-year intervals over a 10-year period showed striking increases for Navy enlisted men from

TABLE 1
Incidence Rates by Year of Enlistment for Alcoholism among Navy Male Enlisted Personnel

Age (in years)	*Year of enlistment*				
	1966–67	*1968–69*	*1970–71*	*1972–73*	*1974–75*
17	—	—	113	282	267
18	15	7	130	173	238
19	9	11	96	150	238
20	10	12	78	132	225
21–22	10	17	63	126	260
23–25	14	30	62	140	289
26–30	31	50	140	452	536
31–35	70	121	258	592	720
36–40	148	228	322	678	701
>40	190	299	437	642	741

Note: Rates per 100,000 strength per year.

age 17 through 40 (table 1). The sharpest increases were evident from 1968–1969 to 1970–1971, the years during which the legislation referred to earlier became effective. Rates have continued to rise, doubling in the subsequent 2-year period (1972–1973) for most age groups. The highest rates were in the most recent time period, 1974–1975. These rates reflect only cases admitted to naval hospitals with diagnoses of alcoholism and do not include individuals treated for alcohol abuse or alcoholism in other programs.

There are a number of possible explanations for the marked increases in observed rates. The simplest would be that alcoholism, or at least alcohol abuse, among Navy personnel actually increased substantially during the decade 1966–1975. Evidence for this position was found in the Second Special Report to the U.S. Congress on Alcohol and Health (1974) which indicated that "the proportion of American youth who drink has been increasing so that, currently, it is almost universal." High scores on an index of problem drinking were obtained for individuals in the 18–20-year-old range, the age range for the majority of first enlistment Navy personnel.

Other explanations are equally possible. The earlier rates, while high in comparison to civilian rates, may have been a conservative estimate for the Navy because alcoholism was viewed so negatively and individuals were not likely to seek treatment unless forced to do so. Further, problems of alcoholism may have been obscured by medical personnel who tended to give diagnoses of transient situational maladjustment or character and behavior disorder because these were considered less damaging to an individual's career than the label alcoholism. The more favorable policies regarding alcoholism and the emphasis on early treatment initiated in the 1970s resulted in an increase in the number of beds available to treat alcoholics. Prior to the establishment of special rehabilitation programs, Navy personnel with alcohol problems were treated, for the most part, on psychiatric services in Navy hospitals, thus vying for beds with all others needing psychiatric care. Alcohol rehabilitation services established in hospital settings made available many beds specifically for this illness group. Rates of alcoholism reported in recent years would be even higher if admissions to alcohol rehabilitation facilities other than those in hospitals were included. The restriction to hospital admissions ensures that individuals counted were diagnosed medically. At the same time the criteria for admission to alcohol rehabilitation centers (nonmedical) are not known to be different from those for admission to alcohol rehabilitation services (medical). Individuals seen in these two types of facilities are equally "ill." Depending on the specific criteria used, many men referred to the less intensive programs in drydocks or men participating in the NASAP educational program could be classified as alcoholics. At best, then, available estimates of alcoholism rates in the Navy have been conservative, failing to accurately reflect the prevalence of alcoholism or of alcohol abuse in the naval population.

Evaluation of Program Effectiveness

A major interest of the Navy since the initiation of rehabilitation programs has been the posttreatment effectiveness of participants and differences in program effectiveness. Posttreatment effectiveness has usually been defined as being on active duty status or in receipt of a favorable discharge from service with a positive recommendation for reenlistment 6 months or more after completing rehabilitation. Information needed to determine this effectiveness criterion is contained in the Naval Career History Data System at the Naval Health Research Center. The most relevant rehabilitation outcome is whether or not the participant can continue to serve on active duty satisfactorily and be recommended for reenlistment at the expiration of his obligated service.

Missing from this criterion, of course, is any direct indication of whether the individual continues to drink or to experience problems in any area of life, on or off duty, because of alcohol. If this information is desired, special studies must be designed and the specific information sought from the individual himself or from others with whom he interacts on the job or socially who are aware of his continued alcohol use and associated behavior. Frequent transfers of Navy personnel to duty assignments worldwide make such studies extremely difficult within existing constraints of time and money. In one followup attempt to reach men discharged from treatment, 2,000 questionnaires were sent out, but only 537 usable responses were returned. Of those 2,000, several hundred questionnaires were returned as undeliverable because the addressees could not be located, even though the envelopes showed they had been forwarded numerous times.

The effectiveness criterion applied to outcome studies of Navy alcoholics essentially reflects disciplinary and performance histories and overall adjustment to the demands of Navy life. With the exception of the posttreatment time factor this is the same criterion that is used to evaluate the performance of any individual in the Navy. From such followup studies of men treated in alcohol rehabilitation facilities it is not actually known to what extent alcohol abuse or alcoholism has affected outcome. Withholding treatment from identified alcohol abusers as a means of testing the effects of rehabilitation on outcome is not ethical. From career histories available on men who became alcoholics in the Navy it was obvious that some of them go through their careers performing skilled work, exercising responsibility, avoiding disciplinary problems, and advancing in pay grade regularly. Finally, the records of some senior personnel with alcohol problems may not accurately reflect their true performance, that is, ineffectiveness can be covered up because of their senior status.

TABLE 2
Differences among Alcohol Rehabilitation Programs on Indicators of Severity of Alcoholism

	Total population				
Indicator	*Centers*	*Services*	*Drydocks*	*NASAP*	F^a
Hospitalized because of drinking	0.27[b]	0.47	0.11	0.06	436.43
Told by doctor to stop drinking	0.28	0.33	0.15	0.06	223.86
Participated in AA	0.58	0.44	0.33	0.11	411.88
Had shakes the "morning after"	0.60	0.62	0.51	0.28	245.92
Had hallucinations	0.18	0.20	0.14	0.07	67.79
Had convulsions	0.09	0.10	0.08	0.04	24.19
Vomited blood	0.18	0.20	0.14	0.06	73.04
Had blackouts	0.81	0.84	0.79	0.53	277.95
Doctor said had pancreatitis	0.02	0.02	0.01	0.00	6.73
Doctor said had liver problems	0.10	0.07	0.03	0.02	50.62
Saw professional to help stop drinking	0.50	0.47	0.36	0.15	263.33
Composite variable: alcoholic by behavioral criteria	0.95	0.83	0.57	0.27	261.40
Prognosis (excellent, good, fair, poor)	1.66	1.84	1.78	1.25	220.88
Posttreatment effectiveness proportion noneffective)	0.21	0.18	0.17	0.09	46.99

[a]All values are significant ($P < 0.05$).
[b]All values are proportions except alcoholic by behavioral criteria and prognosis, which are scores.

Comparisons of Types of Treatment Facilities

Studies comparing outcome by type of facility have been completed for two large populations of rehabilitees during the past five years (Kolb & Gunderson, 1975; Kolb et al., 1978). Differences in posttreatment outcomes among centers, services, and drydocks tended to be related to population differences at the time of admission to the programs rather than to differences among the programs themselves. Posttreatment differences among individual facilities within type generally were not significant, suggesting general similarity among programs of the same type.

Recent investigations involved comparisons between participants in alcohol rehabilitation programs and participants in the NASAP program (Kolb et al., 1979). Higher effectiveness rates were observed for NASAP participants compared with rehabilitation program participants, which was consistent with more favorable population characteristics, less severe alcohol problems, and the concept of early treatment intervention. Further analyses compared the three types of rehabilitation facilities with NASAP participants. Differences in alcohol symptomatology, diagnoses of alcoholism by behavioral criteria, and posttreatment outcomes are shown for the total populations in table 2. Populations of each of these three types of rehabilitation facilities differed from NASAP participants on the majority of drinking-related behaviors and symptoms, whereas the differences among the rehabilitation facilities themselves were less pronounced. Centers and services particularly reflected similarities in the populations treated in these facilities. In general, men treated in drydocks had less severe symptom histories than those treated in centers and services but more severe than NASAP participants. The composite variable Alcoholic by Behavioral Criteria discriminated among all four populations, indicating that men treated at centers had the most severe alcohol problems and men in NASAP programs the least severe problems. These findings show that the various types of programs generally are being used appropriately: men with the most severe alcohol histories are being treated in the longer-term residential programs while men with less severe histories are involved in preventive educational programs; men with moderate alcohol involvement are being treated in outpatient treatment facilities.

A Study of Alcohol-Related Problems

One major study has been conducted to evaluate the effects of alcoholism on the health and performance of career Navy personnel utilizing a cohort approach. Using the medical and service history files maintained at the Naval Health Research Center, the records of a group of men diagnosed alcoholic and those of a control group not medically diagnosed alcoholic were compared over more than a decade. Both groups enlisted during the same 2-year period, and the experimental and control groups were matched on occupation and age at enlistment. Medical and service history observations began after the second enlistment, thus maximizing the probability that subjects would be career-oriented and that their records would be available over an extended period. The alcoholics differed from controls on social and military history variables: Alcoholics less often married and had children than controls and achieved less favorable performance records (table 3). At the same time, alcoholics had higher

TABLE 3
Social and Service History Variables that Discriminated between Alcoholics and Controls

Marital status	*Alcoholics*	*Controls*
Single	16.2[a]	9.1
Married	69.7	84.0
Other	14.1	6.9
Highest number of dependents ever claimed		
None	17.2	9.4
One or two	29.4	33.5
More than two	53.4	57.1
Highest pay grade achieved		
≤ E-4	7.4	3.7
E-5	22.9	18.3
E-6	52.3	50.1
E-7 through E-9	17.4	27.9
Times reduced in pay grade		
None	58.5	85.2
Once	23.8	11.1
More than once	17.6	3.7
Lost time adjustment due to unauthorized absence		
None	74.3	93.7
One	17.1	5.0
≥ Two	8.6	1.4
Ever declared a deserter		
Yes	5.7	1.6
Recommended for reenlistment		
No	13.9	4.3
Number of courts-martial		
None	69.9	80.1
One	5.5	2.5
≥ Two	24.6	17.5
Number of cases	545	1,090

Note: All differences significant by chi-square statistic at 0.001 level.
[a]Percentage

TABLE 4
Admission Rates for Alcoholics and Controls by Major Disease Categories

Major disease categories[a]	*Alcoholics*	*Controls*
Inefective and parasitic diseases	5.64	3.41
Neoplasms	2.92	2.48
Nutritional and metabolic diseases	1.55	0.31
Diseases of blood and blood-forming organs	0.19	0.41
Mental diseases	19.82	3.00
Diseases of the nervous system and sense organs	2.72	2.90
Diseases of the circulatory system	6.61	3.72
Diseases of the respiratory system	11.08	7.86
Diseases of the digestive system	16.52	7.34
Diseases of the genitourinary system	4.66	4.55
Diseases of the skin	7.39	3.62
Diseases of the musculoskeletal system	8.75	5.79
Congenital anomalies	0.58	1.24
Ill-defined conditions	7.58	5.17
Accidents, poisonings, and violence	39.65	15.51
Special Conditions	4.47	2.58
Number of cases	545	1,090

Note: Admission rates are the numbers of new cases per 1,000 men per year (1966–1978).
[a]Primary diagnoses; alcoholism diagnoses are excluded.

hospital admission rates for most categories of disease and injury, particularly mental disorders (other than alcoholism), disorders of the digestive system, and accidents, poisonings, and violence (table 4). It was clear from this study that alcoholism had a deleterious effect on both health and performance among naval career personnel. Health effects of alcoholism have been further detailed in three longitudinal studies (Kolb & Gunderson, 1981a, 1981b, and 1982).

Changes in Treatment Populations Over Time

During the past several years a number of studies of rehabilitation outcomes using the effectiveness criterion described earlier have been completed for Navy enlisted men. A number of important trends have been noted: (1) an increasing proportion of those referred for treatment are younger men; (2) larger proportions of individuals are being treated in less intensive programs (drydocks and NASAP); (3) differences in treatment outcomes tend to be related more to population differences than program differences, and (4) effectiveness rates have tended to improve over time, especially among younger men (age 17–25).

Effectiveness rates have been high for older men since the beginning of special rehabilitation programs (over 80%). While at first glance it might be assumed that increases in effectiveness rates for younger men were due to improvements in the treatment programs, there was little direct evidence to support this assumption. Such improvement was more likely the result of larger numbers of younger men with less severe alcohol problems entering treatment. It may also have been partly due to positive changes in attitudes and behaviors toward men with alcohol problems by supervisory personnel in the fleet. A third possibility is that followup services are better developed now than they were 5 years ago and the individual can more easily find support and assistance in his efforts to control his drinking following treatment and thus can avoid behavior difficulties related to alcohol use. The increase in numbers of younger men being referred to treatment cannot necessarily be attributed to an increase in alcohol abuse among younger sailors, nor can the lower proportion of older men be attributed to a decline in prevalence in that group. For example, a command may feel that it can more easily afford to lose the services of a young, less experienced sailor to the 6 weeks residential rehabilitation program than it can the services of a skilled senior petty officer. This may be especially important aboard ship where maintaining personnel strength, particularly in key positions, is critical to the ship's mission. If a ship is deployed overseas, the loss of the individual's services may well exceed the time spent in treatment.

The treatment of larger numbers of individuals in less intensive programs (drydocks) is an appropriate consequence of ever-expanding services and increasing awareness of alcoholism and alcohol abuse among younger personnel. It also reflects less certainty about the underlying nature of the problem while at the same time providing an opportunity for continued evaluation of the individual and his problem while he remains in a working situation. It is a more economical approach to problems of alcohol abuse than referral to the longer-term residential programs.

Identification of Treatment Subgroups

The presence of increasing numbers of younger personnel in treatment raises the question of how alcoholism is defined.

Many of these younger men evidence histories of antisocial behavior, both related and unrelated to the use of alcohol, and both before and during their naval service. Increasingly, treatment staff see many of these younger men as behavioral problems for whom alcohol abuse is only one symptom. Such men may be referred to treatment primarily because they are management problems for their commands.

Diagnostic criteria for alcoholism are not clearly spelled out at naval rehabilitation facilities and the basis for such a diagnosis is not routinely established. Therefore, it is not always clear why individuals are in treatment. This does not mean that men in treatment have not had serious difficulties with drinking. Men referred for rehabilitation are screened and not all are accepted for treatment—only those who in the opinion of the screening staff have severe alcohol problems. Once accepted for a residential rehabilitation program, however, the treatment staff may find that it requires several weeks of observation before they feel confident that the individual's problem is primarily alcohol rather than a behavior disorder.

From the biographic information provided by rehabilitation participants a composite variable was developed called the Sociopathy Scale. This variable may have some value as an adjunct to the screening and referral process. The items that comprise the scale represent more severe antisocial behaviors, for example, using an alias or wandering without a job for several months. Higher Sociopathy scores were associated with poor response to treatment and with posttreatment ineffectiveness. Because present alcohol rehabilitation programs rest heavily on an Alcoholics Anonymous approach to alcoholism and the majority of the treatment staff are individuals who have experienced severe alcohol problems themselves, neither the program as a whole nor individual staff members may be adequately prepared to treat individuals whose problems are basically characterologic or behavioral. It seems important to clarify this issue. Either present programs should be modified to meet the needs of men with these problems and staff should be given special training to work with persons having behavioral and characterologic problems, or special programs should be created to deal specifically with these types of adjustment difficulties. A third alternative would be to screen such individuals out of alcohol rehabilitation programs and manage them by other administrative procedures. To continue with the present trend of accepting large numbers of young men whose primary difficulties may be other than alcoholism or alcohol abuse can only have a negative impact on current programs and treatment staffs.

Conclusions

The research studies that have been completed at the Naval Health Research Center during the past 10 years on alcohol abuse among Navy personnel have given us a clearer description of the characteristics and life experiences of men treated in hospitals and rehabilitation facilities. These studies have demonstrated that as rehabilitation and education services are expanded younger men with less severe abuse problems are being reached.

The studies have identified areas for further investigation. These areas include the need for more clearly delineating the diagnostic criteria for alcohol abuse and differentiating the alcohol abuser from the behavior-disordered individual.

The methodologies employed in the studies were dictated by the kinds of data available to Naval Health Research Center investigators, that is, archival hospitalization and service history records and questionnaires administered by rehabilitation staff members. Within the past several years the Naval Health Research Center has developed the Naval Career History Data System which permits detailed longitudinal analyses of the interplay between alcoholism or alcohol abuse, health, and individual status in such areas as job assignment, duty station, and marital status. Such studies will permit new approaches to the analysis of dynamic causal factors.

Summary

Special treatment programs for alcoholism and alcohol abuse were established for naval personnel after federal legislation was enacted in 1970–1971. Four types of rehabilitation programs are now available: centers (nonmedical residential), services (medical residential), drydocks or Counseling and Assistance

Centers (outpatient), and the Navy Alcohol Safety Action Program (after-hours educational program).

Survey methods have been used extensively in the Navy to study alcohol use and abuse patterns. The method of choice, however, is prospective cohort analysis using special historical files containing hospitalization and personnel data as well as data pertaining to alcohol history and treatment. This epidemiologic approach facilitates establishing etiological or causal relationships, identifying risk factors for alcoholism and alcohol abuse incidence, and evaluating rehabilitation program effectiveness. Major studies at the Naval Health Research Center, San Diego, utilizing this data system are described and evaluated.

Acknowledgments

Report Number 80-17, supported by the Bureau of Naval Personnel under Project Order Number N0002278F088AFZ and the Naval Medical Research and Development Command, Department of the Navy, under Research Work Unit M0096-PN.001-1034. The views presented in this paper are those of the authors. No endorsement by the Department of the Navy has been given or should be inferred.

References

Cahalan, D., Cisin, I.H., Gardner, G.L. & Smith, G.C. (1973). A study to measure the extent and patterns of alcohol use and abuse in the U.S. Army. Final Report, Information Concepts, Inc.

Department of Health, Education, and Welfare, National Institute on Alcohol Abuse and Alcoholism (1974). *Second Special Report to the U.S. Congress on Alcohol and Health: New Knowledge* (DHEW Pub. No. 1724-00399.) Washington, D.C: U.S. Government Printing Office.

Gunderson, E.K.E. & Schuckit, M.A. (1975). Hospitalization rates for alcoholism in the Navy and Marine Corps. *Dis. Nerv. Sys.* 36:681–684.

Kolb, D., Coben, P. & Gunderson, E.K.E. (1979). *Comparisons of the Navy Alcohol Safety Action Program with Other Alcohol Rehabilitation Programs.* (Report No. 79-58). San Diego, Calif.: Naval Health Research Center.

Kolb, D. & Gunderson, E.K.E. (1975). *Prognostic Indicators for Navy Alcoholics in Rehabilitation Centers and Units*, Report No. 75-16. San Diego, Calif.: Naval Health Research Center.

Kolb, D. & Gunderson, E.K.E. (1977). *A Longitudinal Study of Illness Patterns in Alcoholics AND Matched Controls*, Report No. 77-23. San Diego, Calif.: Naval Health Research Center.

Kolb, D. & Gunderson, E.K.E. (1981a). A longitudinal study of health risks associated with alcohol abuse in young Navy men. *Drug Alcohol Depend.* 8:131–141.

Kolb, D. & Gunderson, E.K.E. (1981b). *Medical Histories of Male Problem Drinkers and Controls during the First Twelve Years of Naval Service*, Report No. 81-14, San Diego, Calif.: Naval Health Research Center.

Kolb, D. & Gunderson, E.K.E. (1982). Alcohol-related morbidity among older Career Navy men. *Drug Alcohol Depend.* 9:181–189.

Kolb, D., Gunderson, E.K.E. & Coben, P. (1978). *Population Differences and Correlates of Post-treatment Effectiveness in Alcohol Rehabilitation Facilities*, Report No. 78-48. San Diego, Calif.: Naval Health Research Center.

System Development Corporation (1975). *Task XI of a study to evaluate Department of Defense (DOD) Alcohol Abuse Control Programs Comprehensive Report, Final Report*, Vol. II, Part 2 (TM 5386/002/01). Santa Monica, Calif.

Chapter 6

Methodologic Issues in the Study of Driver Impairment

ROBERTA G. FERRENCE

Data on the impairment of drivers by alcohol are collected and applied in various contexts for the ultimate purpose of reducing the frequency of driver impairment and associated problems. Most frequently, researchers seek answers to the following questions: What is the prevalence of driving while impaired? What role do alcohol and other factors play in impairment and collisions? What effect do countermeasures and changes in the law affecting the availability of alcohol have on the prevalence of impairment? These questions are often directed at specific groups, such as young drivers. Since data on impairment are available in many forms and from many sources, it is important to link the appropriate population for study with the research question at hand. It is also crucial to be aware of the limitations of particular sources of data, so that validity and reliability are maximized.

This chapter describes and assesses methodologic issues in the study of driver impairment. These involve the selection of subjects, measurement of concepts, research design and procedures, instrumentation, and analysis of findings. The structure of the chapter corresponds to the three questions posed above: the epidemiology of driver impairment; testing hypotheses related to drinking and driving; and assessing the impact of legislative and other formal changes aimed at reducing impaired driving. A case study of a particular legislative change is included to highlight the relevant issues.

It is useful to get a clear idea of what populations are available for study. The identification of "nesting populations" may be helpful here. Beginning with the total adult population in a particular area, we would usually be interested only in those who drive. We may categorize drivers by age, sex, and exposure (that is, miles driven), or we may concentrate only on those who drive late at night or in certain places. To measure impairment, we may wish to obtain chemical measures of alcohol ingestion, or to observe behavior at the wheel or elsewhere. We may operationalize impairment as involvement in collisions or traffic violations. Finally, we may focus on the small proportion of those who drink and drive who are apprehended, or limit our investigation further to recidivists that are officially recorded.

The Epidemiology of Driver Impairment

Impairment of drivers and traffic collisions are comparable to many diseases and other phenomena that can profitably be studied using the methods of epidemiology. They are widely but unevenly distributed in the population; there are many factors that contribute to their occurrence and distribution; and they are potentially amenable to preventive measures.

The term "driver impairment" refers to the impairment by alcohol of certain functions that are involved in operating a vehicle. Theoretically, impairment can only be measured for each individual, separately, comparing performance with and without the prior ingestion of alcohol. In fact, impairment of an individual is often inferred on the basis of comparison with other individuals who have not been drinking.

The concentration of alcohol in the blood (BAC) has been widely adopted as an operational measure of behavioral impairment. Although BAC reliably measures the presence of alcohol in the body, it is not a valid measure of impairment for all individuals, particularly at low levels. Nevertheless, the legal limits of BAC, at least in North America, are associated with at least some degree of impairment among most of the driving population.

Epidemiologic data on driver impairment may be collected at roadside using chemical measures, in household or other types of surveys that rely on retrospective reports of drinking and driving, or from official records of persons charged with alcohol-related driving offences.

Roadside Surveys

Roadside surveys are unique in that drivers are usually selected at random or systematically (for example, every 10th driver) at sites that are selected randomly from feasible survey locations. To the extent that randomization is successful, the study sample will be representative of the population at risk during the times that surveys are conducted, generally late at night and on weekends. The large samples of passing drivers that are usually obtained in such studies (some as high as 10,000) are often sufficient to carry out detailed examinations of several variables simultaneously. Large samples are necessary, however, if drivers at higher BACs are to be examined separately. In many cases, all drivers who are over the legal limit must be grouped together, and separate analyses for those at very high BACs cannot be done.

The concentration of alcohol in the blood can be measured directly with blood tests or indirectly with breath tests. The use of either type of testing results in much greater precision than human estimates or self-reports of previous consumption (Zusman & Huber, 1979). Blood alcohol content is usually expressed as the weight of alcohol per unit volume of blood, for example, 0.08 g per 100 ml or 0.08%. The convenience of using breath tests for live subjects has led to the development of a number of devices based on various principles that have become increasingly reliable with improvements in technology (Dubowski, 1975). Screening devices, such as the Alcohol Level Evaluation Roadside Tester (ALERT), that provide a quantitative measure of blood alcohol concentration, are easily employed at roadside.

In general, both types of devices achieve a level of accuracy that is acceptable for screening or charging impaired drivers (Perrine, 1971; Lovell, 1972; Levett & Karras, 1975). There is some variation between instruments, but the correlation coefficients between breath tests and blood tests and between repeated breath tests generally exceed 0.95 (Noordzij, 1975; Bonnichsen & Goldberg, 1981). Errors are often in the direction of underestimating blood alcohol concentration (Harger, 1975), and failure to obtain a maximum breath sample can further reduce the reading (Levett & Karras, 1975). Some variability is also associated with the phase of alcohol metabolism, with BACs slightly overestimated during the absorption phase and underestimated during the elimination phase (Jones, 1976). As a matter of practice, police officers rarely charge a driver whose test result is less than 25% above the legal limit.

For epidemiologic purposes, the devices appear to provide satisfactory but conservative results. In most studies, data are grouped so minor variations are less likely to make a difference. At this point, variations in BAC readings are mainly a legal issue and have been challenged in the courts where the issue is the occurrence of false positive readings. False negative results, however, are more likely to occur. Significant proportions of false positives have been reported, but these are largely due to the time lapse between the administration of breath and blood tests and to the deduction made at prosecution to account for possible analytical errors (Goldberg, 1981). Incorrect administration of equipment or the presence of other substances such as cigarette smoke can also produce false positive readings.

Although breath tests are a fairly accurate measure of blood alcohol content, the degree of impairment at any particular BAC can vary greatly among individuals. Heavy drinkers, for example, may develop considerable tolerance to alcohol so that they exhibit much less impairment than those who usually drink less (Smart & Schmidt, 1969; OECD, 1978). These considerations are most important at lower levels of blood alcohol content where the variation in response is greater. Even when BACs are at zero, the driver may still experience aftereffects of drinking that impair performance (Wilde, 1974). Alcoholics are also overrepresented in accidents when sober, which may be due to chronic effects of heavy drinking (Smart, 1969) or to personality factors (Zelhart, 1972; Selzer & Vinokur, 1974). Most of those actually charged with driving over the legal limit display rather high BACs at which most or all drivers exhibit at least some signs of impairment.

To what extent do roadside surveys fulfill the requirements of describing the prevalence of driver impairment? Drivers tested in most surveys do not represent the total population of drivers on the road at all times of the day. They are not even necessarily representative of drivers on the road at the time of the survey, because drivers who are on the road for longer periods of time are more likely to be sampled. According to Wolfe (1975), this is not a serious problem, because length of trip is only weakly related to impairment. Generalizability to all times of day and often to other geographic areas is sacrificed, in order to reduce cost and effort, by sampling at times when the proportion of drivers on the road who have elevated BACs is likely to be highest, that is, late at night, on weekends. These data are frequently collected in order to evaluate interventions designed to reduce the proportion of drivers with BACs above the legal limit, but for purposes of descriptive epidemiology, they are limited.

If one is interested in describing the prevalence of legal impairment among different categories of the driving population, such samples are seriously biased. The rate of driving with a BAC that exceeds the legal limit is comparatively low among drivers during the daytime and early evening, but the numbers involved are substantial, because there are many more drivers on the road. In a roadside survey carried out in Canberra, Australia, between 1000 and 0200 hours (Duncan, 1979), late-night drivers who were legally impaired accounted for only 32% of all those who drove over the legal limit. Late-night drivers are clearly at higher risk than those surveyed at other times, but their social and demographic profile is not generalizable to the total group. The types of drivers and the context of driving, particularly with regard to origin and destination, differ considerably from those at other times: male drivers, and young males in particular, are greatly overrepresented. Thus most of the data on legal impairment among drivers on the road are inadequate for establishing age and sex specific rates for driving over the legal limit. When survey data for a 24-hour period are not available, estimates of the true distribution of legal impairment can still be calculated using data from other sources, such as collisions or records of driving habits, to correct for variations in exposure among different categories of drivers.

A potentially serious problem that affects data from roadside surveys, regardless of application, is the rate of refusals or nonresponse among those selected for testing. Refusals often reach 6 percent or more, which may be as great as the proportion of drivers detected who are legally impaired. Attempts have been made to estimate legal impairment among the nonresponse group (Wolfe, 1975), but these probably underestimate the proportion that are impaired. For example, interviewers in a Canadian survey correctly identified 88% of those with BACs less than 0.02%, but only 44% of those who were legally impaired (Smith et al., 1976). Hurst and Darwin (1977) reanalyzed data from U.S. roadside surveys and estimated that the rate of legal impairment (BAC≥.10%) would increase from 5.4% to 10.3% when the nonresponse group was included. Warren and Simpson (1981) used the Hurst and Darwin estimates to produce weights for Canadian data. Their analysis indicated that impairment (BAC≥.08%) would increase from 5.9% to 8.3% with the addition of nonrespondents.

Another method of assessing the effect of nonresponse is to determine the reasons for refusals. In the Canadian 1981 roadside surveys, the most frequent reasons given for failing to provide a breath sample were "in a hurry," "fear of prosecution," and "unable to blow" (Lawson et al. 1982). This information could be combined with observations by interviewers to estimate impairment.

If drivers with BACs above the legal limit are overrepresented in the nonresponse category, estimates of legal impairment among drivers will be low. When measuring prevalence, any underrepresentation will result in underestimates of the magnitude of the problem, and any variation in the extent to which different categories of the population (e.g., age, sex, and socioeconomic categories) are underrepresented will produce biased pictures of legal impairment.

Changes in methods when surveys are repeated can also affect estimates. Lawson et al. (1982) report rates of impairment in three Canadian provinces in 1974 and 1981. In addition to a change in the geographic area surveyed in one province, improvements in design, procedures, and equipment were associated with a lower proportion of refusals and more precise rates of impairment.

These improvements resulted in more accurate data and increased knowledge about variables that affect reporting. For example, more than one respondent was interviewed at a time, which meant that subject drivers could see that other drivers were cooperating and were apparently more likely to respond (Lawson et al., 1982).

The validity of data collected in roadside surveys is enhanced because impairment is measured at the time it occurs. Since it is not always feasible to conduct this type of survey, other methods, which may provide certain advantages, must sometimes be used.

Household and Other Surveys

The population sampled in household surveys differs in many ways from drivers sampled on the road. Household surveys often use the household rather than the individual as the unit of sampling. Thus households with children over the age of 16 might provide three or more drivers, whereas single-person households would provide one at most. If only one driver were selected from each household, older drivers and women would be overrepresented because they are more likely to be at home. Young males are most often missed in household surveys, and persons with drinking problems may be omitted because they are more likely to be institutionalized or have no fixed address. Nonrandom samples, such as populations of students, may also be used to measure driver impairment (e.g., Ennis, 1978; Wechsler & McFadden, 1979).

Respondents may complete mailed questionnaires or be interviewed at home, in person, or by telephone regarding their drinking and driving behavior (e.g., Wolfe & Chapman, 1973). This type of study shares some of the advantages of roadside surveys, such as random sampling and large sample size. In addition, anonymity can be preserved in surveys conducted by mail or telephone, and the purpose may be camouflaged by combining questions about drinking and driving with unrelated questions.

The nature of the data collected in these surveys is different from those obtained at roadside. The investigator must rely on retrospective reports of drinking and driving and collisions. Problems of recall are a major source of inaccurate reporting. Information, such as the number of miles driven annually and the number of years of driving experience, should be obtained to control for variations in exposure, but this is not always done.

In addition to problems of recall, deliberate underreporting of deviant behavior is a problem. Whereas underreporting of undetected drinking and driving may largely be due to difficulties of recall, most underreporting of charges for impaired driving and collisions is probably intentional, because the event is relatively rare and potentially more stigmatizing than undetected drinking and driving.

Attempts to measure the extent of underreporting have met with some success. Bradburn and Sudman (1979) investigated response effects to a question on driving under the influence of alcohol during the previous year. The extent of underreporting ranged from one-third of those using a random response technique to over half of those who completed a questionnaire. The data are useful because they provide correction factors that can be used to produce more accurate rates of driver impairment.

In summary, household and other surveys produce data on legal impairment that are probably less accurate and less representative than those obtained at roadside in 24-hour surveys. Moreover, BAC levels cannot be obtained. There are certain advantages to this method of collecting data, however, that make it preferable in some instances. Since respondents are not in transit, more extensive information can be obtained. The relevant questions can be included in a more general survey at considerable savings. Finally, the household survey can be used to determine drinking and driving histories of individual drivers and to measure the prevalence of legally impaired driving in a community for a given period of time. Some roadside surveys have collected retrospective data in addition to BACs, but these data cannot be used to measure period prevalence.

Epidemiologic data from different societies and jurisdictions are often compared. Aside from differences in consumption, there are other factors that could produce differences in results. These include variations in drinking and driving patterns and in the legal BAC limit, changes over time, variations by time of year, size and characteristics of the nonresponse category, and the use of different testing instruments, in particular the ALERT, which can vary by a BAC reading of 0.02%. Sampling error could be considerable in studies which use a relatively small sample, particularly among subsets of impaired drivers. The use of multistage sampling techniques also increases sampling error substantially.

Driving While Impaired (DWI)

Drivers charged with driving while impaired (DWI) are sometimes used to measure the prevalence of driver impairment. Relevant data can usually be obtained from police records in which specific infractions such as driving over the legal BAC limit, driving while impaired by alcohol, or refusing to take a breath test are recorded. The selection of drivers usually depends on the observation by the arresting officer of driving infractions, erratic or unusual driving behavior, or a collision. Occasionally, impaired drivers are detected in routine checks for other purposes, such as vehicle safety. Once the driver is suspected of being impaired, the officer may administer a simple breath test with a device that is used only for the purpose of screening and, if warranted, refer the driver for a test on more accurate equipment that produces results that are legally admissible. The officer can exercise considerable discretion in deciding which drivers to stop, which to test, and which to charge.

Data on drivers charged with impairment cannot be considered representative of all those who drive while impaired (Whitehead, 1975). First, they represent only a very small fraction of this population, since less than 1% of all episodes of drinking and driving are detected. Second, police manpower is deployed on the basis of the distribution of crime in general. Since crime tends to be concentrated in the core areas of cities where most drinking establishments are located, those who drink at these establishment are more likely to be detected. In most cases, drivers are stopped only when they do something to gain the police officer's attention, and this may be quite unrelated to impairment. Even among those drivers suspected of being impaired, only a small percentage are actually tested (Borkenstein, 1975). There is no evidence that police deliberately pick on drivers who are older, lower class, or members of minority groups (Hyman et al., 1972; Zylman, 1972; Ward & Spronz, 1976), but the effects of selection bias are probably substantial.

Because of the small proportion of legally impaired drivers who are detected and charged, certain changes in enforcement procedures may also produce a sizable change in both the rate of citations and the sociodemographic profile of those cited. For example, the introduction of Alcohol Safety Action Programs in certain communities in the United States resulted in large increases in arrests for DWI (Oates, 1974). Zelhart and Schurr (1977) report that the proportion of DWIs detected as a result of an accident in Nashville, Tennessee decreased from 50% to 15% between 1972 and 1976 when there was at least an eightfold increase in the frequency of citations, apparently due to the addition of mobile testing laboratories for measuring BACs in the field.

Because of their limitations, these data cannot be used to measure the prevalence of legal impairment in a community. There are other situations, however, where data from this source are useful. In some cases, one is interested only in those drivers who have been formally charged with impairment. In other cases, the data on DWIs can usefully be combined with data from other sources, such as roadside surveys, or with data from well-chosen control groups to test specific hypotheses.

Testing Hypotheses Related to Drinking and Driving

Many different strategies have been used to assess the etiologic role of alochol in impairment and associated damage. These range from highly controlled laboratory studies to large-scale quasiexperimental designs, and include a variety of field experiments.

Considerable information about the relationship between alcohol and behavioral responses has been generated by experimental studies carried out under controlled conditions in the laboratory and in the field. In much of this research, validity has been a major issue. For example, there appears to be no correlation between performance on a driving simulator and actual driving behavior (Edwards et al., 1969). Many studies of processes that are believed to be components of driving behavior provide no evidence that there is a relationship (OECD, 1978). Subjects tested in laboratory experiments are often moderate drinkers who do not normally drink and drive and who may react quite differently from those who do. Furthermore, drivers on the road may be more likely to compensate for the effects of alcohol because they are more motivated to avoid detection (OECD, 1978).

Ideally, experimental studies should provide information about the effect of alcohol on specific behavioral functions so that the exact mechanism whereby impairment occurs can be understood. Under controlled conditions, many apparent contributors to driving impairment, such as response time, visual discrimination, and manual dexterity, are affected even at relatively low BACs. Complex tasks that require the simultaneous performance of several functions are affected more (Moskowitz, 1974). These results are sometimes viewed as indicators of the role of alcohol in causing impairment and collisions, but their most valid function is to suggest directions for field experiments in which conditions approach those of actual driving experiences (cf. Wilde, 1974). Closed-course studies of driver impairment provide a closer approximation to real-world driving situations and allow for a greater range of measurements. For example, Attwood et al. (1980) used multivariate functions to discriminate between sober and intoxicated drivers in a closed-course experiment. Multivariate studies in real-life traffic situations are more difficult to carry out, but provide a clearer picture of the relative importance of psychological and social factors, as well as physiological factors, in the occurrence of collisions.

True field experiments are difficult to carry out and few have been attempted, whereas laboratory studies may lack validity because they cannot duplicate real-life situations on the road (Chapanis, 1967; Hurst, 1974; Browning & Wilde, 1975; OECD, 1978). Factors that may be associated with impairment and collisions, such as the social and demographic characteristics of the driver, the driver's motivation to avoid detection, the context of driving, and the condition of the vehicle, are usually controlled in laboratory studies so they cannot be examined as independent variables. Furthermore, the choice of dependent variables may not adequately represent actual behavior on the road. Even field experiments require the imposition of certain controls, and these may result in problems similar to those experienced in laboratory settings. Browning and Wilde (1975) contend that by studying real populations of drinking drivers who are involved in collisions, new knowledge on this subject can best be gained. They conclude that some precision must be sacrificed to achieve validity. Collisions are rare events, however, and may involve a number of factors unrelated to impairment, so that the most fruitful approach is likely to be one that combines the results of both laboratory and field studies.

Useful information can be obtained without benefit of true experimental designs. For example, much epidemiologic knowledge is acquired using case-control studies, which can provide information that is sufficiently detailed to strongly support, though not necessarily confirm, a hypothesized causal relationship.

Case-control studies have been carried out in which previous exposure to an agent among cases characterized by a particular condition is compared with that of a similar group without the condition. To establish the level of risk associated with the previous consumption of alcohol, comparisons can be made between different types of alcohol-involved collisions or between collisions and noncollision controls matched on the basis of the time and place of the crash. Samples of different types can also be compared, for example, drivers selected at random in roadside surveys with drivers involved in fatal collisions. In these studies, data from drivers in each group are used to establish the relative hazard of various BACs.

Comparisons between collisions that vary in severity pose certain problems. The process of investigation by legal agents is different for nonfatal collisions that involve personal injury or property damage and those in which the driver dies. Alcohol involvement in nonfatal collisions can be measured by breath tests, but it is frequently based on the observations of the attending police officer. In fatal collisions, blood tests are usually performed when feasible, and the investigation of the collision may be much more intensive. When drivers involved in collisions are compared with drivers selected at random, similar problems occur with regard to the measurement of impairment.

Traditionally, BACs of drivers involved in collisions were compared with those not involved to produce a measure of relative risk. The increasing difficulty of carrying out roadside surveys has made it more difficult to collect appropriate data on exposure. An alternative method which does not require these data has been suggested by Terhune (1983). "Responsibility Analysis" involves the combining of judgments made by raters as to the contribution of the driver to the accident. The raters are "blind" with regard to the driver's use of alcohol. Although not the method of choice, Responsibility Analysis appears to be a reliable and at least partially valid method of estimating the role of alcohol in collisions.

Modeling techniques can be used to establish factors associated with varying levels of impairment and to clarify the role of alcohol in impairment and collisions. Schliewen (1979) used a nonparametric segmentation technique to identify predictors of BAC level. Norström (1981) developed a more comprehensive causal model that included demographic variables, consumption of alcohol, risk of collisions, impaired driving, as well as items that measured inclination to obey the law. These kinds of approaches are particularly useful, not only because they contribute knowledge about the etiology of driver impairment, but also because they delineate those relationships that require further testing and specification and those that should be discarded.

Evaluation and Legal Impact Studies

The uses of data on driver impairment that are most relevant to prevention and public policy are program evaluation and studies of the effects of changes in laws affecting the availability of alcohol. Two approaches are most common. One is to measure driver impairment in repeated roadside surveys to assess actual changes in the average BACs of drivers. The other is to use samples of drivers involved in traffic collisions, either alone or in combination with estimates of impairment of the drivers involved.

We have discussed many of the methodological problems associated with data collected in roadside surveys. In the context of evaluation research, the lack of representativeness of survey data on nighttime drivers is usually not a problem. Because one is looking at changes in the proportion of drivers that are impaired, rather than absolute numbers, the exclusion of daytime drivers does not significantly affect results. What is critical is that methods of data collection be consistent across surveys and that any nonequivalent control groups used in the study be as similar as possible to the experimental group.

The use of data on traffic collisions poses some of the same problems and many different ones. Reports of drivers involved in collisions are fairly comprehensive, although cases in which little or no damage occurs are not likely to be included. Large numbers of collisions are available for study, and considerable information can be extracted from police records. These data can be used alone in legal impact studies or in combination with other sets of data.

Drivers involved in collisions that are reported to the police may be observed by the officer for evidence of recent drinking.

Most of these drivers are not given a breath test, but many jurisdictions require that the investigating police officer indicate on the collision report whether or not the driver appears to have been drinking or is impaired by alcohol (OECD, 1978). Since the police officer may indicate only that the driver has been drinking, it is not clear what proportion of drivers are legally impaired or what range of BACs is involved. Furthermore, human judgment of blood alcohol levels is known to be unreliable, particularly at moderate levels of impairment when error can reach 50% (Wilde, 1974). In fact, one study has shown, albeit in a less threatening context, that drivers' reports of their own drinking are more accurate than estimates made by interviewers (Zusman and Huber, 1979). Of drivers with BACs≥.10%, interviewers estimated that only 45% had been drinking at all, whereas 68% of these drivers reported drinking. Variability between geographic areas in the coding of impairment can considerably reduce the comparability of data from different areas (Douglass et al., 1974). These problems become less critical, however, if one is making a series of observations within a geographic area.

A different approach is to employ a surrogate measure of alcohol involvement, such as the proportion of late-night, single vehicle collisions involving male drivers (cf. Douglass et al., 1974). This category is known to have a high proportion of legally impaired drivers, and their rate of collisions may be employed as an alternate measure of impairment or as an additional method of verifying results obtained using police observations.

The exclusion of nonreportable collisions may produce some bias, but the direction is not entirely clear. For reportable crashes, rates of alcohol involvement increase with increasing severity of the crash. Nevertheless, there may be a substantial proportion of very minor "fender benders" involving alcohol, in which the driver just leaves the scene. When more than one vehicle is involved, police attention may be more likely, even for cases where damage is minor.

Most fatally injured drivers are given blood tests to determine BAC, when death occurs within 6 hours of the collision. Estimates of rates of legal impairment can be based either on the proportion tested or on the total category of fatalities. Some of the factors that affect the likelihood of a driver being tested, such as severe loss of blood, are fairly independent of other characteristics of the driver. Yet, it appears that those not tested tend to belong to those categories of drivers who are less likely to be legally impaired, for example, adolescents and older drivers, and those involved in multiple vehicle collisions (TIRF, 1975). In addition, BACs are usually not measured until after death occurs. Since this can be up to 6 hours after the collision, some of those who were legally impaired at the time of the collision will produce test results that are below the legal limit (TIRF, 1975). Thus rates that use the total number of fatalities as the population base are conservative but probably more accurate than those based only on the proportion of those who are tested (Simpson et al., 1978).

There are several advantages in using populations of fatally injured drivers. Data based on coroners' reports can be accessed. Most fatal collisions in which the driver is killed are included. Most drivers are tested for BAC, and the assessment is based on blood tests, which are more reliable than human judgment.

The principal limitation is that fatally injured drivers are not representative of those involved in alcohol-related collisions generally, and some of the factors that increase the likelihood that the driver will die are unrelated or only weakly related to impairment, for example, the crashworthiness of the vehicle and the proximity of emergency facilities. This unrepresentativeness is not a relevant issue when one is simply describing the prevalence of legal impairment among fatally injured drivers. It becomes a problem when populations of these drivers are used to represent all drivers in alcohol-related collisions as is often done in evaluation or legal impact studies.

Other factors that increase the risk of death following a collision are highly associated with the use of alcohol. For example, heavy drinkers who are physically deteriorated are less likely to survive serious collisions (Waller, 1979). The use of seatbelts is inversely related to BAC (Interministerial Committee on Drinking-Driving, 1979). Furthermore, intoxicated persons involved in collisions receive less effective medical care than those who are sober (Waller, 1979). These factors inflate the proportion of fatal crashes that are alcohol-related, if one considers only the role of alcohol in causing the collision.

An additional difficulty occurs when rates of legally impaired fatalities are calculated for specific age groups or geographic areas, because the numbers involved may be too small to produce stable rates. International comparisons pose problems as well because the definition of a fatality in different countries may range from those deaths that occur at the site of the crash to those occurring within a year as a result of injuries sustained in the crash (Waller, 1975).

The biases associated with incomplete testing of fatally injured drivers and the absence of any tests for those who survive collisions in which passengers may have died are apparently minimal (Traffic Injury Research Foundation, 1975), especially when compared to the unrepresentativeness of the entire category of fatalities. These biases could be reduced by using estimates based on attributes of cases in which testing was carried out (Kannemann & Warren, 1980).

The Effect of Changes in the Legal Drinking Age on Driver Impairment

The importance of methodologic considerations in research on driver impairment is apparent when we consider specific examples. One type of research that well illustrates the issues concerns the effect of changes in the legal drinking age. A large body of literature deals with the effect of lowering the drinking age on the rate of alcohol-related collisions (Whitehead, 1977; Wechsler, 1980). A growing number of studies are evaluating the subsequent raising of the drinking age in many jurisdictions (Wagenaar et al., 1981; Hingson et al., 1983; Williams et al., 1983). This discussion will focus on an example of this latter body of research.

Many of the problems of design that plagued earlier work on the raising of the drinking age have been eliminated. Most recent studies use sophisticated designs that control for the important threats to validity. Even so, findings are not uniformly consistent, and in at least one case there are conflicting results (Hingson et al., 1983).

Wagenaar et al. (1981) examined the effect of raising the legal drinking age on alcohol-related collisions among young drivers in Michigan and Maine. A nonequivalent multiple-time series design was used, which included comparisons between two sets of jurisdictions, four age groups, and between collisions that involved alcohol and those that did not. Two independent measures of alcohol involvement were used.

Several features of this design control for most of the major threats to validity (Wagenaar et al., 1981). Time-ordered measurement establishes the direction of causality; multiple comparisons control for other events, such as economic changes, that might affect the rate of collisions, and for possible changes in instrumentation that may occur in some areas. The use of a time-series reduces the chances of misinterpreting the effect of developmental changes or of a regression to the mean from an unusually high or low point. Multiple measures of alcohol involvement, including a surrogate measure, control for possible bias in the selection of cases. The diffusion effect of the change in the drinking age on underage drinkers is dealt with by examining several age groups.

Even with a careful design that eliminated most competing hypotheses, some methodologic problems remain. The surrogate measure of alcohol involvement would tend to underestimate the effect of the intervention because it is only an approximate indicator. Although the authors do report positive findings, failure to do so might not indicate the lack of a relationship. Chemical tests of impairment would provide a more reliable measure, but these are not usually done for victims of nonfatal crashes.

The proportion of missing data was close to 10% in some jurisdictions, and there were variations in the way police reported impairment. In one state, a major change occurred in the regulations for reporting collisions involving property damage. The inclusion of less serious crashes would probably increase the proportion of those that were alcohol-related, which would tend to diminish the hypothesized relationship. Changes in patterns of use of seat belts would also overrepresent alcohol-related collisions because impaired drivers are less likely to use them.

Most of these problems are fairly minor and at least would not inflate the effect of the legal change. Even the best designs cannot fully circumvent the problems of quasi-experimental research, and researchers should attempt to "know the enemy" and measure the effect of these sources of bias.

What distinguishes much of this research, particularly in comparison with some of the earlier studies, is the consistent use of "triangulation," the employment of two or more independent measures of the concepts involved. This approach greatly reduces the likelihood of slippage between the concept being measured and the operational definition. For example, a surrogate measure of impairment, usually the proportion of male drivers involved in fatal nighttime collisions, is included along with police reports of alcohol involvement. Collisions themselves are a measure of impairment and are often treated separately according to severity. The independent variable, the change in the law, is varied when several jurisdictions are studied, because comparisons can be made between areas with different changes in age and with changes affecting different types of beverages.

This multiple confirmation has two effects: it strengthens whatever inferences can be made from the analysis, and it may specify the conditions under which a relationship exists. This specification can be very useful because it provides information about the nature of the relationship, its magnitude, and some of the mechanisms involved. For example, the use of states that changed the drinking age for spirits and not for other beverages reduces the likelihood of finding a relationship because young people prefer beer. When several comparisons are made, however, variations in the results would suggest to the researcher that factors in addition to the change in the law were involved.

The literature on raising the drinking age provides an example for other types of research on driver impairment. The adoption of designs that incorporate multiple-time series, the use of triangulation, and the replication of studies all serve to increase validity and strengthen confidence in the existence and magnitude of the relationships that are reported.

Conclusions

Three types of studies on driver impairment have been examined with regard to the kinds of methodologic problems encountered. Evaluation research and legal impact studies now employ fairly sophisticated methods that eliminate many of the inadequacies of previous work. Those problems that remain will require improvements in the recording of original data used in secondary analysis and further assessment of the magnitude and direction of biases that cannot be avoided.

Studies of the epidemiology of driver impairment should ideally be extended to be more representative of the total population of impaired drivers. The increasing legal and financial difficulties encountered in conducting roadside surveys may require very different approaches to measuring the prevalence of impairment.

The study of etiologic factors in driver impairment is perhaps the least developed, but there are many promising avenues of research. Because of the ethical and logistic problems inherent in conducting true roadside experiments, future research will require imaginative designs that involve unobtrusive measures of impaired driving behavior. The role of physiological, psychological, and social factors that would explain sex differences in risk factors or crashes should be explored. The effects of personality and stress should be tested in controlled studies that use measures of alcohol and psychological traits applicable at the time of the event.

Changes in the structure of the driving population and in drinking and driving patterns may well shift attention from the young male driver to older drivers and women, who are also at excessive risk of crashes when legally impaired. Examining these groups requires either larger overall samples or oversampling of these categories.

The study of driver impairment has expanded and developed greatly in recent years. The challenge for future researchers is to resolve the many problems of method and design that circumscribe this area of applied research.

Acknowledgment

The author expresses her appreciation to Paul C. Whitehead for his valuable contribution to this paper.

References

Attwood, D.A., Williams, R.D. & Madill, H.D. (1980). Effects of moderate blood alcohol concentrations on closed-course driving performance, *J. Stud. Alc.* 41:623–634.

Bonnichsen, R. & Goldberg, L. (1981). Large-scale breath-blood comparisons under field conditions: Methods, evaluation techniques and results. In: *Alcohol, Drugs, and Traffic Safety,* Vol. 1, ed. L. Goldberg. Stockholm: Almqvist & Wiksell International, pp. 796–810.

Borkenstein, R.F., (1975). Problems of enforcement, adjudication and sanctioning. In: *Alcohol, Drugs, and Traffic Safety,* ed. S. Israelstam & S. Lambert. Toronto: Addiction Research Foundation, pp. 655–662.

Bradburn, N.M. & Sudman, S. (1979). *Improving Interview Method and Questionnaire Design.* San Francisco: Jossey-Bass.

Browning, J.J. & Wilde, G.J.S. (1975). *Research in Drinking and Driving, Studies of Safety in Transport.* Kingston, Canada: Queen's University.

Chapanis, A. (1967). The relevance of laboratory studies to practical situations. *Ergonomics* 10:557–577.

Douglass, R.L., Filkins, L.D. & Clark, F.A. (1974). *The Effect of Lower Legal Drinking Age on Youth Crash Involvement.* Washington, D.C.: U.S. Department of Transportation, National Highway Traffic Safety Administration, Report No. DOT HS–801 213.

Dubowski, K.M. (1975). Recent developments in breath-alcohol analysis. In: *Alcohol, Drugs, and Traffic Safety,* ed. S. Israelstam & S. Lambert. Toronto: Addiction Research Foundation, pp. 493–494.

Duncan, J.A. (1979). Report on a survey of the effect of breath testing in Canberra, ACT. In: *Proceedings of the 7th International Conference on Alcohol, Drugs, and Traffic Safety,* ed. I.R. Johnston. Canberra: Australian Government Publishing Service, pp. 481–493.

Edwards, D.S., Hahn, C.P. & Fleishman, E.A. (1969). *Evaluation of Laboratory Methods for the Study of Driver Behavior: The Relation Between Simulator and Street Performance.* Final Report. Silver Spring, Maryland: American Institute for Research.

Ennis, P. (1978). *Drinking and Driving Among Ontario Students in 1977,* Substudy No. 938. Toronto: Addiction Research Foundation.

Goldberg, L. (1981). Random road tests in non-accident-involved drivers: Epidemiological data, differential characteristics and role of alcoholism. In: *Alcohol, Drugs, and Traffic Safety,* Vol. 1, ed. L. Goldberg. Stockholm: Almqvist & Wiksell International, pp. 846–859.

Harger, R.N. (1975). The Hamburg, W. Germany, 1973 report questioning the reliability of breath alcohol instruments for medico-legal use in traffic cases. In: *Alcohol, Drugs, and Traffic Safety,* ed. S. Israelstam & S. Lambert. Toronto: Addiction Research Foundation, pp. 583–596.

Hingson, R., Scotch, N. Mangione, T., Meyers, A., Glantz, L., Heeren, T., Lin, N., Mucatel, M. & Pierce, G. (1983). Impact of legislation raising the legal drinking age in Massachusetts from 18–20. *Am. J. Pub. Health* 73:163–170.

Hurst, P.M. (1974). Epidemiological aspects of alcohol in driver crashes and citations. In: *Alcohol, Drugs and Driving,* ed. M.W. Perrine. Washington, D.C.: National Highway Traffic Safety Administration, Technical Report, DOT HS-801 096.

Hurst, P.M. & Darwin, J.H. (1977). Estimation of alcohol for nonrespondents in roadside breath surveys, *Accid. Anal. Prevent.* 9: 119–123.

Hyman, M.M., Helrich, A.R. & Besson, G. (1972). Ascertaining police bias in arrests for drunken driving. *Quart J. Stud. Alc.* 33:148–159.

Interministerial Committee on Drinking-Driving (1979). *The 1979 Ontario Roadside BAC Survey: Summary Report.* Toronto: Ministry of the Solicitor-General.

Jones, A.W. (1976). Precision, accuracy and relevance of breath alcohol measurements. In: *Alcohol, Drugs and Driving,* ed. M. Mattila. Volume II of *Modern Problems of Pharmacopsychiatry.* Basel: S. Karger.

Kannemann, K. & Warren, R.A. (1980). A method for estimating the BAC distribution among fatally injured drivers. *Accid. Anal. Prevent.* 23:247–257.

Lawson, J.J., Arora, H.R., Jonah, B.A., Krzyzewski, J.W., Smith, G.A., Stewart, D.E. & Hieatt, D.J. (1982). 1981 Night-time surveys of drivers' alcohol use. Paper presented at the 26th Annual Proceedings, American Association of Automotive Medicine, Ottawa, Canada.

Levett, J. & Karras, L. (1975). Errors in current alcohol breath analysis. In: *Alcohol, Drugs, and Traffic Safety,* ed. S. Israelstam & S. Lambert. Toronto: Addiction Research Foundation, pp. 527–532.

Lovell, W.S. (1972). Breath tests for determining alcohol in the blood. *Science* 178:264–272.

Moskowitz, H. (1974). Alcohol influences upon sensory motor function, visual perception, and attention. In: *Alcohol, Drugs and Driving,* ed. M.W. Perrine. Washington, D.C.: National Highway Traffic Safety Administration.

Noordzij, P.C. (1975). Comparison of blood and breath testing under field conditions. In: *Alcohol, Drugs, and Traffic Safety,* ed. S. Israelstam & S. Lambert. Toronto: Addiction Research Foundation, pp. 553–560.

Norström, T. (1981). Drunken driving: A causal model. In: *Alcohol, Drugs, and Traffic Safety,* Vol. III ed. L. Goldberg. Stockholm: Almqvist & Wiksell International, pp. 1215–1230.

Oates Jr., J.F. (1974). *Factors Influencing Arrests for Alcohol-Related Traffic Violations.* Washington, D.C.: National Highway Traffic Safety Administration, Report No. DOT HS-801 230.

Organisation for Economic Co-operation and Development (1978). *Road Research: New Research on the Role of Alcohol and Drugs in Road Accidents.* Paris: O.E.C.D. (September).

Perrine, M.W. (1971). *Methodological Considerations in Conducting and Evaluating Roadside Research Surveys.* Washington, D.C.: National Highway Traffic Safety Administration, Report No. DOT HS-800 471.

Schliewen, R.E. (1979). *1974 National Roadside Survey, Data Analysis and*

Report. Ottawa: Transport Canada, Road and Motor Vehicle Traffic Safety Branch.

Selzer, M.L. & Vinokur, A. (1974). Life events, subjective stress, and traffic accidents. *Am. J. Psychiat.* 131:903–906.

Simpson, H.M., Warren, R.A., Pagé-Valin, L. & Collard, D. (1978). *Analysis of Fatal Traffic Crashes in Canada, 1976. Focus: The Impaired Driver.* Ottawa: Traffic Injury Research Foundation of Canada.

Smart, R.G. (1969). Are alcoholics' accidents due solely to heavy drinking? *J. Safety Res.* 1:170–173.

Smart, R.G. & Schmidt, W. (1969). Physiological impairment and personality factors in traffic accidents of alcoholics, *Quart. J. Stud. Alc.* 30:440–445.

Smith, G.A., Wolynetz, M.S. & Wiggins, T.R.I. (1976). *Drinking Drivers in Canada: A National Roadside Survey of the Blood Alcohol Concentrations in Nighttime Canadian Drivers.* Ottawa: Transport Canada, Road and Motor Vehicle Traffic Safety Branch.

Terhune, K.W. (1983). An evaluation of responsibility analysis for assessing alcohol and drug-crash effects. *Accid. Anal. Prevent.* 15: 237–246.

Traffic Injury Research Foundation (1975). *Analysis of Fatal Traffic Crashes in Canada, 1973. Focus: The Impaired Driver.* Ottawa: Traffic Injury Research Foundation of Canada.

Wagenaar, A.C., Douglass, R.L. & Compton, C.P. (1981). *Raising the Legal Drinking Age in Michigan and Maine.* The University of Michigan Highway Safety Research Institute.

Waller, J.A. (1975). Epidemiologic issues about alcohol, other drugs and highway safety. In: *Alcohol, Drugs, and Traffic Safety,* ed. S. Israelstam & S. Lambert. Toronto: Addiction Research Foundation, pp. 3–12.

Waller, J.A. (1979). Analytic issues in studying the interaction of alcohol and other drugs in highway crashes. In: *Proceedings of the 7th International Conference on Alcohol, Drugs and Traffic Safety,* ed. I.R. Johnston. Canberra: Australian Government Publishing Service, pp. 15–23.

Ward, R.M. & Spronz, W. (1976). A geographical analysis of drunken drivers. *J. Stud. Alc.* 37:997–1002.

Warren, R.A. & Simpson, H.M. (1981). *Effects of Measurement Assumptions on Estimations of Risk of Collisions.* Ottawa: Traffic Injury Research Foundation.

Wechsler, H. (ed.) (1980). *Minimum-Drinking-Age Laws: An Evaluation.* Lexington, Ky.: D.C. Heath and Company.

Wechsler, H. & McFadden, M. (1979). Drinking among college students in New England: Extent, social correlates and consequences of alcohol use. *J. Stud Alc.* 40:969–996.

Whitehead, P.C. (1975). DWI programs: Doing what's in or dodging what's indicated? *J. Safety Res.* 7:127–134.

Whitehead, P.C. (1977). *Alcohol and Young Drivers: Impact and Implications of Lowering the Drinking Age,* Monograph Series, No. 1. Ottawa: Health Protection Branch, Health and Welfare Canada.

Wilde, G.J.S. (1974). *Alcohol and Traffic Accidents: A Review in Quest of Remedies.* Ottawa: Alcohol and Highway Safety, Minister of Transport.

Williams, A.F., Zador, P.L., Harris, S.S. & Karpf, R.S. (1983). The effect of raising the legal minimum drinking age on involvement in fatal crashes. *J. Legal Stud.* 12:169–179.

Wolfe, A.C. (1975). Characteristics of late-night, weekend drivers: Results of the U.S. national roadside breath testing survey and several local surveys. In: *Alcohol, Drugs, and Traffic Safety,* ed. S. Israelstam & S. Lambert. Toronto: Addiction Research Foundation, pp. 41–50.

Wolfe, A.C. & Chapman, M.M. (1973). An analysis of drinking and driving survey data. *HIT LAB Rep.* 4:1–5.

Zelhart, P.F. (1972). Types of alcoholics and their relationship to traffic violations. *Quart. J. Stud. Alc.* 33:811–813.

Zelhart, P.F. & Schurr, B.C. (1977). People who drive while impaired, a review of research on the drinking-driving problem. In: *Alcoholism: Physiological and Psychological Bases,* ed. N. Estes & E. Heinemann. St. Louis: Mosby.

Zusman, M.E. & Huber, J.D. (1979). Multiple measures and the validity of response in research on drinking drivers. *J. Safety Res.* 11:132–137.

Zylman, R. (1972). Race and social status discrimination and police action in alcohol-affected collisions. *J. Safety Res.* 4:75–84.

Chapter 7

Heavy Alcohol Consumption and Physical Health Problems: A Review of the Epidemiologic Evidence[1]

ROBERT E. POPHAM
WOLFGANG SCHMIDT
STEPHEN ISRAELSTAM

The epidemiologic evidence respecting the physical health problems associated with chronic heavy alcohol use derives mainly from studies of (*a*) the drinking histories of persons suffering from a particular disease or trauma; *(b)* the prevalence of physical health problems in samples of heavy drinkers; *(c)* the mortality experience of such drinkers; *(d)* the drinking histories of persons who have died from a particular cause; *(e)* regional and temporal variation in cause-specific daath rates in relation to variation in indexes of the prevalence of heavy drinking; and *(f)*, more recently, the morbidity and mortality experience of general population groups followed for a number of years and characterized at entry according to alcohol consumption. There have also been many experimental studies, but insofar as human subjects have been involved, these have necessarily been short-term and confined to acute effects presumed to be relevant to the disease conditions of interest.

Until recently, morbidity studies—especially those falling into the first two categories—have rarely included control sam-

1. Reprinted from: *Research Advances in Alcohol and Drug Problems, Vol. 8,* ed. R. G. Smart et al. (New York: Plenum, 1984), pp. 149–182. We thank our colleague, Dr. Mary Jane Ashley, for a critical reading of the manuscript and many useful suggestions.

ples, and as a result, seldom provide the data required to calculate risk factors. However, such studies taken as a whole present a reasonably consistent picture respecting the types of physical health problems likely to be encountered among heavy drinkers. Typically found are (1) certain diseases of the nervous system such as peripheral neuropathy and various indications of brain damage; (2) certain diseases of the digestive system, especially of the liver, acute and chronic gastritis, peptic ulcers, and pancreatitis; (3) certain respiratory diseases, especially chronic bronchitis, pneumonia, and tuberculosis; (4) certain heart and vascular diseases, especially cardiomyopathy and hypertension; (5) certain cancers, especially those of the upper respiratory and upper digestive tracts; and (6) injuries resulting from motor vehicle and other accidents. For recent reviews of the literature on morbidity see Kissin and Begleiter (1974), Lelbach (1974), Seixas et al. (1975), Fallon and Lesesne (1978) and Eckardt et al. (1981). The morbidity picture for clinical alcoholics is well illustrated by the data of Ashley et al. (1977) for a sample of admissions to a voluntary inpatient treatment unit in Toronto, Canada (table 1). It is noteworthy that, contrary to a currently popular notion, the female alcoholics in this population apparently did not exhibit greater morbidity than the males.

The incidence of the various diagnoses listed may be influenced by patient selection and thoroughness of physical examination, among other factors. However, the kinds of illness and trauma encountered would seem to be typical.

General Mortality

As might be expected in view of the morbidity data, mortality studies have consistently revealed significantly elevated death rates in samples of alcoholics and other heavy drinkers. In all but one case, the studies tabulated in table 2 found a ratio of observed over expected mortality approaching 2 or higher. The variations in the ratio reflect mainly differences in type and size of sample, length of followup and source of expected value. There is also a consistent difference in the size of the ratios for males and females. This difference will be discussed in the section on sex differences in cause of death. A satisfactory explanation cannot be offered for the departure of Dahlgren's ratio from

TABLE 1
Prevalence at Admission of Various Disease Entities, Complications, and Trauma in a Clinical Sample of Alcoholics

	Men (N = 736)		*Women (N = 135)*	
	No.	*%*	*No.*	*%*
Fatty liver	351	47.7	37	27.4
Chronic obstructive lung disease	89	12.1	8	5.9
Trauma (all)	88	11.4	10	7.4
Hypertension	64	8.7	9	6.7
Malnutrition	57	7.7	12	8.9
Gastritis	45	6.1	4	3.0
Fractures	42	5.7	5	3.7
Peripheral neuritis	34	4.6	3	2.2
Hiatus hernia	33	4.5	8	5.9
Cirrhosis	32	4.4	4	3.0
Anemia (all)	31	4.2	18	13.3
Peptic ulcer	30	4.1	5	3.7
Chronic brain damage	27	3.7	4	3.0
Obesity	23	3.1	8	5.9
Ischemic heart disease	23	3.1	0	0.0
Cardiomyopathy	20	2.7	6	4.4
Pneumonia	19	2.6	3	2.2
Epileptic disorders	19	2.6	1	0.7
Diabetes	18	2.4	1	0.7
Gastrointestinal hemorrhage	17	2.3	3	2.2
Urinary tract infection	12	1.6	4	3.0
Acute brain syndromes	12	1.6	1	0.7
Pancreatitis	6	0.8	1	0.7

Source: Ashley et al., 1977.

that obtained in all other studies. This is particularly puzzling since his compatriot, Dahlberg—whose sample likewise comprised Swedish Temperance Board cases—found considerable excess mortality.

An important question respecting the generality of these findings concerns the possibility that excess mortality is greater among heavy drinkers who seek treatment than among those who do not. Schmidt and de Lint (1972) found that a relatively high death rate occurred in the first year after clinic admission. This would suggest that some of their pateints sought treatment as a consequence of a seriously deteriorated state of physical health. Although omitting first-year deaths reduced the ratio by less than 5%, this does not allow for the possibility that some

TABLE 2
The Ratio of Alcohol to Expected Mortality in Samples of Alcoholics and Other Heavy Drinkers

Reference	*Country*	*Source of sample*	*Sex*	*Size of sample*	*No. of deaths*	*Followup period*	*Exposure (years)*	*Source of expected values*	*Ratio*
Gabriel[a] (1935)	Austria	Admissions to a mental hospital alcoholism treatment facility.	M	1,107	148	1922–35	?	Male mortality for the age group 21–70 in Austria 1932.	2.5
Kendall & Staton (1966)	U.K.	Untreated referrals to an alcoholism treatment facility.	M&F	59	11	1950–63	?	Age-sex-specific mortality in the U.K.	5.2
Gorwitz et al. (1966)	U.S.A.	Admissions for alcoholism to mental hospitals.	M	1,355	70	1961–64	n.a.	Age-sex-specific mortality in Maryland.	6.0
			F	298	15	1961–64	n.a.		9.0
Brenner (1967)	U.S.A.	Admissions to alcoholism treatment facilities.	M&F	1,343	217	1954–61	7,289	Age-sex-specific mortality in California.	3.0
Sundby (1967)	Norway	Admissions for alcoholism to a psychiatric facility.	M	1,722	1,061	1925–62	34,951	Age-specific male mortality in Oslo.	1.7
Babigian & Odoroff (1969)	U.S.A.	Admissions for alcoholism to psychiatric facilities.	M	?	362	1960–66	?	Age-sex-specific mortality in Monroe County, N.Y.	2.8
			F	?	78	1960–66	?		4.9

Gillis (1969)	South Africa	Admissions to an alcoholism treatment facility.	M	707	81	1959–64	3,080	Age-sex-specific mortality of Whites in South Africa.	3.9
			F	95	9	1959–64	399		4.5
Lindelius & Salum (1972)	Sweden	Admissions to a hospital ward for the treatment of acute alcoholic psychosis.	M	1,021	275	1956–66	?	Age-specific male mortality in Stockholm.	3.6
Lindelius et al. (1974)	Sweden	Admissions for alcohol abuse to a psychiatric facility.	M	139	25	1962–71	910	Age-sex-specific mortality in Stockholm.	2.3
			F	118	19	1962–71	761		3.9
Nicholls et al. (1974)	U.K.	Admissions for alcoholism to mental hospitals.	M	678	233	1953–67	?	Age-sex-specific mortality in the U.K.	2.7
			F	257	76	1953–67	?		3.1
de Lint & Levinson (1975)	Canada	Admissions to an alcoholism treatment facility.	M	154	20	1969–74	584	Age-sex-specific mortality in Ontario.	3.6
			F		2	1969–74	167		3.9
Ciompi & Medvecka (1976)	Switzerland	Admissions for alcoholism to a psychiatric facility.	M	1,229	968	1915–62	?	Age-sex-specific mortality in Switzerland.	1.7
			F	155	110	1915–62	?		2.2
Dahlgren & Myrhed (1977)	Sweden	Admissions for alcoholism to a hospital department of alcoholic diseases.	M	100	16	1963–75	713	Age-sex-specific mortality in Stockholm.	3.0
			F	100	18	1963–75	791		5.6
Robinette et al. (1979)	U.S.A.	Admissions for alcoholism to V.A. hospitals.	M	4,401	1,438	1946–74	112,244	Age-specific mortality of male patient control group.	1.9

TABLE 2 (*continued*)

Reference	*Country*	*Source of sample*	*Sex*	*Size of sample*	*No. of deaths*	*Followup period*	*Exposure (years)*	*Source of expected values*	*Ratio*
Thorarinsson (1979)	Iceland	Treated alcoholics listed in the Psychiatric Register.	M	2,863	573	1951–74	37,200	Age-specific male mortality in Iceland.	2.2
Schmidt & Popham (1980)	Canada	Admissions to an alcoholism treatment facility.	M	9,889	1,823	1951–71	85,641	Age-sex-specific mortality in Ontario.	1.9
			F	2,158	296	1951–71	17,805		3.0
Menge (1950)	U.S.A.	Insurance policy holders classed as sub-standard due to alcohol habits.	Mostly M	?	758	1931–48	72,658	Standard male mortality risk for insurance policy holders.	3.1
Dahlgren (1951)	Sweden	Cases recorded by Malmö and Malmöhus Temperance Boards.	M	10,616	564	1939–47	?	Age-, marital status-, and residence-specific male mortality in Sweden.	1.1
Dahlberg[b] (1952)	Sweden	Cases recorded by Stockholm Temperance Board.	M	2,365	?	?	?	Age-specific male mortality in Stockholm.	1.0–1.9
Davies (1965)	U.S.A.	Insurance policy holders classed as sub-standard due to alcohol habits.	Mostly M	2,582	140	1940–62	?	Standard male mortality risk for insurance policy holders.	2.7

Newman[c] (1965)	Canada	Case finding survey of one county.	Mostly M	339	84	1953–64	3,594	Age-specific average male mortality in Ontario 1953–64.	1.8
Giffen et al. (1971)	Canada	Persons arrested for drunkenness 3 or more times within a year.	M	343	191	1940–61	4,214	Age-specific male mortality in Ontario.	2.3
Pell & D'Alonzo[d] (1973)	U.S.A.	Alcoholic employees of one industry.	M	842	96	1965–69	n.a.	Age-sex-specific mortality of fellow-worker control group.	3.1
			F	57	6	1965–69	n.a.		
Dyer et al. (1981)	U.S.A.	Problem drinker employees of one industry.	M	38	20	1958–73	n.a.	Age-specific male mortality of fellow-worker cohort.	2.6
Dyer et al. (1981)	U.S.A.	Consumers of 6 or more drinks per day among the employees of one industry.	M	78	32	1957–74	n.a.	Age-specific male mortality of fellow-worker cohort.	2.7

[a]In the calculation of the mortality rate, Gabriel did not take into account the number of years of exposure to the risk of death. As a consequence, his ratio of actual to expected mortality was erroneously inflated. On the assumption that the admissions and deaths were evenly distributed over Gabriel's observation period, an estimate of exposure years could be obtained. The ratio shown in the table was calculated on the basis of this estimate.

[b]A risk ratio for all age groups combined was not reported. For those up to 65 years of age, the reported ratios ranged from 1.4 to 1.9; for the older groups, from 1.0 to 1.2.

[c]The ratio of 1.0 reported in this study resulted from a misapplication of life tables and a faulty comparison of the sample with the general population. Thus, number of survivors rather than number of deaths was employed in the comparison. This is particularly unjustified when the number of exposure years is small.

However, the primary data provided in the report permitted calculation of the ratio shown in the table in accord with accepted methods.

[d]The alcoholic sample comprised persons identified by the company physician as "recovered," "suspected," or "known" alcoholics.

persons who sought help were suffering from chronic diseases not immediately fatal. On the other hand, the last nine studies in table 2 employed essentially nonclinical samples and show—with the exception noted—significantly high ratios. A mean could not be calculated for Dahlberg's sample, but the ratios for most of his age groups ranged from 1.4 to 1.9. As in other studies, only those aged 65 and older failed to exhibit a notable excess mortality.

The ratio of 1.8 based on the study of Newman (1965) is of special interest since his largely male sample was secured through a casefinding survey in Ontario employing many different sources in addition to hospitals and physicians. The followup period overlaps that of Schmidt and Popham (1980) who found a male ratio of 1.9 for their sample of clinic alcoholics drawn from the same province.

The ratios for samples of industrial workers (Pell and D'Alonzo, 1973; Dyer et al., 1981) and for insurance policy holders (Menge, 1950; Davies, 1965) would also seem to indicate that elevated death rates are not confined to clinically identified heavy drinkers. The samples of policyholders included not only persons with a history of alcoholism treatment or frequent episodes of intoxication, but also "steady free users" without a history of drunkenness and persons with only occasional episodes of intoxication. When the several categories of heavy alcohol users were examined separately, both authors found mortality ratios of 2 or higher in every case. Moreover, care was taken to ensure that the excess mortality was not attributable to selection factors resulting from the insurance risk categories used for comparison. Indeed, Davies' study was restricted to a comparison of groups differing only with respect to alcohol habits.

Although many earlier mortality studies used insurance data (see Pearl, 1926, for a review of these), the typical approach was to contrast abstainers with nonabstainers. The abstainer group always lived longer, but it would be erroneous to conclude that drinking in any amount shortens life expectancy. Among nonabstainers, there is bound to be a proportion of habitually heavy drinkers whose unfavorable mortality experience adversely affects the picture for the group as a whole. The studies of Menge and Davies, on the other hand, employed standard risks for comparison, and these reflected the mortality experience of both abstainers and moderate drinkers.

We must emphasize our agreement with Room and Day

(1974) that samples of the type described cannot be assumed a priori to be representative of all heavy drinkers. Certainly, in the case of those identified as "alcoholic" the mortality ratio might be expected to exceed that which would be found in a suitable population sample of heavy drinkers. However, that a significantly elevated death rate probably does characterize the latter, is indicated by the work of Pearl (1926) and Room and Day (1974) who determined the death rates of drinkers identified through studies of general population samples in the United States. In both studies, heavy users were found to have higher death rates than moderate users and abstainers. The findings differed in that the group for which Room and Day found elevated mortality comprised only 2%–3% of the total sample (probably around 4%–5% of the drinkers). In contrast, the proportion of all drinkers found by Pearl to have an elevated risk seems to have been at least three times as great. The two studies were conducted at quite different periods, appear to have used somewhat different definitions of "heavy drinking," and used different techniques to ensure the accuracy and comprehensiveness of the data on drinking habits. Furthermore, Pearl's sample was, in effect, a random sample of the white working-class population of a single city (Pearl, 1923); that of Room and Day was more generally representative of the national population.

A prospective study of the employees of an industry in Chicago also found elevated death rates among the heavy drinkers (5 or more drinks/day) as compared with the moderate drinkers and abstainers (Dyer et al., 1977). In addition, the abstainers were found to have a slightly higher mortality rate than the moderate drinkers. Such a difference was also reported by Pearl (1926) and by Room and Day (1974), but only Pearl attempted to control for the possibility that the difference might be due to factors not connected with alcohol use. He selected from his original records pairs of brothers in which one had been a moderate drinker throughout his life, and the other, an abstainer. Under these conditions, the difference in mortality rates disappeared.[2]

2. Another possible explanation for such a difference is that, even when an effort is made to avoid the difficulty, some persons for whom drinking has been contraindicated on health grounds (including former heavy drinkers) are recorded as abstainers. Certainly where a distinction has been made (e.g., Dyer et al., 1977, 1981), former drinkers are found to have a substantially higher mortality rate than abstainers and moderate drinkers.

Our conclusions are: (1) that chronic heavy users of alcohol—whether identified in a clinical situation, through a casefinding survey, on the basis of drunkenness arrest record, or through reported drinking habits—have a substantially elevated risk of premature death; and (2) that there is no convincing evidence that moderate consumption has an adverse effect on life expectancy or that a lifetime of abstinence has a beneficial effect.

Hazardous Consumption Levels[3]

Clearly these conclusions beg a question of very great practical importance: at what point is consumption "heavy" in that there is a significant reduction in life expectancy? In the studies reviewed, heavy consumption was either implied a priori (e.g., in studies of clinic alcoholic samples) or defined without reference to a minimum volume of intake. A valid quantitative estimate of the upper limit of safe consumption (from a public health rather than an individual standpoint) has yet to be made. Of several early attempts perhaps the best known is that of Anstie. He concluded (1870, p.222), from observations of essentially acute effects, that a daily intake of 1.5 ounces (4.4 cl) of absolute alcohol was "about the limit of what can be habitually taken . . . without provoking symptoms of chronic malaise indicative of actual alcohol poisoning." Later, Becker (1908) postulated the safe level to be 15 g (1.9 cl). This represented the daily equivalent of the average lifetime intake of a sample of men over 90 years of age.

More recently, Schmidt and de Lint (1970) approached the problem from the standpoint of the lower limit of consumption of clinic alcoholics. They found that a daily intake at or above 15 cl of absolute alcohol encompassed the reported consumption of 96% of the alcoholics in their sample. Moreover, the mean for the sample was in remarkably close agreement with that for

3. Quantities of alcohol consumed have been expressed in a variety of ways by the authors whose work is cited in this review. However, in the interest of comparability we have translated all quantities reported into centiliters (cl) of absolute alcohol. For the benefit of those who prefer to think in terms of "drinks," a 1.5 ounce drink of distilled spirits at 40% alcohol by volume contains 1.7 cl of absolute alcohol. This amount is also contained in a 12-ounce bottle of 5% beer or a 5-ounce glass of 12% table wine.

samples in several other countries (Schmidt, 1973). Given the mortality data reviewed in the previous section, and the reasonable assumption that clinical alcoholics are among the heaviest of heavy drinkers, there can be little doubt that, as a group, drinkers of such quantities have a markedly elevated risk of premature death. However, it is evident from the results of retrospective studies that this is very unlikely to be the lowest point at which a significant increase in the risk of alcohol-related disease occurs. thus, Péquignot (1974) showed that an average daily intake of 40–60 g (5 – 7.5 cl) was potentially cirrhogenic, and similar levels have been implicated in the development of certain cancers. For example, Tuyns et al. (1977) reported that the same consumption level carries a significant risk of cancer of the esophagus. Keller and Terris (1965) found a strong positive association between the consumption of 35 g (4.4 cl) of absolute alcohol per day, when combined with cigarette smoking, and the occurrence of carcinomata of the mouth and pharynx.[4] And Wynder and Mabuchy (1972) found that the risk of carcinomata of the larynx and mouth rose significantly among drinkers of seven or more ounces of whisky per day (about 8 cl of absolute alcohol).

It should be noted that the daily averages to which we have been referring simply represented the total volume of alcohol consumed over a given period of time divided by the number of days involved. Clearly, such a measure does not take into account differences in pattern, for example, whether the drinking is steady or intermittent. However, with respect to most alcohol-related organic complications, the pattern appears to be irrelevant except in so far as it affects the total amount of alcohol consumed. The crucial variables appear to be the duration of drinking and the volume of alcohol consumed (Lelbach, 1974).

On the other hand, it is evident that the pattern of drinking is highly relevant to the acute problems of alcohol use. Here the issue is the concentration of alcohol in the body at a given point in time rather than the amount consumed over a long period. Only in the field of vehicular accidents have attempts been made to establish risk levels. It is generally agreed that blood alcohol concentrations in drivers below 0.05% are safe.

4. Risk ratios calculated from the Keller and Terris data by Rothman (1980) suggest an elevated risk among nonsmokers at even lower alcohol consumption levels.

Above this level, risk rates increase exponentially with blood alcohol concentration.

In summary, the lowest level of alcohol consumption that constitutes a significant hazard to longevity has yet to be determined. It is almost certainly substantially less than a daily equivalent of 15 cl and quite possibly below 7.5 cl. The derivation of a valid estimate of this point is a critical problem for future research. The task is unusually difficult, among other reasons, because of the apparent inability of current survey techniques to elicit accurate quantitative data on volume of consumption. Accordingly, as we have noted elsewhere (Popham & Schmidt, 1978), the most promising route would seem to be through a combination of animal mortality studies and controlled retrospective studies of persons who are suffering or have died from alcohol-related trauma or disease.

Mortality by Cause

Another question posed by the occurrence of a higher death rate among heavy drinkers is the relative etiologic significance of the alcohol consumption and frequently associated factors such as heavy smoking, emotional problems, and personal neglect. Clearly the issue is of considerable importance to the planning of preventive action. It may be approached through examination of the specific causes of death that have a higher than expected frequency among such drinkers. These are shown for various samples in table 3. Although "alcoholism" is a commonly reported cause of death, especially in clinical samples of heavy drinkers, it has not been included because the role of alcohol is self-evident, and because coincident pathologies are typically present and its selection as the primary cause is therefore usually an arbitrary decision. An indication that the causes listed are those mainly responsible for the overall excess mortality is provided by the relatively small size of the ratio for deaths from all other causes (except alcoholism) found by Schmidt and de Lint (1972). These residual deaths comprised 11% of the total mortality. The ratio, calculated from the data reported by the authors, was 1.3. That it exceeded 1.0 can be attributed to the inclusion of deaths from several rare causes such as homicide, nutritional diseases, and epilepsy, which also occur more often than expected among heavy drinkers (Riddick & Luke, 1978; Schmidt & Popham, 1981).

Tuberculosis

The excess mortality from tuberculosis, observed in several samples, is in accord with morbidity data indicating an apparently higher than expected rate of alcoholism among tubercular patients (Feingold, 1976; Bailey et al., 1978), and of tuberculosis among heavy drinkers (Lyons & Saltzman, 1974). However, with one notable exception (Robinette et al., 1979), for which we cannot offer an explanation, there were few deaths from this cause, especially in the recent samples. For example, Schmidt and de Lint (1972) found no deaths from tuberculosis, and Schmidt and Popham (1981) found only five deaths from this cause in their much larger sample of the same population. Doubtless this reflects both the general decline in the incidence of tuberculosis and the very marked decline in the likelihood of a fatal outcome. The excess mortality found seems to be at least partly attributable to factors often associated with chronic heavy drinking, such as poor food habits, living in close contact with high-risk groups, heavy smoking, and failure to seek or persist in treatment (Brown & Campbell, 1961; Doll & Hill, 1964; Sundby, 1967). Whether or not chronic alcohol use exerts an additional independent effect remains open to question.

Cancer

Excess mortality from cancer involves only a limited number of sites, namely, the lung and upper digestive and upper respiratory tracts. Hepatic carcinoma has frequently been found at autopsy in association with cirrhosis (Parker, 1957; Leevy et al., 1964; Lee, 1966), and Tuyns (1979) suggests in his recent review that 5%–30% of all cirrhosis cases also show liver cancer. However, hepatic carcinoma has rarely been reported as a cause of death in mortality studies of heavy drinkers. It may be that it is overlooked in the absence of an autopsy or that the associated cirrhosis tends to be favored as the primary cause for purposes of death certification. Another possibility is suggested by Purtilo

TABLE 3

The Ratio of Actual to Expected Mortality by Cause in Male Samples of Alcoholics and Other Heavy Drinkers

	Clinical samples						
Cause of death	*Gabriel 1935*[b]	*Sundby 1967*[c]	*Lindelius & Salum 1972*[d]	*Nicholls et al. 1974*[e]	*Robinette et al. 1979*[f]	*Thorarinsson 1979*[g]	*Schmidt & Popham 1981*[h]
Tuberculosis	4.1	2.8	2.2[a]	3.0[a]	10.2		
All cancers	2.5	1.7	1.8	1.7	1.2	1.5	1.3
Upper digestive and upper respiratory tract		4.2					3.9
Cardiovascular diseases	2.2	1.1			1.3	1.8	1.4
Cerebrovascular lesions		1.6			1.3	1.1	1.2
Pneumonia	1.9	1.9			2.3	3.3	2.8
Peptic ulcers							2.8
Cirrhosis of the liver	4.0[a]	3.6	14.8		2.1	11.3	11.1
Suicide	9.0	5.8	9.4		2.0	4.4	5.8
All accidents		2.8	8.2		3.4	4.0	3.6
All causes	2.5	1.7	3.6	2.7	1.9	2.2	1.9

	Nonclinical samples				
Cause of death	*Menge 1950*[i]	*Dahlgren 1951*[j]	*Davies 1965*[k]	*Giffen et al. 1971*[l]	*Dyer et al. 1981*[m]
Tuberculosis	1.7	0.8			
All cancers	2.7	1.2	2.3	1.4	3.7
Upper digestive and upper respiratory tract					
Cardiovascular diseases	4.1	0.9	2.6		1.9
Cerebrovascular lesions		0.5			
Pneumonia					
Peptic ulcers					
Cirrhosis of the liver	14.0	3.0			
Suicide	4.0	3.2	2.7[a]		
All accidents	3.2	2.5	4.7		
All causes	3.1	1.1	2.8	2.3	2.7

[a] Actual frequency less than six deaths.
[b] See Note a, Table 2.
[c] The ratios based on Oslo mortality were taken in all instances. Those for tuberculosis and all cancers were for the 1951-62 sub-sample. All other ratios were for the total (1925–62) sample. The ratio for pneumonia was obtained from Table 42, for general mortality from Table 5, and for all other causes from Table 17 of Sundby.
[d] The ratios were based on the data provided in Table 35 of Lindelius and Salum.
[e] The ratios were taken from Table 1 of Nicholls *et al.*
[f] The ratios were taken from Table 3 of Robinette *et al.*
[g] The ratios were taken from Table 2 of Thorarinsson.
[h] The ratios were taken from Table 2 of Schmidt and Popham.
[i] The ratios were calculated from the percentage in Table VI of Menge using the general mortality ratio provided by the author.
[j] The ratios were taken from Table 4 of Dahlgren except that for cerebrovascular lesions which was calculated on the basis of data for cerebral hemorrhage given in the text.
[k] The ratios were taken from Table 3 of Davies.
[l] The ratios were taken from Table XIII-16 of Griffen *et al.*
[m] The ratios were taken from Table 10 of Dyer *et al.*

and Gottlieb's (1973) observation that hepatic carcinoma typically appears about 8 years after cirrhotic damage is first discerned. Given the extremely heavy alcohol consumption characteristic of the clinical samples in table 3, and the notoriously low rate of success of efforts to induce the alcoholic to remain abstinent, it is conceivable that many do not live long enough after the onset of cirrhosis to develop cancer of the liver. Some support for this explanation was recently advanced by Schmidt and Popham (1981). Cirrhosis deaths among their alcoholic patients occurred some 5 years, on the average, after the disease was first diagnosed.

Carcinomata at the other sites mentioned clearly contribute to the elevated death rate. In the case of lung cancer, it would now seem that the excess mortality is entirely attributable to heavy smoking (Schmidt & Popham, 1981). On the other hand, in the development of carcinomata of the oral cavity, pharynx, larynx and esophagus, most workers contend that alcohol consumption and smoking each have an independent effect, and a synergistic effect when combined (Keller & Terris, 1965; Rothman & Keller, 1972; Kissin & Kaley, 1974; Tuyns et al., 1977, 1978; Rothman, 1978; McMichael, 1979). However, Wynder (1978), who pioneered research on this question, maintains that heavy alcohol use in the absence of smoking does not increase the risk of these cancers.

Mortality studies of alcoholics are probably not capable of resolving this issue. Our impression, which is supported by at least one systematic study (Dreher & Fraser, 1967), is that nearly all alcoholics are more or less heavy smokers. The consequence is that the effects of the heavy drinking alone cannot be isolated. Schmidt and Popham (1981) compared the mortality experience of their alcoholics with that of nonalcoholic veterans who were equally heavy smokers. Although much reduced, there remained a significant excess mortality from cancers of the head and neck with smoking thus controlled. While this result confirms that heavy alcohol use elevates the smoking-related risk, the question remains as to whether the effect is additive or synergistic, and for that matter, as to whether or not there is an independent alcohol effect. An unexpected outcome of the comparison was the finding that the two study populations did not differ in their overall cancer death rates. In other words, while heavy alcohol use enhanced the smoking-related risk of cancer at certain sites, it apparently did not increase the risk of neoplastic disease in general. This finding is somewhat easier to reconcile with Wynder's view that heavy alcohol use alone may not be carcinogenic than with the contention that there is an independent alcohol effect.

Cardiovascular Diseases

Deaths due to cardiovascular diseases account for a large proportion of the total excess mortality in most samples in table 3. For example, of the 862 extra deaths in the Schmidt and Popham (1981) sample, 175 were ascribed to this causal category. An excess of deaths from cerebrovascular lesions (apoplexy) was also found in two of the samples (Sundby, 1967; Robinette et al., 1979). However, with the exception of alcoholic cardiomyopathy (Burch & Giles, 1974)—a comparatively rare cause of death —there is as yet no clear evidence that heavy alcohol consumption as such is or is not of etiologic importance in the development of these conditions (Sundby, 1967; Knott & Beard, 1972). Heavy smoking has been clearly implicated in the development of arteriosclerotic heart disease (Weir & Dunn, 1970), the most common cause of death in the category; but it has been shown in at least three studies that, although much reduced, there remains a significant excess mortality from cardiovascular disease in heavy drinkers when smoking is controlled (Tibblin et al., 1975; Dyer et al., 1981; Schmidt & Popham, 1981).

It is not unlikely that lack of exercise, other neglect of personal health care, and dietary factors also contribute to the excess cardiovascular mortality. In this regard, it is noteworthy that an excess was not found in Sundby's (1967) subsample of homeless alcoholics. Possibly, a relatively lower intake of food by this type of heavy drinker—who is likely to be notably underweight (Olin, 1966)—reduces the risk of developing certain cardiovascular diseases. Another possibility, currently under debate, is that at least moderate doses of alcohol have a protective function in regard to ischemic heart disease (see, for example, Klatsky et al., 1979). This has been rendered plausible by the results of experimental and clinical research indicating an enhancing effect of alcohol on coronary blood flow (Bing & Tillmans, 1977) and on high-density lipoprotein levels (Williams et al., 1979), and supported by the findings of several prospective, case control, and other epidemiologic studies. The relevant literature has been thoroughly reviewed by M.J. Ashley (1984).

Pneumonia

While pneumonia is no longer one of the most common causes of death among heavy drinkers—owing to the introduction of antibiotics—it is evident from the ratios in table 3 that a substantial excess of observed over expected deaths continues to be found. Moreover, studies of pneumonia victims indicate a more prolonged course of illness, a greater frequency of complications, and a higher death rate from the disease when there is a history of heavy alcohol consumption (Lyons & Saltzman, 1974). Both acute and chronic effects of alcohol are probably involved. Acute effects are probably involved in the sense that heavy drinkers often display a chracteristic form of pneumonia resulting from frequent aspiration of foreign matter into the lungs, and which may be especially severe if the foreign matter contains alcohol (Lyons & Saltzman, 1974). Chronic effects are probably involved in the sense that chronic heavy alcohol consumption appears to lower resistance to infections, for example, through reduction in the number of leukocytes and impairment of their mobilization (Lindenbaum, 1974). Specific toxic effects of alcohol on respiratory symptoms and pulmonary function have also been suggested (Emirgil et al., 1974; Emirgil & Sobol, 1977), and recently shown to obtain even when smoking and other risk factors were taken into account (Lebowitz, 1981). In addition, it is clear that associated heavy smoking (Rankin et al., 1969; Weir & Dunn, 1970), delays in seeking treatment, neglect of personal hygiene, and environmental hazards are also implicated (Chomet & Gach, 1967).

Peptic Ulcer

Comparatively few deaths from peptic ulcers have been reported in any mortality studies, but in one an excess mortality was clearly substantiated and shown to remain significant with smoking controlled (Schmidt & Popham, 1981). The evidence from morbidity data as to whether or not the frequency of ulcers exceeds that in the general population is inconclusive (Bingham,

1960; Engeset et al., 1963). It is probably safe to assume that chronic heavy alcohol consumption and commonly associated behaviors such as smoking, poor food habits and other neglect of personal care will increase the likelihood of a fatal outcome once an ulcer has occurred. However, whether or not heavy drinking can be the cause of such an ulcer in the first instance has yet to be demonstrated (Lorber et al., 1974).

Cirrhosis

It is evident from table 3 that a very substantial excess mortality from liver cirrhosis has been consistently found. Indeed, the disease is one of the leading causes of death among heavy drinkers. For example, it ranked second only to cardiovascular diseases in contribution to total excess mortality in the Schmidt and Popham (1981) sample. The etiologic importance of long-term heavy alcohol intake per se would seem to have been established beyond doubt. In addition to a large body of epidemiologic and clinical evidence (Lelbach, 1976; Schmidt, 1977; Thaler, 1977), recent experimental work has convincingly shown that a direct hepatotoxic effect of alcohol is mainly responsible rather than a nutritional deficiency (Rubin & Lieber, 1974; Israel et al., 1975). However, malnutrition when present may well heighten susceptibility to the alcohol effect.

Suicide

Generally, suicide is also found to be one of the more frequent causes of death among chronic heavy drinkers, and, conversely, a high proportion of alcoholics among suicide cases has been reported (Robins et al., 1959; Dorpat & Ripley, 1960; Riddick et al., 1978). The studies in table 3 consistently reported a high ratio of actual to expected deaths from this cause. This excess mortality has usually been attributed to predisposing personality factors and to the emotional consequences of progressive dissolution of primary social ties associated with a history of heavy drinking (Rushing, 1969; Lundquist, 1970). On the other hand, Schmidt and de Lint (1972) considered that insufficient attention had been given to the possibility of a direct effect of alcohol. They noted the high rates of suicide among publicans, restaurateurs, and hoteliers who have in common a very high exposure to alcoholic beverages. There would seem to be little reason to suppose that these occupations have more than their share of persons with personality traits predisposing to suicide. However, as Ignev's (1979) study suggests, this does not rule out the effect of social deterioration resulting from heavy drinking.

Accidents

The data in table 3 clearly indicate an excess mortality from accidents. Brenner (1967) and Schmidt and de Lint (1972) found the principal types to be vehicular accidents, poisonings, fires, and falls. Traumatic injuries, as shown in table 1, were among the more common diagnoses in the sample of alcoholic patients studied by Ashley et al. (1977). And various investigators, for example, Goldberg (1955) and Schmidt et al. (1962), have shown that impaired accident drivers frequently have a history of excessive drinking, and that clinical alcoholics constitute a high-risk group with respect to such accidents. Perhaps an elevated death rate from accidental injury is hardly surprising given the well-known impairing effects of large doses of alcohol on judgment and motor functions. Schmidt et al. (1962) argued that the high frequency of such acute impairment was a sufficient explanation for the elevated vehicular accident rate of alcoholics, but Selzer (1975) and McLean and Campbell (1979) considered that personality traits were also of etiologic significance. With respect to accidental poisoning, Schmidt and de Lint (1972) found that acute alcohol intoxication was mentioned on the death certificate in half their cases, and Schmidt and Popham (1980) noted that such deaths commonly involved alcohol and another psychoactive drug, usually a barbiturate. Careless smoking was the commonly recorded contributing cause in deaths due to fires (Schmidt & de Lint, 1972). Other factors probably include the greater likelihood of fires and accidental falls in the deteriorated rooming house areas where heavy drinkers may often live, and the greater likelihood of a fatal outcome due to a generally poorer state of health (Brenner, 1967; Hudson, 1978).

Table 4 summarizes the foregoing discussion of the principal factors which may account for the mortality data on heavy drinkers. Clearly the tabulation oversimplifies what is probably often a complex picture of interrelated causes in the individual

TABLE 4
The Etiological Significance of Alcohol and Associated Variables in the Excess Mortality of Chronic Heavy Drinkers

Cause of death	*Effects of alcohol*	*Heavy tobacco smoking*	*Emotional problems*	*Poor food habits*	*Other personal neglect*	*Increased environmental hazards*
Tuberculosis		X		X	X	X
Carcinoma of:						
Mouth	XX	XX				
Larynx	XX	XX				
Pharynx	XX	XX				
Esophagus	XX	XX				
Lung		XX				
Alcoholic cardiomyopathy	XX					
Other cardiovascular diseases		XX		X	X	
Pneumonia	XX	XX			XX	XX
Peptic ulcers	XX	X		X	X	
Liver cirrhosis	XX			X		
Suicide	X		XX			
Accidents	XX	XX	X		X	X

Note: X = probably indicated; XX = clearly indicated. Where a space is left blank, the factor is probably either of no significance or its role, if any, is unknown.

case. Therefore, it is important to emphasize that the table refers to the *population* of heavy drinkers, not to the individual drinker, and to what is known about the causes of *elevated death rates* in this population, rather than about the causes of the diseases and behaviors that may lead to death.

Sex Differences in Cause of Death

Schmidt and Popham (1980) found that, generally, the same causes in nearly the same proportions contributed to the excess mortality in male and female alcoholics. This is illustrated in figure 1.

In table 2, the ratios for females are consistently larger than those for males. However, this difference is due to the fact that

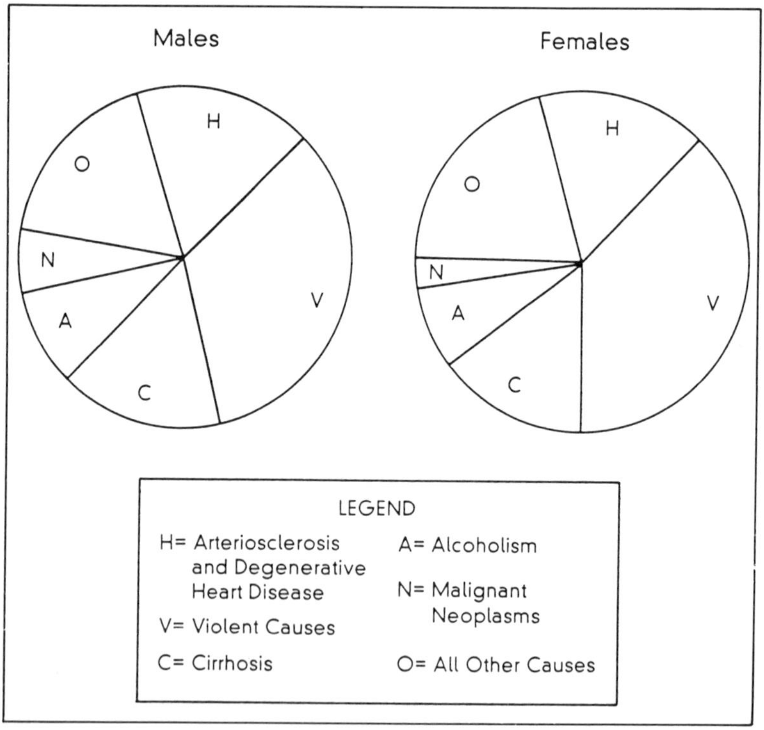

Figure 1: Proportionate contribution of major causes of death to the excess mortality of alcoholics. (From Schmidt and Popham, 1980.)

mortality rates for females in general populations (on which expected values were based) are uniformly much lower than for males. When Schmidt and Popham compared the mortality of female and male alcoholics, the females were found to have a significantly *lower* mortality. The rates did not differ for causes with a clear alcohol etiology such as trauma, liver cirrhosis, and cancer of the esophagus. On the other hand, despite apparently little difference between the two sex groups in duration and amount of smoking (Dreher & Fraser, 1968), the females had substantially lower death rates from lung cancer and heart disease. Schmidt and Popham concluded that these lower death rates reflected a constitutional difference in susceptibility. However, possible contributing factors such as differential exposure to industrial pollutants, stress, and other occupational hazards cannot be ruled out.

The absence of a sex difference in cirrhosis mortality in the Schmidt and Popham samples seems to be at variance with the observation in several morbidity studies (e.g., Wilkinson et al., 1969; Péquignot et al., 1974; Krasner et al., 1977) that females are more susceptible to the disease. However, the lack of agreement is probably attributable to the broader age range of the mortality sample. Thus Schmidt and Popham found a higher rate among females below 50 years of age (the age group emphasized in clinical samples), but also that this was offset by a lower rate among those aged 50 and older.

Beverage Differences in Cause of Death

In the discussion to this point, there has been an implicit assumption that the important variable in alcohol consumption is the intake of ethyl alcohol. Since alcoholic beverages differ substantially in ethanol concentration and in the types and amounts of other substances present, the possible etiologic relevance of the class of beverage consumed cannot be ignored. For example, heavy beer consumption has been seen to have special significance in alcoholic cardiomyopathy (McDermott et al., 1966; Anonymous, 1968), wine consumption in liver cirrhosis (Whitlock, 1974), and distilled spirits in certain cancers (Tuyns, 1970). With respect to diseases of the heart and liver, the case for a specific beverage effect rests mainly on uncontrolled clinical studies and epidemiologic analyses in which total alcohol intake was not adequately taken into account. Following a careful assessment of the experimental, clinical, and epidemiological literature, Lelbach (1974, p. 157) concluded, "no clear-cut evidence has been presented to prove that, if comparable quantities of ethyl alcohol are absorbed, any of the commonly consumed alcoholic beverages exert a more pronounced influence on the production of organic lesions than others."

On the other hand, Lelbach's conclusion may not apply to the development of alcohol-related carcinomata. Here the evidence for a specific beverage effect derives from retrospective clinical studies in which appropriate controls were employed (Wynder et al., 1957; Tuyns, 1970). The findings suggested that whisky drinking predisposed to the development of carcinomata of the head, neck, and esophagus more than beer or wine. Tuyns et al. (1979) argued that the ethanol concentration in the beverage consumed is the relevant factor, although they noted that apple-based alcoholic beverages may carry a risk independent of concentration.

It has also been argued that since beer has a lower intoxication potential than other beverages, it carries a lower risk of causing alcohol-related accidents (Brewers Assoc. of Canada, 1973). The contention rests on the finding of Dussault et al. (1972)—which is consistent with a large body of experimental evidence (see Takala et al., 1957 for a review)—that beer produced less impairment than the same quantity of alcohol consumed in more concentrated form. The issue, dealt with at length elsewhere (Popham et al., 1976), reduces essentially to two questions: Given the experimental conditions imposed by Dussault et al., is their result likely to be applicable to actual drinking situations? Is there any *direct* evidence of a lower risk of accidents when drinking involves beer?

As to the first question, the experiment involved prolonged fasting of the subjects followed by consumption of a single large dose of alcohol in one or another beverage. In this regard, Kalant et al. (1975) showed that under more realistic conditions of progressive drinking, interbeverage differences altogether disappeared. With respect to the second question, little evidence has been gathered to date. Borkenstein et al. (1974) found that drivers in alcohol-related accidents reported beer to be their beverage of choice somewhat more often than nonaccident drivers, and that the proportion of accident drivers reporting beer increased with increasing blood alcohol level. However, to determine with certainty the role of beer would require knowledge of the type of beverage actually consumed prior to the accident. In any event, it would seem that the experimental basis of the argument favoring beer is doubtfully relevant—at least in a North American context—and such direct evidence as exists does not support the inference that beer drinking is less likely to cause traffic accidents.

Conclusions

Our conclusions are that: (1) the acute or chronic effects of alcohol explain a considerable part of the excess mortality of heavy drinkers; (2) the etiologic importance of alcohol is clear with respect to deaths from liver cirrhosis, accidents, and carcinomata of the upper digestive and upper respiratory tracts, and unclear with respect to most cardiovascular diseases; (3) other factors often associated with heavy drinking, such as heavy smoking, emotional problems, poor food habits, personal neglect, and increased environmental hazards are probably largely or entirely responsible for the elevated death rates from tuberculosis, lung cancer, and suicide; certain of these factors also contribute to the excess deaths from cardiovascular diseases; (4) the excess mortality of male and female alcoholics is similarly distributed by cause; however, despite similarity in smoking history, the female has a lower overall mortality rate than the male owing mainly to lower death rates from heart disease and lung cancer; and (5) the class of alcoholic beverage consumed is probably of little etiologic significance in the mortality of heavy drinkers although the ethanol concentration in the beverage consumed may be related to the risk of certain cancers.

Mortality Rate Variation in General Populations

The question now arises as to whether or not the relationship between heavy drinking and elevated death rates is reflected in mortality and consumption statistics for general populations. It has been shown that the rate of heavy alcohol use—however the latter is defined in terms of consumption levels—is likely to rise and fall with the average per drinker consumption in a population (Ledermann, 1956, 1964; de Lint and Schmidt, 1968; Mäkelä, 1971; Skog, 1971). Theoretically, therefore, variation in per capita consumption—either from one region to another or through time in the same region—should be accompanied by similar variation in relevant mortality rates. The extent to which this is actually the case is most likely to be revealed by trends in general mortality, and in death rates for the three causes in which direct effects of alcohol are most clearly implicated, namely carcinomata of the upper digestive and upper respiratory tracts, cirrhosis, and accidents.

It is evident that any dependence of the general mortality level on the amount of alcohol consumption in a population is not likely to be detected through examination of trends in the crude rate of death from all causes. Thus excess deaths resulting from heavy drinking would not be expected to comprise more than a small percentage of all deaths in any given year. For example, Schmidt and de Lint (1973) estimated the proportion for Ontario in 1969 to be about 5.5% of total deaths in the age range 20 to 69 years. This means that any alcohol-related variation in the general mortality rate could be masked by comparatively small fluctuations due to other factors. To overcome the difficulty, Bandel (1930) maximized the variation attributable to alcohol use by focusing only on the mortality of males between 40 and 69 years of age. He reasoned that alcohol-related deaths would be at a peak in middle age, and that the frequency of heavy drinking would be much greater among males than among females. Therefore, the excess of male over female mortality in this age range seemed to be the measure most likely to reflect variation in alcohol consumption.

To test the hypothesis, Bandel examined temporal series for Bavaria, Prussia and Italy. Later, Ledermann (1964) extended the Italian series, added one for France and undertook a more limited analysis of data for Sweden and Denmark. The relationship between the two variables proved remarkably close in nearly all cases, and was especially pronounced in the Bavarian series as illustrated in figure 2. Ledermann noted that many differences between men and women—both constitutional and in life style—might account for excess mortality among men. However, he concluded that none of these, other than differential drinking habits, offered a reasonable explanation for

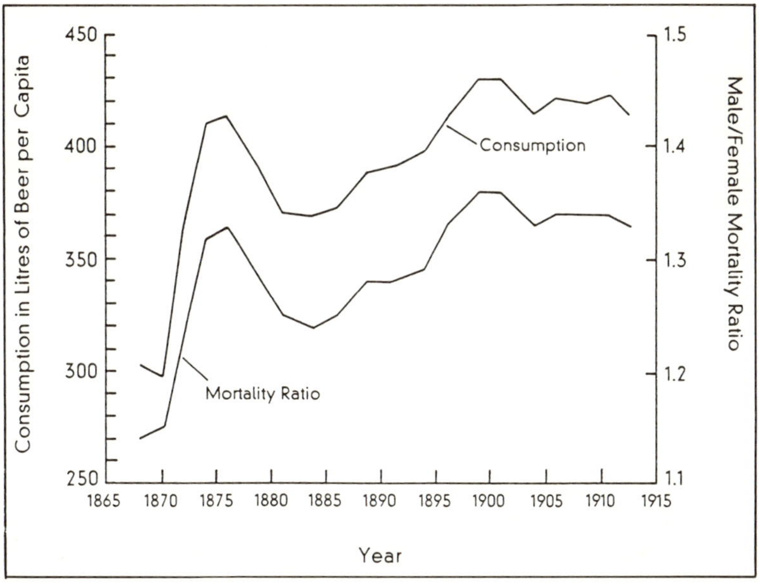

Figure 2: Apparent consumption of beer in liters per capita aged 20 and older and excess mortality of males over females: Bavaria, 1867–1913. (From Ledermann, 1964.)

the covariation of the excess through time with rate of alcohol consumption.

Schoenberg et al. (1971) studied the variation in mortality from esophageal carcinoma among 41 states of the United States, and found significant correlations with differences in per capita sales of both distilled spirits and cigarettes. Schmidt (1974) examined almost the same series, but included total alcohol sales as an independent variable. The latter, however, did not give a better correlation, and the coefficient was reduced to borderline significance when the distilled spirits component was held constant (table 5). On the other hand, the correlation remained significant with the influence of cigarette sales removed. In both studies degree of urbanization was found to be a powerful explanatory variable, although its effect was less marked in Schmidt's data than in the series of Schoenberg et al.

An analysis of variation in mortality rates for 88 French *départements* used the death rate from alcoholism and cirrhosis as the index of the prevalence of heavy drinking (Lasserre et al.,

TABLE 5
Correlation Between Various Cancers and Total Alcohol Consumption: 46 States of the U.S.A. in 1960

Type of coefficient	*Site of Cancer*		
	Larynx	*Oral cavity*	*Esophagus*
Simple	0.50[a]	0.53[a]	0.61[a]
Partial: controlling for the effect of:			
Urbanization	0.42[a]	0.41[a]	0.38
Cigarette sales	0.2	0.23	0.47[a]
Distilled spirits sales	0.12	0.22	0.36

Source: Schmidt, 1974.
[a]Significant at the 0.01 level.

1966). A correlation of +0.70 was found between this variable and rates of death from esophageal carcinoma. In the case of carcinomata of the oral cavity and larynx, the coefficients were 0.44 and 0.40, whereas an analysis of the same variables for 21 countries gave coefficients of 0.68 and 0.80, respectively (Schwartz et al., 1966).

Tuyns and Audigier (1976), in a cohort study of French males born between 1902 and 1916, found that death rates from cancers of the esophagus and larynx—like those from alcoholism and cirrhosis—were responsive to the reduction in availability of alcoholic beverages during World War II. In contrast, mortality from cancers of the lung and pancreas did not show this effect. McMichael (1979) also found death rates from cancers of the esophagus and larynx to be correlated in time series for Australia and Great Britain, and showed that the trends in deaths from these causes differed notably from that in mortality from lung cancer. On the other hand, in Schmidt's series for the United States (table 5), differences in cigarette sales appeared to explain virtually all of the variation in deaths from carcinoma of the larynx, and most of that in deaths from carcinoma of the oral cavity. Evidently, therefore, the matter cannot be considered entirely settled. There are indications of the expected relationship with regard to esophageal carcinoma, but in the case of cancers of the oral cavity and larynx the findings of correlational studies are not consistent.

The expected correlation with per capita alcohol consumption emerges far more clearly in the case of cirrhosis mortality. This is illustrated by the generally high coefficients for various temporal and spatial series shown in table 6. Moreover, Wallgren et al. (1970) and Skog (1980) demonstrated that even higher coefficients could be obtained when the consumption data were taken for a period preceding that of the mortality data. This procedure allows for the latent period between exposure and death from the disease.

An objection to the inference that these correlations reflect a

TABLE 6
Temporal and Regional Correlations Between Rate and Liver Cirrhosis Mortality and Per Capita Alcohol Consumption

Area	*Series*	*Correlation coefficient*	*Probability less than*
Australia	1938–59	0.65	0.005
Belgium	1929–59 (less 1940–45)	0.75	0.001
Canada	1927–60	0.88	0.001
Alberta	1929–60	0.85	0.001
Manitoba	1935–60	0.86	0.001
Nova Scotia	1932–60	0.60	0.001
Ontario	1930–60	0.89	0.001
Quebec	1929–60	0.43	0.05
Saskatchewan	1943–60	0.77	0.001
Canada	9 provinces 1955	0.81	0.01
Finland	1933–57	0.78	0.001
France	1925–58	0.62	0.001
France	23 départements 1950	0.76	0.001
Holland	1927–58	0.57	0.001
Sweden	1926–56	0.45	0.05
United Kingdom	1931–58	0.68	0.001
United States	1934–58	0.60	0.005
United States	45 states 1939	0.61	0.001
United States	48 states 1944	0.78	0.001
United States	46 states 1950	0.76	0.001
United Sates	46 states 1957	0.86	0.001
International	11 countries 1956	0.78	0.005

Source: Popham, 1970.
Note: In all instances, liver cirrhosis mortality was expessed as an unstandardized rate: deaths per 100,000 population aged 20 and older; and the measure of alcohol consumption comprised sales of alcoholic beverages expressed as imperial gallons of absolute alcohol per capita of population aged 15 and older. The International series comprised Australia, Belgium, Canada, Denmark, France, Finland, the Netherlands, Sweden, Switzerland, the United Kingdom, and the United States.

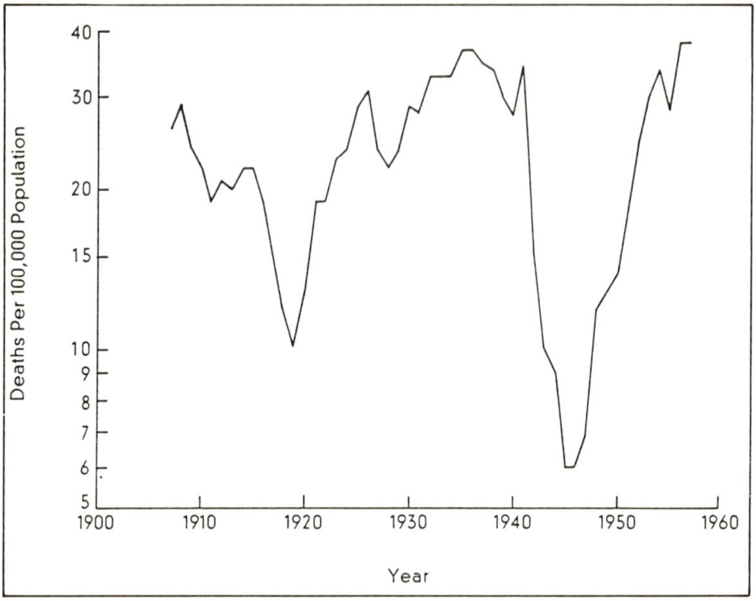

Figure 3: Liver cirrhosis mortality rates: Paris 1907–1956. (Based on data in Ledermann, 1964.)

cause-effect relationship is that several of the time series involve trends that are mainly unidirectional. However, the case is strengthened by the high correlations in the regional series, and by the effect on the mortality trend of a decline in the availability of beverage alcohol. Notable instances of the latter occurred during, and for a period after, World War I when diversion of alcohol to military purposes combined with Prohibition resulted in a severe reduction in supply. In Canada (Popham, 1956), Finland (Bruun et al., 1960) and the United States (Jolliffe & Jellinek, 1941) this was accompanied by a remarkably rapid and very substantial drop in the cirrhosis death rate. In France, extreme shortages occurred during both World Wars with particularly dramatic effects on the mortality trend, as shown in figure 3. For the country as a whole, the decline in the cirrhosis death rate among middle-aged males was of the order of 50%, and for Paris—where there was less possibility to circumvent the rationing system—the decline was more than 80% (Ledermann, 1964).

One probable reason for a more consistent picture with this

disease is that, as Jolliffe and Jellinek (1941) argued many years ago, the rate of cirrhosis mortality *not* attributable to heavy drinking probably varies little in many populations. However, transitory factors unrelated to alcohol use such as the aftermath of an outbreak of epidemic hepatitis, can sometimes distort the trend (Ipsen, 1950). There are also instances where the correlation is weak, and at least one—the United Kingdom—for which a negative coefficient is obtained. The latter may be due to the fact that cirrhosis mortality rates were very low during the period and probably largely attributable to factors other than alcohol. Consequently, there was little more than chance fluctuation in the rate. Under such circumstances, as Popham (1970) suggested, a spurious result might be obtained with Pearsonian correlation analysis. In an examination of U.K. data for a later period, when both cirrhosis and alcohol consumption rates were much higher and changing rapidly, Schmidt (1977) found a highly significant positive correlation. In any case, overall, the results of correlation analyses may be said to confirm the expectation based on morbidity and mortality studies: the rate of death from cirrhosis usually rises and falls with the apparent level of alcohol consumption in general populations. Furthermore, the relationship is evidently curvilinear as shown in figure 4, and Schmidt (1975) has demonstrated that an increase in the cirrhosis death rate is likely to be proportional to the square of the corresponding increase in per capita consumption.

With the exception of motor vehicle mishaps, no attention seems to have been given as yet to the possibility of regional or temporal correlations between accident death rates and apparent alcohol consumption. In a recent study of the effects of a reduction in the legal drinking age in Ontario, Schmidt and Kornaczewski (1975) reported that an increase in per capita alcohol sales to the age group affected was paralleled by an increase in the alcohol-related traffic fatalities of the group. On the other hand, the variation among the states of the United States in rate of motor vehicle accidents reported to have involved drinking could not be statistically explained by differences in either alcohol sales or cirrhosis mortality (Schmidt & Smart, 1963). Similarly, the data in figure 5 give no indication of a relationship on an international basis between apparent consumption and traffic fatalities. This is particularly noteworthy since the importance of

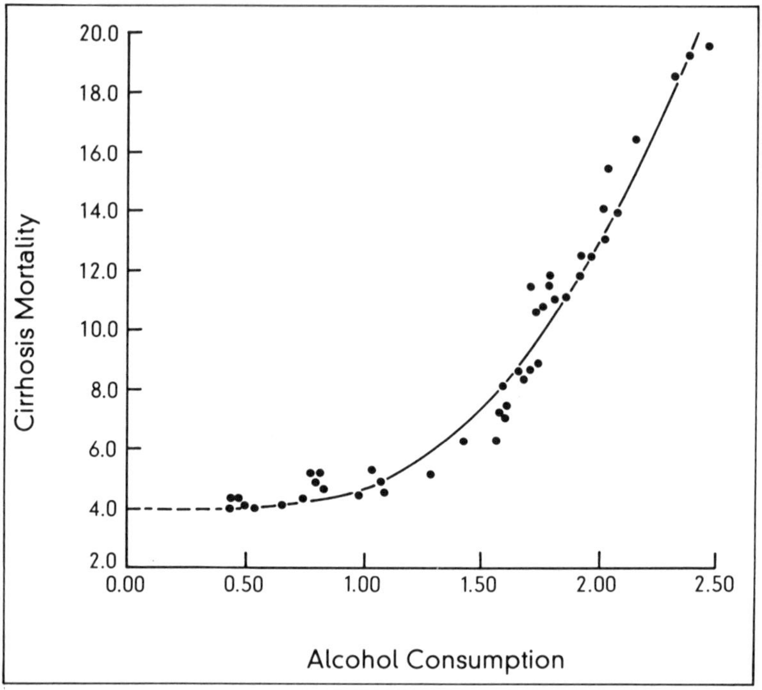

Figure 4: The regression of cirrhosis death rates on per capita alcohol consumption, Ontario data 1932–1974. (From Schmidt, 1977.)

alcohol as a factor in this type of death has been established beyond doubt.

Many sources of considerable variation other than the prevalence of heavy drinking affect accident mortality rates. For example, there are vast differences in traffic density, driver and vehicle safety regulations, and highway engineering from one country to another. Accordingly, it would probably be more surprising to find a significant association between reported accident mortality and per capita consumption than not to do so.

To summarize, the theoretical expectation that the relationship between heavy drinking and excess mortality would be manifested in general populations by covariation of relevant mortality and apparent alcohol consumption rates has been confirmed for cirrhosis mortality. There is highly suggestive evidence that the relationship holds for cancer of the esophagus,

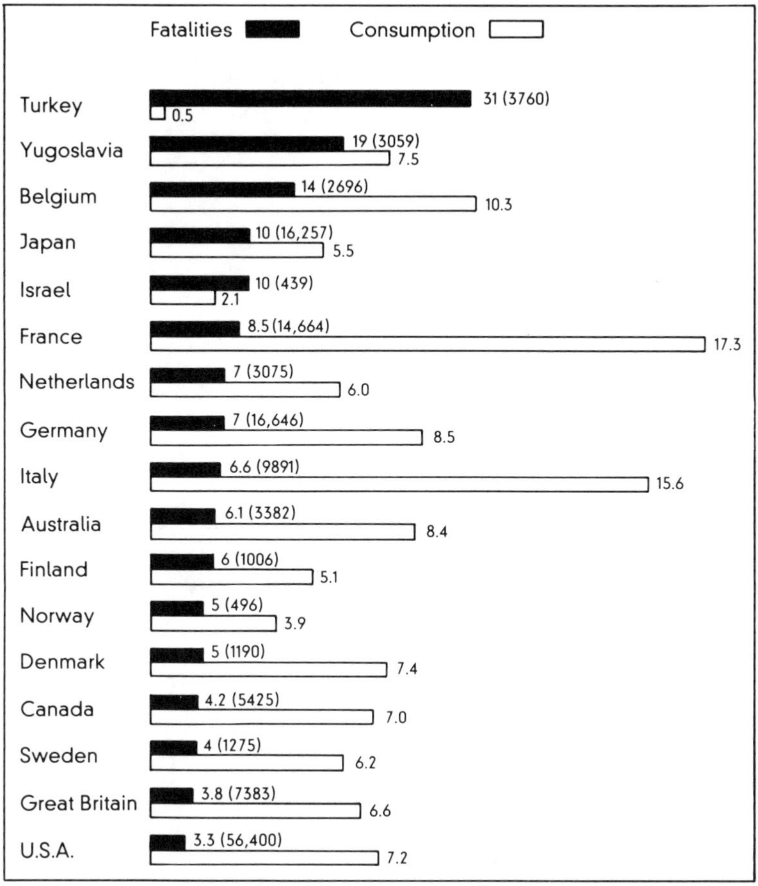

Figure 5: Traffic fatalities per 100 million vehicle kilometers and apparent alcohol consumption in liters per capita. All fatality rates are for 1969 except Israel (1968) and Sweden (1966). Total deaths are shown in parentheses. Data were obtained from Borkenstein (1975). Consumption figures are for 1970 or 1971, and were obtained from Sulkunen (1973).

and that it is reflected in general mortality rates when the excess mortality of males over females in the middle age range is taken as the dependent variable. The correlation data for cancers of the larynx and oral cavity are inconclusive. And with respect to accidental death, the question has only been investigated for traffic fatalities. Here the primarily negative results may be attributable to the many sources of variation other than alcohol consumption, which affect the mortality trend.

General Conclusion

Our primary purpose in this review has been to determine what conclusions respecting the hazards to physical health of chronic heavy alcohol use may be drawn with confidence from morbidity and mortality studies. The evidence would seem compelling that such use carries a risk of premature death greatly exceeding normal expectancy. While the life style typical of many heavy drinkers undoubtedly contributes to this elevated risk in some diseases, it is clear that the chronic and acute effects of alcohol itself are of central importance in others.

The lowest level of intake that may be considered hazardous has yet to be determined. However, it is surely well below the lower limit (15 cl/day) of the range of consumption of most clinical alcoholics. A level of 5–7.5 cl daily appears to increase the likelihood of cirrhosis, and a similar consumption level, when combined with smoking, may enhance the risk of certain cancers. On the other hand, the consumption of comparatively small amounts—quantities commonly identified as "moderate" in the literature—does not seem to adversely affect life expectancy.

The impact of the elevated death rate of heavy drinkers on the population at large is not always easy to detect. The mortality and consumption statistics available for general populations are often subject to other sources of considerable variation that can obscure any effect of changes in the prevalence of heavy drinking. Nevertheless, when per capita alcohol sales is taken as an index of the latter, it is in most cases a highly accurate predictor of the cirrhosis death rate. And the impact on general mortality may be reflected in the covariation, so far observed in several temporal series, of per capita alcohol sales and the excess of male over female mortality in the middle age range. In this regard, a characteristic of mortality in the Western nations during the past generation has been the lack of improvement in middle-aged men as compared to other segments of the population. It is by no means inconceivable that the increase in alcohol consumption over the same period has been a contributing factor.

Finally, we must echo Pearl (1926, p.222) and "disclaim any responsibility" for the application of these conclusions to the individual case. As he so aptly put it "it will be the part of wisdom to remember that a conclusion which is on the average true for a large statistical aggregate may not be so for a particular individual in that aggregate". There will always be the octogenarian who has consumed heavily most of his life; there will be those who seem unable to tolerate the smallest quantities. But such variability in individual susceptibility need not concern us here. The relevant public health objectives are to delineate, for the drinking population as a whole, the risks of disease and premature death associated with different levels of alcohol consumption, and to seek means to minimize the number of drinkers in the hazardous range.

References

Anonymous (1968). Heart disease and beer drinking. *Public Health Rep.* 83: 998.

Anstie, F.E. (1870). On the dietetic and medicinal uses of wine. *Practitioner* 4:219–224.

Ashley, M.J. (1984). Alcohol consumption and ischemic heart disease: The epidemiologic evidence. In: *Research Advances in Alcohol and Drug Problems, Vol. 8* ed. R.G. Smart, et al. New York: Plenum.

Ashley, M.J., Olin, J.S., le Riche, W.H., Kornaczewski, A., Schmidt, W. & Rankin, J.G. (1977). Morbidity in alcoholics. Evidence for accelerated development of physical disease in women. *Arch. Intern. Med.* 137:883–887.

Babigian, H.M. & Odoroff, C.L. (1969). The mortality experience of a population with psychiatric illness. *Am. J. Psychiatry* 126:470–479.

Bailey, W.C., Sellers, C.A., Sutton, F.D., Sheehy, T.W. & Maetz, H.M. (1978). Tuberculosis and alcoholism: A partial solution through detection. *Chest* 73:183–185.

Bandel, R. (1930). Die spezifische Männersterblichkeit als Masstab der Alkoholsterblichkeit. In: *Ergebnisse der Sozialen Hygiene und Gesundheitsfürsorge, Bd. II.* Leipzig: Georg Thieme Verlag, pp. 424–492.

Becker, W.H. (1908). Eine maximaldosis des alkohols. *Therap. Monatsch.* 22:444–458.

Bing, R.J. & Tillmans, H. (1977). The effect of alcohol on the heart. In:

Metabolic Aspects of Alcoholism, ed. C.S. Lieber. Baltimore: University Park Press, pp. 117–134.

Bingham, J.R. (1960). Precipitating factors in peptic ulcer. *Can. Med. Assoc. J.* 83:205–211.

Borkenstein, R.F. (1975). Problems of enforcement, adjudication and sanctioning. In: *Proceedings of the 6th International Conference on Alcohol, Drugs, and Traffic Safety,* ed. S. Israelstam & S. Lambert. Toronto: Addiction Research Foundation, pp. 655–662.

Borkenstein, R.F., Crowther, R.F., Shumata, R.P., Ziel, W.B. & Zylman, R. (1974). The role of the drinking driver in traffic accidents (The Grand Rapids Study). In: *Blutalkohol, Volume II, Supplement 1,* ed. R.F. Borkenstein. Bloomington: Indiana University, pp. 1–132.

Brenner, B. (1967). Alcoholism and fatal accidents. *Quart. J. Stud. Alc.* 28:517–528.

Brewers Association of Canada (1973). *Beer, Wine and Spirits: Beverage Differences and Public Policy In Canada.* Ottawa: Alcoholic Beverage Study Committee.

Brown, K.E. & Campbell, A.H. (1961). Tobacco, alcohol and tuberculosis. *Brit. J. Dis. Chest* 55:150–158.

Bruun, K., Koura, E., Popham, R.E. & Seeley, J.R. (1960). *Liver Cirrhosis as a Means to Estimate the Prevalence of Alcoholism,* Publication No. 8. Helsinki: Finnish Foundation for Alcohol Studies.

Burch, G.E. & Giles, T.D. (1974). Alcoholic cardiomyopathy. In: *The Biology of Alcoholism, Volume 3,* ed. B. Kissin & H. Begleiter. New York: Plenum Press, pp. 435–460.

Chomet, B. & Gach, B.M. (1967). Lobar pneumonia and alcoholism: An analysis of 37 cases. *Am. J. Med. Sci.* 253:300–304.

Ciompi, L. & Medvecka, J. (1976). Etude comparative de la mortalité à long terme dans les maladies mentales. *Arch. Suisses Neurol. Neurochir. Psychiat.* 118:111–135.

Dahlberg, G. (1952). Dodlighet bland alkoholister. *Svenska Lakartidningen* 49:112–118.

Dahlgren, K.C. (1951). On death rates and causes of death in alcohol addicts. *Acta Psychiat. Neurol. Scand.* 26:297–311.

Dahlgren, L. & Myhred, M. (1977). Alcoholic females II. Causes of death with reference to sex difference. *Acta Psychiat. Scand.* 56:81–91.

Davies, K.M. (1965). The influence of alcohol on mortality. *Proc. Home Office Life Underwriters Assoc.* 46:159–179.

de Lint, J. & Levinson, T. (1975). Mortality among patients treated for alcoholism: A 5-year follow-up. *Can. Med. Assoc. J.* 113:385–387.

de Lint, J. & Schmidt, W. (1968). The distribution of alcohol consumption in Ontario. *Quart. J. Stud. Alc.* 29:968–973.

Doll, R. & Hill, A.B. (1964). Mortality in relation to smoking: Ten years' observation of British doctors. *Brit. Med. J.* 1:1399–1410, 1460–1467.

Dorpat, T.L. & Ripley, H.S. (1960). A study of suicide in the Seattle area. *Compr. Psychiat.* 1:349–359.

Dreher, K.F. & Fraser, J.G. (1967). Smoking habits of alcoholic outpatients. I. *Int. J. Addict.* 2:259–270.

Dreher, K.F. & Fraser, J.G. (1968). Smoking habits of alcoholic outpatients. II. *Int. J. Addict.* 3:65–80.

Dussault, P., Burford, R. & Chappel, C. (1972). *Studies of Alcoholic Beverages: Physiological Effects.* Montreal: Brewers Association of Canada, Bio-research Laboratory.

Dyer, A.R., Stamler, J., Paul, O., Berkson, D.M., Lepper, M.H., McKean, H., Shekelle, R.B., Lindberg, H.A. & Garside, D. (1977). Alcohol consumption, cardiovascular risk factors and mortality in two Chicago epidemiological studies. *Circulation* 56:1067–1074.

Dyer, A.R., Stamler, J., Oglesby, P., Berkson, D.M., Shekelle, R.B., Lepper, M.H., McKean, H., Lindberg, H.A., Garside, D. & Tokich, T. (1981). Alcohol, cardiovascular risk factors and mortality: The Chicago experience. *Circulation* 64 (Suppl. III):20–27.

Eckardt, M.J., Harford, T.C., Kaelber, C.T., Parker, E.S., Rosenthal, L.S., Ryback, R.S., Salmoiraghi, G.C., Vanderveen, E. & Warren, K.R. (1981). Health hazards associated with alcohol consumption. *J.A.M.A.* 246:648–666.

Emirgil, C. & Sobol, B.J. (1977). Pulmonary function in former alcoholics, *Chest* 72:45–51.

Emirgil, C., Sobol, B.J., Heymann, B. & Shibutani, K. (1974). Pulmonary function in alcoholics. *Am. J. Med.* 57:69–77.

Engeset, A., Lygren, T. & Idsoe, R. (1963). The incidence of peptic ulcer among alcohol abusers and non-abusers. *Quart. J. Stud. Alc.* 24: 622–626.

Fallon, H.J. & Lesesne, H.R. (1978). Medical complications of excessive drinking. In: *Drinking—Alcohol in American Society,* ed., J.A. Ewing & B.A. Rouse. Chicago: Nelson-Hall, pp. 63–69.

Feingold, A.O. (1976). Association of tuberculosis with alcoholism. *South. Med. J.* 69:1336–1337.

Gabriel, E. (1935) Über die Todesursachen bei Alkoholikern. *Zbl. Ges. Neurol. Psychiat.* 153:385–406.

Giffen, P.J., Oki, G., Lambert, S., Timothy, E. & Maxwell, J. (1971). *The Chronic Drunkenness Offender: Ages and Causes of Death of the Chronic Drunkenness Offender Population,* A.R.F. Substudy No. 418. Toronto: Addiction Research Foundation.

Gillis, L.S. (1969). The mortality rate and cause of death of treated alcoholics. *S. Afr. Med. J.* 43:230–232.

Goldberg, L. (1955). Drunken drivers in Sweden. In: *Proceedings of the 2nd Conference on Alcohol and Road Traffic.* Toronto: Garden City Press, pp. 112–127.

Gorwitz, K., Bahn, A.K., Klee, G. & Solomon, M.S. (1966). Release and return rates for patients in state mental hospitals of Maryland. *Public Health Rep.* 81:1095–1108.

Hudson, P. (1978). The medical examiner looks at drinking. In: *Drinking—Alcohol in American Society,* ed. J.A. Ewing & B.A. Rouse. Chicago: Nelson-Hall, pp. 71–92.

Ignev, I. (1979). Reasons for suicides and attempted suicides among chronic alcoholics. In: *Proceedings of the 10th International Congress for Suicide Prevention and Crisis Intervention.* Ottawa: International Association of Suicide Prevention, p. 224.

Ipsen, J. (1950). An epidemic of infectious hepatitis, predominantly of adults, and highly fatal for elderly women. *Am. J. Hyg.* 51:255–263.

Israel, Y., Kalant, H., Orrego, H., Khanna, J.M., Videla, L. & Phillips, J.M. (1975). Experimental alcohol-induced hepatic necroses suppression by propylthiouracil. *Proc. Nat. Acad. Sci.* USA 72:1137–1141.

Jolliffe, N. & Jellinek, E.M. (1941). Vitamin deficiencies and liver cirrhosis in alcoholism. VII, Cirrhosis of the liver. *Quart. J. Stud. Alc.* 2: 544–583.

Kalant, H., LeBlanc, A.E., Wilson, A. & Homatidis, S. (1975). Sensorimotor and physiological effects of various alcoholic beverages. *Can. Med. Assoc. J.* 112:953–958.

Keller, A.Z. & Terris, M. (1965). The association of alcohol and tobacco with cancer of the mouth and pharynx. *Am. J. Public Health.* 55: 1578–1585.

Kendall, R.E. & Staton, M.C. (1966). The fate of untreated alcoholics. *Quart. J. Stud. Alc.* 27:30–41.

Kissin, B. & Begleiter, H. (eds.) (1974). *The Biology of Alcoholism, Clinical Pathology, Volume 3.* New York: Plenum Press.

Kissin, B. & Kaley, M.M. (1974). Alcohol and cancer. In: *The Biology of Alcoholism, Volume 3,* ed. B. Kissin & H. Begleiter. New York: Plenum Press, pp. 481–511.

Klatsky, A.L., Friedman, G.D. & Siegelaub, A.B. (1979). Alcohol use, myocardial infarction, sudden cardiac death, and hypertension. *Alc. Clin. Exp. Res.* 3:33–39.

Knott, D.H. & Beard, J.D. (1972). Changes in cardiovascular activity as a function of alcohol intake. In: *The Biology of Alcoholism, Volume 2,* ed. B. Kissin & H. Begleiter. New York: Plenum Press, pp. 345–365.

Krasner, N., Davis, M., Portman, B. & Williams, R. (1977). Changing pattern of alcoholic liver disease in Great Britain: Relation of sex and signs of autoimmunity. *Brit. Med. J.* 1:1497–1500.

Lasserre, O., Flamant, R., Lellouch, J. & Schwartz, D. (1966). Alcool et cancer: Etude de pathologie géographique portant sur les Départements Français. *Bull. Instit. Nat. Santé* 22:53–60.

Lebowitz, M.D. (1981). Respiratory symptoms and disease related to alcohol consumption. *Am. Rev. Respir. Dis.* 123:16–19.

Ledermann, S. (1956). *Alcool, Alcoolisme, Alcoolisation: Données Scientifiques de Caractère Physiologique Economique et Social,* Institut National d'Etudes Démographiques. Paris: Presses Universitaires de Françe, Travaux et Documents, Cahier No. 29.

Ledermann, S. (1964). *Alcool, Alcoolisme, Alcoolisation: Mortalité, Morbidité, Accidents du Travail,* Institut National d'Etudes Démographiques, Paris: Presses Universitaires de Françe, Travaux et Documents, Cahier No. 41.

Lee, F.I. (1966). Cirrhosis and hepatoma in alcoholics. *Gut* 7:77–85.

Leevy, C.M., Gellene, R. & Ning, M. (1964). Primary liver cancer in cirrhosis of the alcoholic. *Ann. N.Y. Acad. Sci.* 114:1026–1040.

Lelbach, W.K. (1974). Organic pathology related to volume and pattern of alcohol use. In: *Research Advances in Alcohol and Drug Problems, Volume 1,* ed. R.J. Gibbins et al. New York: John Wiley and Sons, pp. 93–198.

Lelbach, W.K. (1976). Epidemiology of alcoholic liver disease. *Prog. Liver Dis., N.Y.* 5:494–515.

Lindelius, R. & Salum, I. (1972). Mortality. In: *Delirium Tremens and Certain Other Acute Sequels of Alcohol Abuse, Supplement 235,* ed. I. Salum. Stockholm: *Acta Psychiat. Scand.* pp. 86–100.

Lindelius, R., Salum, I. & Agren, G. (1974). Mortality among male and female alcoholic patients treated in a psychiatric unit. *Acta Psychiat. Scand.* 50:612–618.

Lindenbaum, J. (1974). Hematologic effects of alcohol. In: *The Biology of Alcoholism, Volume 3,* ed. B. Kissin & H. Begleiter. New York: Plenum Press, pp. 461–480.

Lorber, S.H., Dinoso, V.P. & Chey, W.Y. (1974). Diseases of the gastrointestinal tract. In: *The Biology of Alcoholism, Volume 3,* ed. B. Kissin & H. Begleiter. New York: Plenum Press, pp. 339–357.

Lundquist, G.A.R. (1970). Alcohol dependence and depressive states. Paper presented at the 16th International Institute on the Prevention and Treatment of Alcoholism, Lausanne.

Lyons, H.A. & Saltzman, A. (1974). Diseases of the respiratory tract in alcoholics. In: *The Biology of Alcoholism, Volume 3,* ed. B. Kissin & H. Begleiter. New York: Plenum Press, pp. 403–434.

Mäkelä, K. (1971). Concentration of alcohol consumption. *Scand. Stud. Criminol.* 3:77–78.

McDermott, P.H., Delaney, R.L., Egan, J.D. & Sullivan, J.F. (1966). Myocardosis and cardiac failure in men. *J.A.M.A.* 198:253–256.

McLean, N.J. & Campbell, I.M. (1979). The drinking driver: A personality profile. In: *Proceedings of the 7th International Conference on Alcohol, Drugs, and Traffic Safety,* ed. I.R. Johnson. Canberra: Australian Government Publishing Service.

McMichael, A.J. (1979). Laryngeal cancer and alcohol consumption in Australia, *Med. J. Aust.* 1:131–134.

Menge, W. (1950). Mortality experience among cases involving alcohol habits. *Proc. Home Office Life Underwriters Assoc.* 31:70–93.

Newman, A.F. (1965). Alcoholism in Frontenac County: A survey of the characteristics of an alcoholic population in its native habitat. Ph.D. Thesis, Queen's University, Kingston.

Nicholls, P., Edwards, G. & Kyle, E. (1974). Alcoholics admitted to four hospitals in England. II. General and cause-specific mortality. *Quart. J. Stud. Alc.* 35:841–855.

Olin, J.S. (1966). "Skid row" syndrome: A medical profile of the chronic drunkenness offender. *Can. Med. Assoc. J.* 95:205–214.

Parker, R.G.F. (1957). The incidence of primary hepatic carcinoma in cirrhosis. *Proc. Roy. Soc. Med.* 50:145–147.

Pearl, R. (1923). Alcohol and mortality. In: *Action of Alcohol on Man*, ed. E.H. Sterling. London: Longmans, Green, pp. 213–286.

Pearl, R. (1926). *Alcohol and Longevity*. New York: Alfred A. Knopf.

Pell, S. & D'Alonzo, A. (1973). A five-year mortality study of alcoholics. *J. Occup. Med.* 15:120–125.

Péquignot, G. (1974). Les problèmes nutritionnels de la société industrielle. *Vie Mèd. Canad. France* 3:216–225.

Péquignot, G., Chabert, C., Eydoux, H. & Courcoul, M.A. (1974). Augmentation de risque de cirrhose en fonction de la ration d'alcool. *Rev. Alcool.* 20:191–202.

Popham, R.E. (1956). The Jellinek alcoholism estimation formula and its application to Canadian data. *Quart. J. Stud. Alc.* 17:559–593.

Popham, R.E. (1970). Indirect methods of alcoholism prevalence estimation: A critical evaluation. In: *Alcohol and Alcoholism*, ed. R.E. Popham. Toronto: University of Toronto Press, pp. 294–306.

Popham, R.E. & Schmidt, W. (1978). The biomedical definition of safe alcohol consumption: A crucial issue for the researcher and the drinker. *Brit. J. Addict.* 73:233–235.

Popham, R.E., Schmidt, W. & de Lint, J. (1976). The effects of legal restraint on drinking. In: *The Biology of Alcoholism, Volume 4*, ed. B. Kissin & H. Begleiter. New York: Plenum Press, pp. 579–625.

Purtilo, D.T. & Gottlieb, L.S. (1973). Cirrhosis and hepatoma occurring at Boston City Hospital 1917–1968. *Cancer* 32:458–462.

Rankin, J.G., Hale, G.S., Wilkinson, P., O'Day, D.M., Santamaria, J.N. & Babarzy, G. (1969). Relationship between smoking and pulmonary disease in alcoholism. *Med. J. Aust.* 1:730–733.

Riddick, L. & Luke, J.L. (1978). Alcohol associated deaths in the District of Columbia—a postmortem study. *J. Forensic Sci.* 23:493–502.

Robins, E., Murphy, G.E., Wilkinson, R.J., Gassner, S. & Kayes, J. (1959). Some clinical considerations in the prevention of suicide based on a study of 134 successful suicides. *Am. J. Public Health.* 49:888–899.

Robinette, C.D., Hrubec, Z. & Fraumeni, J.F. (1979). Chronic alcoholism and subsequent mortality in World War II veterans. *Am. J. Epidemiol.* 109:687–700.

Room, R. & Day, N. (1974). Alcohol and mortality. In: *Second Special Report to the U.S. Congress: Alcohol and Health,* ed. M. Keller. Washington, D.C.: U.S. Government Printing Office, pp. 104–123.

Rothman, K.J. (1978). The effect of alcohol consumption on risk of cancer of the head and neck. *Laryngoscope* 88 (No. 1, Pt. 2, Suppl. 8):51–55.

Rothman, K.J. (1980). The proportion of cancer attributable to alcohol consumption. *Prevent. Med.* 9:174–179.

Rothman, K. & Keller, A. (1972). The effect of joint exposure to alcohol and tobacco on risk of cancer of the mouth and pharynx. *J. Chron. Dis.* 25:711–716.

Rubin, E. & Lieber, C.S. (1974). Fatty liver, alcohol hepatitis and cirrhosis produced by alcohol in primates. *N. Engl. J. Med.* 290:128–135.

Rushing, W.A. (1969). Suicide and interaction of alcoholism (liver cirrhosis) with the social situation. *Quart. J. Stud. Alc.* 30:93–103.

Schmidt, W. (1973). Analysis of alcohol consumption data: The use of consumption data for research purposes. In: *Proceedings of the Epidemiology of Drug Dependence: Report on a Conference.* Copenhagen: World Health Organization Regional Office for Europe, pp. 57–66.

Schmidt, W. (1974). Unpublished report. Toronto: Addiction Research Foundation.

Schmidt, W. (1975). Agreement, disagreement in experimental, clinical and epidemiological evidence on the etiology of alcoholic liver cirrhosis: A comment. In: *Alcoholic Liver Pathology,* ed. J.M. Khanna, Y. Israel, & H. Kalant. Toronto: Addiction Research Foundation, pp. 19–30.

Schmidt, W. (1977). Cirrhosis and alcohol consumption: An epidemiological perspective. In: *Alcoholism: New Knowledge and New Responses,* ed. G. Edwards & M. Grant. London: Croom Helm Ltd. Publishers.

Schmidt, W. & de Lint, J. (1970). Estimating the prevalence of alcoholism from alcohol consumption and mortality data. *Quart. J. Stud. Alc.* 31:957–964.

Schmidt, W. & de Lint, J. (1972). Causes of death of alcoholics. *Quart. J. Stud. Alc.* 33:171–185.

Schmidt, W. & de Lint, J. (1973). The mortality of alcoholic people. *Alc. Health and Res. World,* Experimental Issue:16–20.

Schmidt, W. & Kornaczewski, A. (1975). The effect of lowering the legal drinking age in Ontario on alcohol-related motor vehicle accidents. In: *Proceedings of the 6th International Conference on Alcohol, Drugs, and Traffic Safety,* ed. S. Israelstam & S. Lambert. Toronto: Addiction Research Foundation, pp. 763–770.

Schmidt, W. & Popham, R.E. (1980). Sex differences in mortality: A comparison of male and female alcoholics. In: *Research Advances in Alcohol and Drug Problems, Volume 5,* ed. O.J. Kalant. New York: Plenum Press, pp. 365–384.

Schmidt, W. & Popham, R.E. (1981). The role of drinking and smoking in mortality from cancer and other causes in male alcoholics. *Cancer* 47:1031–1041.

Schmidt, W. & Smart, R.G. (1963). Drinking-driving mortality and morbidity statistics. In: *Alcohol and Traffic Safety,* ed. B.H. Fox & J.H. Fox. Public Health Service Publication No. 1043, Washington, D.C.: U.S. Government Printing Office, pp. 27–43.

Schmidt, W., Smart, R.G. & Popham, R.E. (1962). The role of alcoholism in motor vehicle accidents. *Traff. Safety Res. Rev.* 6:21–27.

Schoenberg, B.S., Bailar, J.C. & Fraumeni, J.F. (1971). Certain mortality patterns of osophageal cancer in the United States, 1930–67. *J. Nat. Cancer Inst.* 46:63–73.

Schwartz, D., Lasserre, O., Flamant, R. & Lellouch, J. (1966). Alcool et cancer:Etude de pathologie géographique portant sur 19 pays, *Europ. J. Cancer* 2:367–372.

Seixas, F.A., Williams, K. & Eggleston, S. (eds.) (1975). *Medical Consequences of Alcoholism* (Annals of the N.Y. Academy of Sciences, Volume 252). New York: New York Academy of Sciences.

Selzer, M.L. (1975). Alcoholics and social drinkers: Characteristics and differentiation. In: *Proceedings of the 6th International Conference on Alcohol, Drugs, and Traffic Safety,* ed. S. Israelstam & S. Lambert. Toronto: Addiction Research Foundation, pp. 13–20.

Skog, O-J. (1971). *The Distribution of Alcohol in a Population.* Oslo: National Institute for Alcohol Research.

Skog, O-J. (1980). Liver cirrhosis epidemiology: Some methodological problems. *Brit. J. Addict.* 75:227–243.

Sulkunen, P. (1973). *On International Alcohol Statistics, Reports from the Social Research Institute of Alcohol Studies No. 72.* Helsinki: Finnish Foundation for Alcohol Studies.

Sundby, P. (1967). *Alcoholism and Mortality, National Institute for Alcohol Research, Publication No. 6.* Oslo: Universitetsforlaget.

Takala, M., Pihkanen, T.A. & Markkanen, T. (1957). *The Effects of Distilled and Brewed Beverages, Publication No. 4.* Helsinki: Finnish Foundation for Alcohol Studies.

Thaler, H. (1977). Alcohol consumption and diseases of the liver. *Nutr. Metab.* 21:186–193.

Thorarinsson, A.A. (1979). Mortality among men alcoholics in Iceland 1951–74. *J. Stud. Alc.* 40:704–718.

Tibblin, G.T., Wilhelmsen, L. & Werko, L. (1975). Risk factors for myocardial infarction and death due to ischemic heart disease and other causes. *Am. J. Cardiol.* 35:514–522.

Tuyns, A.J. (1970). Cancer of the oesophagus: Further evidence of the relation to drinking habits in France. *Int. J. Cancer* 5:152–156.

Tuyns, A.J. (1979). Epidemiology of alcohol and cancer. *Cancer Res.* 39:2840–2842.

Tuyns, A.J. & Audigier, J.C. (1976). Double wave cohort increase for oesophageal and laryngeal cancer in France in relation to reduced alcohol consumption during the second world war. *Digestion* 14:197–203.

Tuyns, A.J., Jensen, O.M. & Péquignot, G. (1977). Le cancer de l'oesophage en Ille-et-Vilaine en fonction des niveaux de consommation d'alcool et de tabac: Des risques qui se multiplient. *Bull. Cancer* 64:45–60.

Tuyns, A.J., Péquignot, G. & Jensen, O.M. (1978). Nutrition, alcohol and oesophageal cancer. *Bull. Cancer* 65:59–64.

Tuyns, A.J., Péquignot, G. & Abbatucci, J.S. (1979). Oesophageal cancer and alcohol consumption: Importance of type of beverage. *Int. J. Cancer* 23:443–447.

Wallgren, H., Kosunen, A. & Nikander, S. (1970). *Alkoholhaittojen Kytkeytyminen Juoman Laatuun.* Helsinki: Alkon Kesjuslaboratorio, Seloste 8065.

Weir, J.M. & Dunn, J.E. Jr. (1970). Smoking and mortality: A prospective study. *Cancer (Brussels)* 25:105–122.

Whitlock, F.A. (1974). Liver cirrhosis, alcoholism and alcohol consumption. *Quart. J. Stud. Alc.* 35:586–605.

Williams, P., Robinson, D. & Bailey, A. (1979). High-density lipoprotein and coronary risk factors in normal men. *Lancet* 1:72–75.

Wilkinson, P., Santamaria, J.N. & Rankin, J.G. (1969). Epidemiology of alcoholic cirrhosis. *Australasian Ann. Med.* 18:222–226.

Wynder, E.L. (1978). The epidemiology of cancers of the upper alimentary and upper respiratory tracts. *Laryngoscope* 88:50–51.

Wynder, E.L., & Mabuchy, K. (1972). Etiological and preventive aspects of human cancer. *Prevent. Med.* 1:300–334.

Wynder, E.L., Bross, I.J. & Feldman, R.M. (1957). A study of etiological factors in cancer of the mouth. *Cancer (N.Y.)* 10:1300–1323.

Chapter 8

The Prevalence of Alcoholism in Medical and Surgical Patients

ROBERT A. MOORE

At this time, knowledge about the prevalence of alcoholism in medical and surgical patients, as well as in the general population, is rudimentary. Medical and surgical patients are, after all, part of the general population and the vast majority of the general population will at some time in their lives become medical or surgical patients. Does alcohol consumption make it more or less likely one will become a medical or surgical patient? If so, how much is required? And, if so, with what illnesses or diseases? Will alcohol consumption cause or contribute to the cause of their illnesses or diseases or will some of their illnesses or diseases cause or encourage alcohol consumption? Does alcohol consumption reduce the likelihood of having certain diseases and, if so, at what level of consumption?

If we have any hope of approaching this topic, we must have some limits to our subjects. Therefore, we will consider the relationship of alcoholism, to be defined below, to medical and surgical illnesses and diseases as encountered in a hospital.

Definition

Critical to any epidemiologic study is a clear and agreed-to definition of the disorder to be studied. Unfortunately, such a definition has not been unanimously adopted for alcoholism so is not always possible to make comparisons between studies. As a result, prevalence rates vary widely and, as stated by Keller (1979), "We have yet to develop a reliable epidemiology of alcoholism." This is understandable since most often we use rather general definitions, such as: "Alcoholism is an illness characterized by significant impairment that is directly associated with persistent and excessive use of alcohol. Impairment may involve physiological, psychological or social dysfunction." (AMA, 1977). What constitutes "significant impairment" and "persistent and excessive" may be variously interpreted. The National Institute on Alcohol Abuse and Alcoholism, hindered by that title, has trouble defining the disorder. In their *First Special Report* (Secretary of HEW, 1971), after listing certain impairments as in the AMA definition, they call this "—alcohol abuse—and may raise a strong inference of alcoholism." In the *Second Special Report* (Secretary of HEW, 1974), they simply state, "Clear definitions of problem drinking and alcoholism do not exist." This does not prevent them from estimating that, "as many as 10,000,000 people" may be involved. This and other such estimates "seem to have been derived by a new system of statwistics or mythematics" (Keller, 1979). Reviewing epidemiologic data, Keller (1975) estimated alcoholism (those addicted to alcohol) to afflict about 5.5 million with another 5.0 million showing significant impairment without addiction. To confuse our terminology, these last 5.0 million are often called alcohol abusers, troubled drinkers, impaired drinkers, or problem drinkers but in many surveys are included with the narrower definition of alcoholism.

To get around this roadblock to epidemiologic advances, Feighner and his associates (1972) established a set of criteria that are worthy of duplication here. A "definite" diagnosis of alcoholism requires a symptom in 3 of the 4 groups below; a "probably" diagnosis requires a symptom in 2 groups; a "suspected" diagnosis requires a symptom in 1 group.

The groups are:

Group I: (1) any manifestation of alcohol withdrawal such as tremulousness, convulsions, hallucinations, or delerium; (2) history of medical complications; (3) alcoholic blackouts; (4) more than one alcoholic binge or "bender" (48 hours or more of drinking associated with default of usual obligations).

Group II: (1) patient has not been able to stop drinking when he wanted to; (2) patient has tried to control drinking by allowing himself to drink only under certain circumstances; (3) drinking before breakfast; (4) drinking nonbeverage forms of alcohol.

Group III: (1) arrests for drinking; (2) traffic difficulties associated with drinking; (3) trouble at work because of drinking; (4) fighting associated with drinking.

Group IV: (1) patient thinks he drinks too much; (2) family objects to his drinking; (3) loss of friends because of drinking; (4) other people object to his drinking; (5) patient feels guilty about his drinking.

Using these criteria, Winokur and Tsuang (1978) studied an Iowa population and found a lifetime morbidity risk in men of 5.4% definite; 6.7% definite or probable; and 7.2% definite, probable, or suspected. Very surprisingly, for women the figures were 0.0%, 0.4%, and 0.4%. It is unknown whether these figures would hold nationwide. Further, their data reflect not only the situation now but also in the past. Do usual prevalence rates include alcoholism long in the past or only alcoholism now? Interestingly, the same criteria found definite alcoholism in 3% to 5% of European men and 0.1% to 1% of women (Goodwin, 1976).

Whether the "Feighner criteria" are the best ones we have or not, it is imperative we agree to something if we are to seriously attempt to study the epidemiology of alcoholism.

Making the Diagnosis

Even with agreed upon criteria, problems remain. Someone has to make the diagnosis. Since we are looking for prevalence rates in hospitals, can physicians, nurses, and other professionals make the diagnosis? They can't, apparently, or at least they won't. At as sophisticated a medical center as the University of Minnesota, "physicians and nurses do not currently obtain even minimal information regarding use of drugs and alcohol among hospital patients" (Westermeyer, et al., 1978). In fact, after identifying probable alcoholics from the Michigan Alcoholism Screening Test (Selzer, 1971), two-thirds of the patients did not have their alcoholism considered in treatment planning. Perhaps the physician is on the side of the patient in his denial of alcoholism (Lisansky, 1974) and the negative attitude of professionals toward alcoholics is well known. (Sowa & Cutter, 1974; Wallston, et al., 1976). Fortunately, one study (Fisher, et al.,

1976) demonstrated that family practice residents show an increase in positive concern for alcoholics through proper education and this is followed by a large increase in the frequency of making the diagnosis.

To assist in raising diagnostic suspicion, various screening tests have been developed such as the MAST previously alluded to, the Short Michigan Alcoholism Screening Test (Selzer, et al., 1975), the CAGE (Ewing, 1970), the Self-Administered Alcoholism Screening Test (Swenson & Morse, 1975), the Alcohol Problem Score (Page, 1979), and others. As screening tests, they will overstate the prevalence (Moore, 1972) and there remains the problem previously discussed of confusion between the present condition and that in the distant past. One study (Fisher et al., 1976) by using weighted scores on medical disorders frequently associated with alcoholism could correctly classify 75% of alcoholics and combining with CAGE raise the accuracy to 87%.

A committee of alcoholism experts, brought together by the National Council on Alcoholism, developed an extensive list of criteria for the diagnosis, 86 in total. These were divided into major and minor and further into physiological, clinical, behavioral, psychological, and attitudinal (NCA, 1972). A study done in Germany (Ringer et al., 1977), found that 38 criteria did not differentiate alcoholics from controls and that four variables gave 90% of the variance. These were gross tremor, blackouts, morning drinking, and regressive defense mechanisms, only one of which is directly observable. Their findings have been rather severely criticized, however, by a number of respondents in the *Journal of Studies on Alcohol* 38:1830–1837, 1977. The major problem raised was the lack of knowledge of how many alcoholics were among the control subjects. While these criteria have yet to establish themselves as an accurate diagnostic scheme, they are valuable in raising the sensitivity of physicians toward the possibility of alcoholism.

Guze's (1980) response to a study by Jones (1979), which revealed that 10% of patients admitted to a London hospital via the psychiatric emergency clinic were found to be alcoholic and only half of them were recognized by the psychiatrist, is worth quoting in full:

> "He who knows syphilis, knows medicine" is one of the famous Oslerian adages reflecting the protean manifestations of syphilis. Today, the

> more "relevant" adage would be "he who knows alcoholism, knows medicine." No organ system is immune to the consequences of alcohol abuse, least of all the brain. It is no wonder then that alcoholism must be considered in the differential diagnosis of nearly all neurological *and* psychiatric disorders. Just as physicians were trained to "suspect" syphilis in many clinical situations, so must they today be alerted to the possibility of alcoholism in many clinical situations. What this report makes clear is that psychiatrists are like other physicians in this matter.

My only addition to this is to add "medical" where he states "neurological *and* psychiatric."

The Prevalence of Alcoholism in General Hospitals

Having discussed the problems of definition and diagnosis of alcoholism, we move to prevalence rates in medical and surgical patients in general hospitals, specifically excluding psychiatric patients which is another subject in itself. Now, in addition to diagnostic and definitional variations, we face a compounding and uncontrolled variable—great differences in populations under study. They have in common only that they find themselves identified as patients in a general hospital. The studies are presented in the order of their publication.

Pearson (1962) found 29% of the 100 white male patients in a North Carolina hospital and tuberculosis sanitorium to be alcoholic and 9% "probable" alcoholics. This was based upon 4 positive responses to 6 questions about alcohol effects.

Green (1965) studied 841 patients in a Melbourne, Australia, hospital by asking about their drinking habits. The male to female ratio was 1.2:1.0 and the patients came from a low income area. Of the men, 12.1% were diagnosed as alcoholic.

Nolan (1965) gave an alcohol history questionnaire to 900 consecutive admissions to a community hospital in Connecticut with a male to female ratio of 1.4:1.0. The questionnaire identified 15.3% of the men and 9.9% of the women as alcoholic. Eleven percent of the male alcoholics were black and there was no age difference with the nonalcoholic men. Of the women alcoholics, 32.5% were black and the alcoholic women were significantly younger than the nonalcoholic women.

Kearney et al. (1967) studied medical records of 416 patients in a community general hospital also in Connecticut, 90% of whom were middle class or above. Using the personal knowledge of the investigators plus a history of treatment for alcoholism or a complication of alcoholism, they arrived at a prevalence rate of 8.7%. Kearny also noted (1969) the reluctance of physicians to use the word "alcoholism" in the medical records of their private patients.

Barchha et al. (1968) interviewed 392 adult admissions to a teaching hospital in St. Louis. Among men, 27% were diagnosed as alcoholic and 7% as questionably alcoholic, though at the time of admission 13% of the 34% were in remission. Black men had a rate double that of white men.

McCusker et al. (1971), using an "alcohol abuse scale," interviewed 118 patients at a hospital in Harlem, New York City. Ninety-one percent were black; 60% of the men and 34% of the women were alcoholic.

Moore (1971) reviewed the medical records and gave the MAST (Selzer, 1971) to 200 patients in a community general hospital in San Diego, 87% of whom were private patients. Two-thirds of the patients were women with 5.5% alcoholic and 1.5% questionable; of the men, 18% were alcoholics and 7% questionable. As to medical and surgical conditions, 75% of the liver diseases were in the alcoholic group, 50% of gastrointestinal disorders, 26% of traumatic conditions, and 25% of malignancies. These groups of disorders, in total, were found in 52% of the alcoholic patients but in only 22% of the nonalcoholic group.

Chakerian and Schenkel (1973), at a Veterans Administration Hospital in New Mexico, checked all 351 patients on a given day and using their recorded diagnosis and the opinions of ward staff estimated that 23.8% were "hospitalized for a physical problem that could be traced to alcohol abuse." Of 197 patients admitted to Medical Intensive Care for a 6-month period, 35% were "known alcoholics."

Abbott et al. (1974) estimate that 70% of admissions to the Medical Service of San Francisco General Hospital are alcoholic based upon National Council on Alcoholism criteria (NCA, 1972). Further, of 16 patients studied who had acute pancreatitis, 14 had a history of alcoholism.

Gomberg (1975) at a Veterans Administration Hospital in Michigan used personal interviews and a modified questionnaire from Barchha et al. (1968) in studying 173 medical and surgical patients. Twenty-six percent were problem drinkers by Keller's impairment definition (1962) and 29% had been so in the past. This latter point addressed the issue raised by Winokur and Tsuang (1978). Thirteen percent of the patients were black with a rate of current problem drinkers of 32% compared to 23% of the white patients. When comparing diagnostic groupings, rates were high for alcoholic patients in the respiratory and digestive areas but lower than the controls in the neurological, cardiovascular, and urogenital areas.

Schuckit and Miller (1976) in 113 consecutive elderly medical and surgical admissions to a Veterans Administration Hospital in California, used a structured interview and found 20% had been alcoholic at one time in their lives, 9% currently. Schuckit and Pastor (1978) also estimate rates in nursing homes for the elderly as high as 20%.

Jarman and Kellett (1979) report a six times greater prevalence of alcoholism in a general hospital in London than in the general population. They did not find the alcoholics had differing patterns of medical and surgical disorders from the nonalcoholic patients; in fact, 88% of them had diseases not usually associated with alcoholism.

Table 1 attempts to aggregate this probably unaggregatable data. Because of missing or noncomparable data, the totaled results are approximations at best. While the 3,801 patients in total have an alcoholism prevalence rate of 16%, the range is 9%–70% for the whole group. Broken down by sex when known, the prevalence for males is 9%–60% and for females, 5.5%–34%.

Do these studies provide the basis for any firm statements about the prevalence rates in medical and surgical patients? Obviously not! Yet the techniques to gather such data are available. What is required is an agreed on definition, a common diagnostic approach, and careful delineation of population samples by sex, race, other ethnicity, socioeconomic status, type of hospital, and types of medical and surgical patients treated.

The Prevalence of Alcoholism by Medical and Surgical Diagnoses

Now we venture into an even more murky area; yet it is this type of data that would be invaluable in understanding alcohol's

TABLE 1
Prevalence Rates in Medical-Surgical Patients

Author	*Number*	*Male*[a]	*Female*[a]	*Percent Alcoholic*			*Hospital characteristics*
				Total	*Male*	*Female*	
Pearson (1962)	100	100	0	29	29		North Carolina Hospital & TB San.
Green (1965)	841	459	382	12.1			Melbourne, Australia
Nolan (1965)	900	525	375	13	15.3	9.9	Community Hospital, Connecticut
Kearney et al. (1967)	416			8.7			Community Hospital, Connecticut
Barchha et al. (1968)	392			27			Teaching Hospital, St. Louis
McCusker et al. (1971)	118				60	34	Harlem Hospital, New York City
Moore (1971)	200	66	134	9.5	18	5.5	Community Hospital, California
Chakerian & Schenkel (1973)	351	351		23.8	23.8		V.A. Hospital, New Mexico
	197	197		35	35		Medical intensive care at above hosp.
Abbott et al. (1974)				70			San Francisco General Hospital
Gomberg (1975)	173	173		26	26(29 in past)		V.A. Hospital, Michigan
Schuckit & Miller (1976)	113	113		9	9(11 in past)		V.A. Hospital California, elderly patients
Jarman & Kellett (1979)				6 times general population			Hospitals in London, England
Total	3801			16			

[a]When known.

role in physical disease and in alcoholism casefinding by physicians. A caveat is necessary: because many alcoholics have a particular disease does not mean the prevalence of alcoholism among those that have the disease will be unusually high, especially if the disease is widespread. To put it in the extreme to make the point, all alcoholics will die but most people who die are not alcoholic. Even a statistically significant prevalence of alcoholism in a very widespread disease may not be large enough to attract diagnostic attention.

Table 2, taken from the *First Special Report* (Secretary HEW, 1971) lists alcohol-related disorders. These are conditions believed to be due, at least in part, to the effects of heavy alcohol consumption. Thus it is reasonable to expect that there would be a high prevalence of alcoholism in people with these diagnoses. A Canadian study of 1,000 alcoholics (Ashley et al., 1981) found that only 6.5% were free of physical disease, 68.6% had nonincapacitating or nonsymptomatic disease, and 24.9% were incapacitated to varying degress. Diseases of the gastrointestinal, respiratory, liver and biliary, and nervous systems accounted for three-fourths of the diagnoses.

A study of 63 alcoholics and 63 nonalcoholics matched by age and sex in a family practice clinic were compared for the number of conditions they had in various organ systems (Fisher et al., 1976). Alcoholics had 1.17±0.09 conditions in the respiratory system compared to 0.56±0.08 in the controls, gastrointestinal was 0.60±0.10 versus 0.29±0.07, skin 0.16±0.05 versus 0.05±0.03, bone and joint 0.29±0.07 versus 0.16±0.05, and cardiovascular 0.62±0.10 versus 0.49±0.10.

Brody (1977), head of the NIAAA's Epidemiology and Special Studies Branch, states that alcoholics are more likely to have acute liver disease, chronic respiratory diseases, peripheral neuropathy, hypertension, gastritis, trauma, cirrhosis, and epilepsy. Their mortality rates tend to be double the normal by age, and their longevity is reduced from 8 to 12 years. Fifty percent have cardiovascular deaths at double the expected rate and 10 years earlier. Traumatic deaths claim 20%, and deaths by pneumonia or cancer of the upper gastrointestinal and respiratory tracts occur more frequently. While death by cirrhosis, 30,000 a year, is dramatic, this is only 20% of the number of cardiovascular deaths.

The President's physician (Lukash, 1979) estimates 40%–50%

TABLE 2
Alcohol-Related Disorders (From *First Special Report*)

Gastrointestinal
Esophagitis
Esophageal carcinoma
Gastritis
Malabsorption
Pancreatitis
Fatty liver
Alcoholic hepatitis
Cirrhosis (may lead to cancer of the liver)
Chronic diarrhea
Cardiac
Alcoholic cardiomyopathy
Beriberi
Skin
Rosacea
Telangiestasia
Rhinophyma
Cutaneous ulcers
Neurologic and psychiatric
Peripheral neuropathy
Convulsive disorders
Alcoholic hallucinosis
Delirium tremens
Wernicke's syndrome
Korsakoff's psychosis
Marchiafava's syndrome
Muscle
Alcoholic myopathy
Hematologic
Megaloblastic anemia
Vitamin deficiency disease
Beriberi
Pellagra
Scurvy
Metabolic
Alcoholic hypoglycemia
Alcoholic hyperlipemia

of the problems seen in a digestive disease clinic are caused or aggravated by excess use of alcohol and 25%–50% of hospital patients have medical problems associated with alcohol use. Gitlow (1979) states that alcohol-related conditions are the leading cause of death in the population aged 15 to 45. A previously quoted study by Moore (1971) revealed a higher incidence of liver disease, gastrointestinal disorders, trauma, and malignancies in alcoholics. Gomberg's study (1975), previously cited, showed a higher incidence of diseases of the respiratory and digestive tracts but lower incidence of neurological, cardiovascular, and urogenital disorders.

The AMA's *Medical Complications of Alcohol Abuse* (1973) lists the major surgical problems associated with alcoholism as cirrhosis, trauma, body surface burns, chronic pancreatitis, gastritis with hemorrhage, Mallory-Weiss syndrome (mucosal tear at the gastroesophageal junction due to forceful vomiting), tears in the lower esophagus, and bleeding esophageal varices (cause of one-third of deaths from cirrhosis).

Pathology of the liver, especially cirrhosis, is directly correlated with alcohol consumption. Ten percent of alcoholics will develop cirrhosis, the third cause of death in those from age 25 to 65 in New York City (Secretary HEW, 1971). Cirrhosis deaths are associated in 85%–90% of the cases with alcoholism, though the death certificates so state in only 30% of cases (AMA, 1973). This report also gives a greater importance to cirrhosis as a cause of death than Brody (1977), saying 40,000 deaths are directly the consequence of cirrhosis yearly, with another 20,000 deaths due to the consequences of cirrhosis.

Cardiac problems may be related to thiamin deficiency, or beriberi heart, or cardiomyopathy not related to a deficiency but to the alcohol itself (Secretary HEW, 1971). However, the *Second Special Report* (Secretary HEW, 1974) highlighted data that were surprisingly contradictory to expectation relative to coronary artery disease. The Framingham, Tecumseh, and Los Angeles longitudinal studies showed that both light and heavy drinkers had no more coronary disease than abstainers and much less than drinkers who quit. This even held true for "high risk" persons—hypertensives, smokers, and those with elevated cholesterol levels. This was confirmed in a later report (Hennekens, et al., 1979) who found in 568 men who died of coronary heart disease compared to a 568 matched control group that up to 2 ounces of ethanol daily was inversely related to coronary death. Whether this is related to alcohol leading to increased high-density lipoprotein factor in cholesterol or its simple correlation with personality types (A and B) and their use of alcohol is unknown. The *First Special Report* (Secretary HEW, 1971) had pointed out also that blood alcohol concentrations up to 65 mg%

increased coronary blood flow. All this data shows the problems of trying to relate alcoholism prevalence with cardiac disease. A review by Ashley and Rankin (1980) reveals that most, but not all, data attribute higher morbidity and mortality rates to heavy alcohol consumption, but it is unclear how much this is caused by alcohol or other living and nutritional habits associated with heavy alcohol use.

Since the skin is readily seen, this could be an organ system that gives early indicators of alcoholism. Those disorders most frequently seen in alcoholics are seborrhea capitis, seborrheic dermatitis, acne rosacea, dermatophytosis, psoriasis, acne vulgaris, black hairy tongue, dyshidrotic eczema, intratriginous eczema, leukoplakia, neurodermatitis, rhinothyma, and nummular eczema (AMA, 1973). Unfortunately, from an epidemiologic standpoint, none are specific for alcoholism.

Similarly, hemotologic changes associated with alcoholism are not specific. These include interference with folate utilization and pyridoxine metabolism leading to a decrease in erythopoiesis and megaloblastic anemia, and decreased iron metabolism leading to the finding of ringed sideroblasts. All these findings are usually prevented by an adequate diet, whatever the alcohol consumption may be. (AMA, 1973).

Except for data on the prevalence of alcoholism in patients with cirrhosis, and except for those disorders specifically caused by alcohol such as alcoholic hepatitis, there are inadequate prevalence data available for all these medical and surgical disorders. As stated in a previous caveat, knowing that alcohol or alcoholism plays a role in the genesis of certain conditions does not provide us with data of value for epidemiologic studies.

Alcohol and Cancer

The relationship between heavy alcohol consumption and cancer has been long noted, the first report being made in France in 1910 (Secretary HEW, 1974), showing an association between the drinking of absinthe and carcinoma of the esophagus. A 10–15 year followup of 935 alcoholics admitted to four English hospitals (Nichols et al., 1974) showed more than twice the expected mortality for men and over three times for women.

Neoplasms accounted for 10.9% of the excessive mortality at all sites, but especially in the upper gastrointestinal and respiratory tracts. Accidental and violent deaths (with suicide 25 times the expected rate) accounted for 42.1% of the excessive mortality while diseases of the respiratory system accounted for 16.6% and of the circulatory system 15.9%. Another study demonstrated a rate for head and neck cancer in alcoholics of 286.5/100,000 versus 53.9/100,000 expected (Kissin et al., 1973).

Because of the great concern with tobacco smoking and cancer, the effects of alcohol were not given much attention, especially since it was not carcinogenic from animal studies. Since alcoholics are heavy smokers, 93% of the men and 91% of the women in one study (Dreher and Fraser, 1968), it was not easy to separate their individual contribution. This was accomplished in a study by Rothman and Keller (1972) showing both cigarettes and alcohol contribute alone and synergistically. Oral cancer rates are increased to 2.33 times normal when more than 1.5 ounces of absolute alcohol is consumed by nonsmokers daily but this increases to 9.59 times in smokers of 20 to 39 cigarettes daily and to 15.5 in those who smoke over 40. Similarly, nondrinkers increase their rate to only 2.43 in smoking 40 or more cigarettes daily. One authority (Fraumeni, 1979) states that alcohol and tobacco contribute to 75% of all head and neck cancer and another (Fink, 1979) that squamous cell carcinoma of the oral cavity, pharynx, larynx, and esophagus "would be uncommon in most industrialized countries without exposure to tobacco and alcohol."

Most interesting from an epidemiologic standpoint are the studies by Schwartz and associates in the *Second Special Report* (Secretary HEW, 1974). The results from their study of 3,937 French cancer patients are shown in table 3, which was produced in the *Second Special Report*. While the control group of noncancer patients has a high rate of alcohol consumption and alcoholism, the significant differences are striking. Several other studies showing the higher rates of cancer in these areas among alcoholics confirm those reported here.

There is much less certainty about the relationship of alcoholism or heavy alcohol consumption and cancer at other sites. Tuyns (1979) believes that pulmonary carcinoma in alcoholics may be due to their excessive smoking, an opinion shared by

TABLE 3

Alcohol Consumption and Percentage of Persons with Alcoholism Among Cancer Patients and Noncancer Control Group (workers in the Paris Area)

		Quantity consumed				Percentage with alcoholism			
				Significance adjusted for:				Significance adjusted for:	
Site of cancer	*Number of cases*	*(Oz. absolute alcohol daily*	*Gross significance (P)*	*Tobacco (P)*	*Tobacco and age (P)*	%	*Gross significance (P)*	*Tobacco (P)*	*Tobacco and age (P)*
Tongue	43	5.2	0.001	0.05		74	0.001	0.001	0.001
Buccal cavity	23	5.4	0.01	0.05	0.05	83	0.001	0.001	0.01
Oropharynx	34	4.9	0.01			56			
Hypopharynx		5.5	0.001	0.05	0.05	62	0.01	0.05	0.05
Larynx	63	5.4	0.001	0.01	0.05	61	0.01	0.05	0.01
Esophagus	100	5.3	0.001	0.01	0.01	58	0.01	0.05	0.05
Control group	366	4.0				43			

Source: Schwartz et al., 1962, in *Second Special Report* (Secretary HEW, 1974).

Lieber et al. (1979). On the other hand, a number of studies have shown a correlation between beer consumption and rectal cancer. However, Tuyns reports that a long-term study of 14,313 Danish brewery workers who were provided with 6 free pints of beer a day did not show an excess of rectal cancer.

Hepatoma, primary cancer of the liver, in 60%–90% of cases occurs in cirrhotic livers (Tuyns, 1979). Looking at it in reverse, 5%–30% of patients with cirrhosis will develop hepatoma. In one U.S. study (Lee, 1966), it was found that the incidence was 30% in those with alcoholic cirrhosis but only 11% in those with cirrhosis from other causes. Studies reported in the *Second Special Report* (Secretary HEW, 1974) show that hepatomas characteristically develop when there is cellular regeneration and more commonly in mild and healed alcoholic cirrhosis than during acute stages of development. Tuyns (1979) suggests since alcohol is not carcinogenic that the causative agent may be fusel oils or nitrosamines or nutritional factors. Lieber and colleagues (1979) speculate that alcohol damages the hepatocyters through the toxic effects of acetaldehyde in the endoplasmic reticulum, mitrochondria, and microtubules, or that accumulation of fat and protein causes distention of the cells.

Not only is it unclear how alcohol relates to liver cancer, it is not known how it works its effects in all types of cancer. McCoy and Wynder (1979) suggest such possibilities as alcohol's role as a solvent, causing alteration in epithelial cells, and its possible role in either enhancing or decreasing the liver's capacity to metabolize other substances. As in other areas of the study of carcinogenesis, much remains to be learned about alcohol.

Summary

The field of alcoholism studies is attempting to develop a base of strong epidemiologic data. These data will be invaluable in learning more about the etiology of the alcoholisms and in alerting health professionals, social scientists, and the general public to new methods of prevention and early casefinding. Serious problems, not yet resolved, are delaying the gathering of sound data.

The definition of alcoholism is controversial. Broad impairment definitions are widely used and, while having the value of bringing more excessive drinkers into treatment, have the disadvantage of being hard to measure. A more rigid, measurable research definition is needed that can be accepted by all in the field. Even with a resolution of the definition problem, there remains a great reluctance to make the diagnosis of alcoholism among health professionals. There is hope this will be remedied by better education about alcoholism.

Prevalence studies of rates of alcoholism among medical/surgical patients in general hospitals show a variation of 9%–70% with an average of 16% for 12 studies. Because of different definitions, diagnostic techniques, types of hospitals, and patient samples, these studies are not easily compared and the question is far from answered.

Prevalence of alcoholism among specific medical and surgical diagnoses is even less well understood. There is strong evidence that alcoholics have an excess of certain types of cancer and illnesses associated with the gastrointestinal and respiratory tracts and are overrepresented among those impaired or subject to violence (especially suicide). The relationship of alcohol and alcoholism to cardiovascular diseases is less clear. There is an expected very high prevalence of alcoholism among those with alcoholic hepatitis, a high prevalence among those with cirrhosis, and an elevated prevalence for those with upper GI and respiratory tract carcinoma. There are not sufficient data to estimate prevalence rates for alcoholism among other medical/surgical diagnoses.

References

Abbott, J.A., Goldberg, G.A. & Becker, C.E. (1974). The role of a medical audit in assessing management of alcoholics with acute pancreatitis. *Quart. J. Stud. Alc.* 35:272–276.

American Medical Association (1973). *Medical Complications of Alcohol Abuse.* Chicago: American Medical Association.

American Medical Association (1977). *Manual on Alcoholism.* Chicago: American Medical Association.

Ashley, M.J. & Rankin, J.G. (1980). Hazardous alcohol consumption and diseases of the circulatory system. *J. Stud. Alc.* 41:1040–1070.

Ashley, M.J., Oliln, J.S., leRiche, W.H., Kornaczewski, A., Schmidt, W., Corey, P.N., & Rankin, J.G. (1981). The physical disease characteristics of inpatient alcoholics. *J. Stud. Alc.* 42:1–14.

Barchha, R., Stewart, M.A. & Guze, S.B. (1968). The prevalence of alcoholism among general hospital ward patients. *Am. J. Psychiat.* 125: 681–684.

Brody, J.A. (1977). Medical Surveillance program of the new Epidemiology and Special Studies Branch of NIAAA. An approach to an epidemiological program on alcohol abuse and alcoholism. *Alc. Clin. Exp. Res.* 1:349–354.

Chakerian, A. & Schenkel, J. (1973). In support of a consolidated alcoholism treatment program. *V.A. Newslett. Res. Ment. Hlth. and Behav. Sci.* 15:37–41.

Dreher, K.F. & Fraser, J.G. (1968). Smoking habits of alcoholic outpatients. *Int. J. Addict.* 2:259–270, 1967; 3:65–80.

Ewing, J.A. (1970). Identifying the "hidden alcoholic". *Int. Congr. Alc. Drug Depend.*, Abst 29th, p. 18.

Feighner, J.P., Robins, E., Guze, S., Woodruff, R.A., Winokur, G. & Munoz, R. (1972). Diagnostic criteria for use in psychiatric research. *Arch. Gen. Psychiat.* 26:57–63.

Fink, D.J. (1979). Cancer overview. *Cancer Res.* 39:2819–2821.

Fisher, J.C., Mason, R.L. & Fisher, J.V. (1976). A diagnostic formula for alcoholism. *J. Stud. Alc.* 37:1247–1255.

Fisher, J.V., Fisher, J.C. & Mason, R.L. (1976). Physicians and alcoholics: Modifying behavior and attitude of family practice residents. *J. Stud. Alc.* 37:1686–1693.

Fraumeni, J.F. (1979). Epidemiological opportunities in alcohol-related cancer. *Cancer Res.* 39:2851–2852.

Gitlow, S.E. (1979). The disease of alcoholism. *Cancer Res.* 39:2836–2839.

Gomberg, E.S. (1975). Prevalence of alcoholism among ward patients in a Veterans Administration Hospital. *J. Stud. Alc.* 36:1458–1467.

Goodwin, D.W. (1976). Adoptive studies of alcoholism. *J. Opl. Psychiat.* 7:54–63.

Green, J.R. (1965). The incidence of alcoholism in patients admitted to medical wards of a hospital. *Med. J. Aust.* 1:465–466.

Guze, S.B. (1980). Recognition of alcoholism. *Psychiat. Cap. Comm.* 2:1.

Hennekens, C.H., Willett, W., Rossner, B., Cole, D.S. & Mayrent, S.L. (1979). Effects of beer, wine and liquor in coronary deaths. *J.A.M.A.* 242:1973–1974.

Jarman, C.M.B. & Kellett, J.M. (1979). Alcoholism in the general hospital. *Brit. Med. J.* 2:469–472.

Jones, G.H. (1979). The recognition of alcoholism by psychiatrists in training. *Psychol. Med.* 9:789–791.

Kearney, T.R., Bonime, H.B. & Cassimatis, G. (1967). The impact of alcoholism on a community general hospital. *Community Ment. Hlth. J.* 3:373–376.

Kearney, T.R. (1969). Alcohol and general hospital patients. *Am. J. Psychiat.* 125:157–158.

Keller, M. (1962). The definition of alcoholism and the estimation of its prevalence. In: *Society, Culture and Drinking Patterns,* ed. D.J. Pittman & C.R. Snyder. New York: Wiley, pp. 310–329.

Keller, M. (1975). Problems of epidemiology in alcohol problems. *J. Stud. Alc.* 36:1442–1451.

Keller, M. (1979). A historical overview of alcohol and alcoholism. *Cancer Res.* 39:2822–2829.

Kissin, B., Kaley, M.M., Su, W.H. & Lerner, R. (1973). Head and neck cancer in alcoholics; the relationship to drinking, smoking and dietary patterns. *J.A.M.A.* 224:1174–1175.

Lee, F.I. (1966). Cirrhosis and hepatoma in alcoholics. *Gut.* 7:77–85.

Lieber, C.S., Seitz, H.K., Garro, A.J. & Worner, T.M. (1979). Alcohol related diseases and carcinogenesis. *Cancer Res.* 39:2863–2886.

Lisansky, E.T. (1974). Alcoholism: the avoided diagnosis. *Md. St. Med. J.*, Aug. pp. 26–31.

Lukash, W.M. (1979). The family physician and confrontation in alcoholism. *Cancer Res.* 39:2834–2835.

McCoy, G.D. and Wynder, E.L. (1979). Etiological and preventive implications in alcohol carcinogenesis. *Cancer Res.* 39:2844–2850.

McCusker, J., Cherubin, D.E. & Zimberg, S. (1971). Prevalence of alcoholism in general municipal hospital population. *N.Y. State J. Med.* 71:751–754.

Moore, R.A. (1971). The prevalence of alcoholism in a community general hospital. *Am. J. Psychiat.* 128:638–639.

Moore, R. A. (1972). The diagnosis of alcoholism in a psychiatric hospital: a trial of the Michigan Alcoholism Screening Test (MAST). *Am. J. Psychiat.* 128:1565–1569.

National Council on Alcoholism, Criteria Committee (1972). Criteria for the diagnosis of alcoholism. *Am. J. Psychiat.* 129:127–135.

Nichols, P., Edwards, G. & Kyle, E. (1974). Alcoholics admitted to four hospitals in England. II. General and cause-specific mortality. *Quart. J. Stud. Alc.* 35:841–855.

Nolan, J.P. (1965). Alcohol as a factor in the illness of university service patients. *Am. J. Med. Sci.* 249:135–142.

Page, J.B. (1979). Identifying drinking problems in Veterans Administration Hospital patients. *J. Stud. Alc.* 40:447–456.

Pearson, W.S. (1962). The "hidden" alcoholic in white male patients admitted for unrelated medical complaints. *N.C. Med. J.* 23:6–10.

Ringer, C., Kufner, H., Antons, K. & Feuerlein, W. (1977). The N.C.A. criteria for the diagnosis of alcoholism: an empirical study. *J. Stud. Alc.* 38:1259–1273.

Rothman, K. & Keller, A. (1972). The effect of joint exposure to alcohol and tobacco on risk of cancer of the mouth and pharynx. *J. Chronic Dis.* 25:711–716.

Schuckit, M.A. & Miller, P.L. (1976). Alcoholism in elderly men: a survey of a general medical ward. *Ann. N.Y. Acad. Sci.* 273:558–571.

Schuckit, M.A. & Pastor, P.A. (1978). The elderly as a unique population: alcoholism. *Alc. Clin. Exp. Res.* 2:31–38.

Secretary, HEW (1971). *First Special Report to the U.S. Congress on Alcohol and Health.* Washington, D.C.: U.S. Government Printing Office.

Secretary, HEW (1974). *Second Special Report to the U.S. Congress on Alcohol and Health.* Washington, D.C.: U.S. Government Printing Office.

Schwartz, D., Lellouch, J., Flamant, R. & Denoix, P.F. (1962). Alcool et cancer; resultants d'une enquete retrospective. *Rev. Fr. Etude Clin. Biol.* 7:590–604. (Cited in *Second Special Report.*)

Selzer, M.L. (1971). The Michigan Alcoholism Screening Test: the quest for a new diagnostic instrument. *Am. J. Psychiat.* 127:1653–1658.

Selzer, M.L., Vinokur, A. & Van Rooijen, L. (1975). A self-administered Short Michigan Alcoholism Screening Test (SMAST). *J. Stud. Alc.* 36:117–126.

Sowa, P.A. & Cutter, H.S. (1974). Attitudes of hospital staff toward alcoholics and drug addicts. *Quart. J. Stud. Alc.* 35:210–214.

Swenson, W.M. & Morse, R.M. (1975). The use of a self-administered alcoholism screening test (SAAST) in a medical center. *Mayo Clin. Proc.* 50:204–208.

Tuyns, A.J. (1979). Epidemiology of alcohol and cancer. *Cancer Res.* 39:2840–2843.

Wallston, K.A., Wallston, B.S. & DeVellis, B.M. (1976). Effects of negative stereotype on nurses' attitudes toward an alcoholic patient. *J. Stud. Alc.* 37:659–665.

Westermeyer, J., Doheny, S. & Stone, B. (1978). An assessment of hospital care for the alcoholic patient. *Alc. Clin. Exp. Res.* 2:53–57.

Winokur, G. & Tsuang, M.T. (1978). Expectancy of alcoholism in a midwestern population (Iowa). *J. Stud. Alc.* 39:1964–1967.

Afterword: Psychosocial Research on Alcohol Problems from an International Perspective

IRVING ROOTMAN

The chapters in this volume focus almost entirely on developed countries. There are a number of reasons why this is so, including the fact that all of the authors are based in North America. However, perhaps the main reason why developing countries are overlooked is that there is not a great deal of published material from developing countries to draw upon in discussing psychosocial research on alcohol problems.

Such research is limited in developing countries in part because of special difficulties in carrying out epidemiologic work on alcohol problems in such circumstances. Added to the many methodologic problems discussed in this volume are unique problems such as absence or unreliability of background information, inaccessible regions, linguistic differences, inadequacy of data processing facilities, shortage of appropriately trained personnel, and difficult interviewing circumstances.

Although these difficulties are indeed daunting, as demonstrated by the current World Health Organization project on community response to alcohol-related problems (WHO, 1983) they are by no means unresolvable. For example, when project collaborators in Mexico did not have adequate maps from which to select a sample for a general population survey, hand-drawn maps were prepared by interviewers. Similarly, the Zambian collaborators managed to successfully translate and back-translate interviews into and from several languages. Guidelines were also developed and used to try to minimize the disruption of interviewing in situations where others were present. While it could not be claimed that all of the special difficulties of epidemiologic research in developing countries were eliminated, at least it was demonstrated that with thought and effort it is possible to deal with them constructively. If nothing else, this project and others like it suggest that it is indeed possible to carry out useful and high-quality psychosocial research on alcohol problems in developing countries.

This, however, raises the question of what should be the priorities of such research in situations of limited resources such as exist in developing countries. In such circumstances, it surely is not possible to pursue *all* of the excellent questions suggested in recent reviews of priorities in this field (Institute of Medicine, 1980; Keller, 1979).

While the establishment of such priorities must of necessity be a national responsibility, and will therefore vary from country to country, some obvious candidates come to mind if one takes the extent to which such research may be useful for improving responses to alcohol-related problems as the prime criterion for establishing priorities.

The first would be the extent and nature of alcohol problems in the country and in particular subgroups of the population. Although such information is fundamental to planning national and local responses to alcohol problems, it is sadly lacking or inadequate in most developing countries. This is unfortunate and unnecessary in view of the fact that there are a number of techniques such as key informant studies that could be applied with minimal cost and effort (Liban & Smart, 1980). The experience of the community response project may be helpful to countries wishing to improve the quality of their information on the magnitude and nature of their alcohol problems (Rootman & Moser, 1984).

The second would be an attempt to answer the question of how the country, or various communities in it, actually responds to alcohol-related problems. Information along these lines is critical to determining how adequately the country and communities are responding and in pointing to possibilities for improving responses. Again, the community response project may be helpful in suggesting approaches to this question (Rootman & Moser, 1984).

A third priority question for developing countries might be the organization of and trends in beverage production, distribution, marketing, and control in the country. Such information is important in establishing policies that could effectively reduce the extent of alcohol problems since the evidence suggests that the relative availability of alcohol is a prime determinant of levels of consumption and consequent problems. The International Study of Alcohol Control Experiences (ISACE) project (Mäkelä et al., 1981) as well as the community response project (Rootman & Moser, 1984), may provide models for adaptation to developing countries in this regard.

Finally, it seems critically important for developing countries to have information on the impact of policies and programs on alcohol-related problems. Such information would be extremely important in directing countries to appropriate modifications of their intervention approaches should they prove to be ineffective. The community response project also developed techniques for assessing the impact of such interventions and may once again be a useful model for developing countries (Rootman & Moser, 1984).

Although the four areas of inquiry suggested as priorities for developing countries here are not the only ones that could have been suggested, they are clearly worth considering when countries begin to establish priorities for epidemiologic research on alcohol problems. Information in these areas is essential to the development and implementation of effective responses to alcohol-related problems. But what about priorities for cross-national collaborative alcohol research in psychosocial epidemiology?

There are two recently completed projects of this type, both of which have been mentioned above—the WHO community response to alcohol-related problems project and the ISACE project (which also has WHO involvement). Both of these projects, in addition to making contributions to our knowledge about alcohol problems, have had additional equally important benefits such as providing training opportunities for young investigators and facilitating communication and problem-solving among workers in the alcohol field. Thus such projects clearly have much to recommend them and deserve to be encouraged in their own right.

Assuming limited resources for the support of such projects, however, what should the priority topics for research be? If one again takes the improvement of responses to alcohol problems as the prime criterion, a couple of possibilities come to mind.

The first, which flows logically out of the ISACE project, would be a collaborative study of the public health impact of the international alcohol trade. Such a project might examine the impact of international trade agreements on alcohol production and trade and on national alcohol controls. It might also study multinationality in the organization of beverage production and trade and the implications of trends in multinationality for national and international systems of control. It could provide extremely useful information to countries and international agencies to enable them to take appropriate action to prevent and reduce alcohol-related problems through limiting availability. It would certainly be in keeping with several recommendations of the recent WHO Expert Committee on problems related to alcohol consumption (WHO, 1980).

A second priority topic that would be in support of the recommendation of the Expert Committee that "prevention should be given clear priority" might be alcohol problems among young people. It could begin with an international review of knowledge and experience leading to collaborative research. Such research would be expected to lead to the development of appropriate policies and programs and their subsequent evaluation. It could be done following the model used in the community response project, involving countries expressing a particular concern about alcohol problems among their young people.

A third topic, again consistent with recommendations of the Expert Committee, would be programs on alcohol problems in employment settings. Such a project could first review experiences of countries in this area and perhaps undertake collaborative assessment of promising programs. It could lead to the development of guidelines and materials that could be used by countries to establish such programs. The WHO and ILO have embarked on a project along these lines.

Other psychosocial topics that might profitably be studied collaboratively include repercussions and management of alcohol problems in the family setting, prevention of alcohol-related traffic accidents, alcohol problems and socioeconomic change, and treatment and management of the alcohol-dependence syndrome at the primary health level. These topics are, in fact, among the priority topics for the expanded WHO program on alcohol problems. It is our hope that their pursuit will enable countries and the international community to deal better with the problems associated with the use of alcohol.

References

Institute of Medicine (1980). *Alcoholism, alcohol abuse and related problems; Opportunities for research.* Washington, D.C.: National Academy of Sciences.

Keller, M., ed. (1979). Research priorities on alcohol. *J. Stud. Alc., Suppl. 8,* pp. 248–322.

Liban, C.B. & Smart, R.G. (1980). *The value of the informant method for studying drinking habits.* Toronto: Addiction Research Foundation.

Mäkelä, K., Room, R., Single, E., Sulkunen, P., Walsh, P., Bunce, R., Cahannes, M., Cameron, T., Giesbrecht, N., deLint, J., Makinen, H., Morgan, P., Mosher, J., Moskaliewicz, J., Muller, R., Osterberg, E., Wald, L. & Walsh, D. (1981). *Alcohol, Society and the State, Vol. 1.* Toronto: Addiction Research Foundation.

Rootman, I. & Moser, J. (1984), *Guidelines for investigating alcohol problems and developing appropriate responses.* Geneva, offset publication no. 81.

World Health Organization (1980), *Expert Committee Report on problems related to alcohol consumption,* Geneva, WHO Techn. Rep. Ser., No. 650.

World Health Organization (1983), *Final Report: Community response to alcohol-related problems; Phase I.* Geneva, World Health Organization Document, 1983.

About the Contributors

MARC A. SCHUCKIT, Professor of Psychiatry at the University of California, San Diego, is internationally known for his research on alcohol and other substance abuse. Prior to his present post as Director of the Alcoholism Research Center of the Veterans Administration Hospital in San Diego, he was Director of the Alcoholism and Drug Abuse Institute at the University of Washington, Seattle. He has won a number of awards and honors for his research including the coveted Hofheimer Award of the American Psychiatric Association. He is on the Editorial Boards of the *Journal of Studies of Alcohol, Alcoholism, American Journal of Drug and Alcohol Abuse* and the *Journal of Clinical Psychiatry*. Dr. Schuckit is a member of a number of research and honorary societies including the Royal College of Psychiatrists, and the American College of Neuropyschopharmacology; he is also a fellow of the American Psychiatric Association and a past member of the National Advisory Council on Alcohol Abuse and Alcoholism of the Alcohol, Drug Abuse, and Mental Health Administration, and the Research Society on Alcoholism. He has published over two hundred papers and chapters in books. His book *Drug and Alcohol Abuse: A Clinical Guide to Diagnosis and Treatment* (Plenum Press, 1984) is widely used by those working in the alcohol field. Dr. Schuckit's address is the San Diego Veterans Hospital, 3350 La Jolla Village Drive, San Diego, California 92161.

ROBERTA G. FERRENCE is a Scientist at the Addiction Research Foundation, Toronto, Canada.

E.K. ERIC GUNDERSON is Head of the Environmental Medicine Department of the Naval Health Research Center, San Diego, and Adjunct Clinical Professor of Psychiatry in the School of Medicine, University of California, San Diego.

STEPHEN ISRAELSTAM is in the Epidemiology Section of the Addiction Research Foundation, Toronto, Canada.

CHARLES T. KAELBER is Chief of the Laboratory of Epidemiology and Population Studies at the National Institute on Alcohol Abuse and Alcoholism, Rockville, Maryland.

DOUGLAS KOLB is Executive Director of Oak Glen, Inc., and was formerly Head of the Psychiatric Effectiveness Program, Naval Health Research Center, San Diego.

RUTH E. LITTLE is Director of the Alcoholism and Drug Abuse Institute and Associate Professor of Epidemiology at the University of Washington, Seattle.

ROBERT A. MOORE is Vice-President for Clinical Programs of the Vista Hill Foundation and Clinical Professor of Psychiatry in the School of Medicine of the University of California, San Diego.

ELIZABETH R. MORRISSEY is Assistant Professor, Department of Sociology & Criminal Justice, Old Dominion University, Norfolk, VA.

J. MICHAEL POLICH is a Senior Behavioral Scientist at the Rand Corporation, Santa Monica, California.

ROBERT E. POPHAM is Director Emeritus of the Social and Biological Studies Division of the Addiction Research Foundation, Toronto, Canada.

IRVING ROOTMAN is Chief of Health Promotion Studies, Health Promotion Directorate, Health and Welfare, Canada, Ottawa. He was formerly with the Division of Mental Health, World Health Organization, Geneva.

WOLFGANG SCHMIDT is Director of Social Policy Research at the Addiction Research Foundation in Toronto, Canada.

ANN PYTKOWICZ STREISSGUTH is Professor of Psychiatry in the Department of Psychiatry and Behavioral Sciences of the University of Washington, Seattle.